THE Family Circle HINTS BOOK

From the Readers of *Family Circle*
Edited by Erika Douglas

NYT
Times
BOOKS

This book is dedicated to that special group
of *Family Circle* readers
whose hints find their way regularly into the
READERS' IDEA EXCHANGE.

Special Project Staff

Editor: Erika Douglas
Assistant Editor: Betsy Lawrence
Designed by Robert Bull

General Manager: John Jaxheimer

Project Manager: Annabelle Arenz

Design Consultant: Joseph Taveroni
Production Consultant: Kathy Reilly
Type Supervisor: Wendy Hylfelt

Assistants: Ilene Browning
Beth Rochford
Beverly Brown
Andy Shinn

Published by TIMES BOOKS, a division of
Quadrangle/The New York Times Book Co., Inc.
Three Park Avenue, New York, N.Y. 10016
Published simultaneously in Canada by
Fitzhenry & Whiteside, Ltd., Toronto

Library of Congress Catalog Card Number 82-50049
ISBN 0-8129-1016-8

Manufactured in the United States of America
10 9 8 7 6 5 4 3 2 1

Foreword

We at *Family Circle* are delighted and proud to bring this exceptionally comprehensive hints book to you. And we' re particularly proud because THE FAMILY CIRCLE HINTS BOOK was "written"—literally—by our readers. These include homemakers and career women (and men!)—all determined to make life easier for themselves and for those around them. They send us over 4,000 hints a month, giving us their most valuable ideas on saving time, money, energy, headaches. The best appear in our Readers' Idea Exchange column, consistently the most widely read feature in *Family Circle*.

Erika Douglas, who edits Readers' Idea Exchange, selected the most compelling hints for publication in this book. With an unerring sense of what people need most in their daily lives, she has appraised thousands of problem-solvers and chosen over 1,800 solid-gold winners. Her collection constitutes a mini-encyclopedia for the '80s, with insightful and exciting advice concerning family relations, food, health, clothes, budgeting, decorating, child care and much, much more. Most important, all the hints have been tested and proven effective. They're all useful, do-able, they really work.

For example, we tell you an amazingly simple way to make sure every guest meal is a smash. We pass on an ingenious device for getting your children's friends home on time. We tell you how a dot of red nail polish saves money and electricity. We give you brilliant tips on removing black heel marks from linoleum floors, using the last drop of shampoo, erasing unwanted hem lines, removing corn silk fast.

Truly, if you ever wanted a complete, pre-tested, proven reference collection of tips and ideas to make your life easier...this is it.

THE FAMILY CIRCLE HINTS BOOK is the widest-ranging, highest-quality collection of hints in print today. There is perhaps only one hint missing: that you get an extra copy for a close friend.

Arthur Hettich
Editor, *Family Circle*

TABLE OF CONTENTS

One

244 WAYS TO SAVE TIME, ENERGY, AND MONEY

COUPONING

Speedy checkout

Clip coupons for grocery items to help your budget. To save time at the checkout line, mark the expiration date with a colorful pen so that it is visible to both you and the cashier.

Snip extra savings

With scissors left near your favorite reading spots (nightstand, couch, breakfast table, or even the bathroom), you can clip coupons from newspapers and magazines as you run across them. If you have youngsters, though, make sure the scissors are out of their reach!

Get your money's worth

Before going shopping, file coupons in the order the products appear in the grocery aisle, and indicate the price you usually pay. That way you know if the coupon item is a good buy.

Coupon holder

Use an old checkbook cover to carry coupons. The pockets on each side will hold a nice assortment.

Weekly shopping list

Attach the weekly grocery list to the refrigerator door with a magnet. This way, everyone in your family can add items as needed. Also, add cash-off and refund coupons that are dated for that week.

DO IT YOURSELF AND SAVE

Just like new

Give andirons and fireplace tools a new lease on life by removing rust with a scouring pad, then coating them with heat-resistant black paint.

For small paint jobs

For a quick touch-up paint job, there is nothing handier than a piece of foam rubber. Paint not only goes on evenly but gets into all the nooks, and you just throw away the rubber when finished. Also, no messy brushes to clean.

Painting partners

When using an oil-base paint, keep a bottle of nail polish remover handy. Dabbed on a cotton ball, the remover cleans up spatters and leaves a pleasant scent.

After painting...

Cleaning your hands following a painting session is no problem if you remember to rub them with a little cooking oil before giving them a thorough washing with soap and water. Kinder to the skin than paint remover!

Cheer up dingy closets

Do the insides of your closets look cave-like even with a light? To brighten them up, paint closet interiors with a high-gloss white enamel.

Paint pipes

Paint plumbing shut-off valves and part of the pipeline with bright colors. Red for hot water, blue for main line, green for waste, and so forth. This saves time when an emergency arises—no matter which line gives you trouble, you have a quick way of eliminating the flow. Just in case, keep a list of what each color represents.

Tips and gadgets to help you paint

Stretch a strong rubber band vertically around your paint can. Use the band to catch excess paint from the brush and keep the can's side and rim paint-free.

Are you painting your ceilings? Try tying a plastic dry cleaning bag around each chandelier and hanging light fixture to protect against drips and spatters of paint.

After finishing a painting project, draw a line with your brush on the outside of the can at paint level. This will show you both the color and amount left in the can. Make a note of the date, too.

If you have a hard time visualizing those small paint samples on an entire wall when trying to decide on a wall color, buy a small amount first and paint a posterboard. The painted area is large enough to give a good idea of the color, and by moving the board to different areas of the room you can see how various lighting conditions might affect the color. The small investment is well worth avoiding the frustration of living with a color that you are not happy with.

When using spray paint for small items, protect your hands by slipping them into plastic bags which can be thrown away when the job is done.

To prevent spattering hinges and knobs when painting a door, rub a little petroleum jelly on them first. Paint will come off easily.

Snip the bottom from a cone-shaped paper cup for a handy disposable paint funnel.

Save empty nail polish bottles and clean them thoroughly. Whenever you paint a room or piece of furniture, fill a bottle with some of the paint used. Small scratches and marks can be easily fixed.

Glue a paper plate to the bottom of your paint can to catch drips and slips.

If you want to be able to use your stairway while painting it, try painting every other step, letting them dry, then painting the rest. You'll get good exercise walking up and down two stairs at a time!

An old hand-held eggbeater or whisk makes a perfect paint mixer. It does the job faster than a stick, and the color mixes evenly and smoothly.

When using a rubber-base paint on the walls of a room, paint the inside of window shades the same color. After they are dry, reroll them—and they will look like new: even pinholes are filled, and the shades are still flexible.

Soft brushes

When washing paintbrushes, use fabric softener in the final rinse. It helps keep them soft and pliable.

Clean and soften hardened paintbrushes by simmering them in boiling vinegar for a few minutes and then washing them in soapy water.

Hints for wallpapering

Doing your own wallpapering? Use a paint roller to apply the paste for a smooth and efficient job.

Hanging prepasted wallpaper is easier if you keep the water in a baby's bathtub. Move it along as you go and you will save many steps and much time.

Soak wallpaper that you're planning to remove. Use a paint roller dipped in hot water, then roll it up and down the wall. Let the paper soak 15 minutes, then scrape it off.

Add a bit of food coloring to wallpaper paste—it helps to see whether or not you've covered the paper to the very edge.

After wallpapering a room, make a penciled notation of the amount used on the wall behind a picture. Then, when the room needs re-papering, the information on the quantity to purchase will be right there.

Cover-up job!

Scratches on your white enamel? Brush white nail polish on the offending areas. It does a fine cover-up job.

Nonrusting garbage cans

Extend the life of your metal garbage cans by preventing rusty bottoms. Spray the base and all the sides up to 4″ or 5″ with leftover (or new) rust-preventive paint.

Protect ice skates

Instead of buying skate guards to protect your ice skates while storing, cut a piece of garden hose the length of the blade, split down the middle, and insert over blade.

Repairing a handbag

When the fabric lining of a purse becomes torn or frayed before the outside wears out, strengthen the lining with strips of iron-on patching material.

Double the use

Cut an inexpensive piece of wood to fit on top of your dining table and glue on a piece of felt. It serves as a great cutting board for sewing projects. Leave it on the table at all times and just remove the tablecloth when needed. All other times it is a nice table pad.

Taking care of your washing machine

Clean your washing machine periodically by filling the tub with warm water and pouring a gallon of distilled vinegar into it. Run it through the entire cycle; the vinegar will cleanse the hoses of soap residue.

Make your own curtain rods

Wooden curtain rods look attractive, but they can be quite expensive. Here is a way to make your own at a fraction of the cost. Purchase long 1½" wooden dowels at a local hardware store, cut them to the needed length, and screw a wooden drawer knob into each end. Then stain them and hang curtains with either wooden or fabric loops. Looks terrific!

Restoring old picture frames

Faded natural wood picture frames can be restored in a matter of minutes. Just apply paste-wax shoe polish to the wood and buff with a soft cloth. The shoe polish not only darkens the faded wood but also gives it a rich, mellow luster.

Cutting plywood

When cutting plywood with a hand saw, put a strip of masking tape over the outline and saw through it to help prevent splintering.

Open doors

Doors on such furniture as hutches, armoires, and china closets that won't stay closed because of warping may be held in place by several magnets attached to the doors and cabinet. You can even purchase magnetic tape and apply it.

Easy pull

You can open a chest drawer that has lost its pulls by using a suction cup or plumber's rubber plunger.

Air conditioner care

Your room air conditioner, like all appliances, needs some care if it is to perform properly. Keep your owner's manual handy, and use it when you turn the unit on at the beginning of the season and off at the end. Not every fan motor is permanently lubricated, so check your manual, and oil if necessary. Wash the filter, if it is a permanent one, about once a month while you use the conditioner. If the filter isn't permanent and must be replaced, check it and get a fresh one before it is overly clogged with dirt.

Many manufacturers do not recommend covering the outside of a unit during the seasons when it's not in use. Warm air from indoors gradually filters out and hits the cold outside cover. The moisture in the air condenses on the cover and will mildew or rot it as well as damage the surfaces of the conditioner.

When you're cleaning the surfaces, use mild suds. Avoid strong cleaning agents: they may discolor the finish or mar it.

Restore a tennis table

Renew those half-obliterated lines on a table-tennis table with white masking tape. First wash the table to remove any dust, then apply over the old lines.

Oil job

Some electric fans require occasional oiling. Slip a large paper bag over the fan blade guard after completing the job, turn on the fan and let it run for a few minutes, then remove the bag. This prevents the spattering of any excess oil.

Getting rid of a squeak!

Remedy a squeaky hinge by applying several drops of odorless salad oil. Blot excess with paper towels or facial tissue to keep it from soiling your floors.

Decorative nailheads

When hammering in decorative nailheads, preserve their finish by covering the head of your hammer with a precut adhesive bandage.

To ease the job

Always rub a little oil or petroleum jelly on screws or bolts before inserting them in any unassembled items you buy. This will make the job easier if the article needs to be taken apart one day.

Loose knobs on dresser drawers?

Just detach and dip the screw portion in colorless nail polish or shellac before resetting. When the shellac or polish hardens, the screws will be set tightly.

Save on paper napkins

Don't save cloth napkins just for special occasions! For a touch of elegance and economy you can use napkins made with permanent-press fabric every day. It is easy to throw them in almost any washload and have them ready for use again right out of the dryer! Assign each family member his own napkin color, or use distinctive rings. To store: Provide a special drawer or keep in a basket within easy reach.

Fashion update

Crochet a lacy collar from leftover yarn to give last fall's sweater a new look.

Miniature clamps

To hold small glued objects in place while they are drying, use an old pair of screw-on earrings. They make a naturally small clamp.

Floor care

Slate, flagstone, or brick flooring in your entryway, hall, or living or dining area should be treated with a penetrating sealer containing tung oil. This will keep the flooring bright, make it moisture-resistant, and help prevent the sanding-off of mortar between the stones. Use a flat hard-bristle brush to scrub the sealer into the floor. Wipe off any surplus with a lintless cloth. The surface can then be washed with suds and water when soiled. For outdoor patios and walks, use a penetrating floor sealer designed for exterior use.

Seal it up!

A small cup hook makes a good seal for an open tube of glue, cement, or wood putty. Screw the hook into the opening with the flange part of the hook turned flush against the top of the tube. This also furnishes a convenient way to hang the tube on a wall or shelf.

Fix it

Before you replace that torn vacuum cleaner bag, see if it can be fixed with iron-on patches.

Mending upholstery

Tears can be mended almost invisibly: Place fabric tape on the reverse side of upholstery, shiny side of the tape face down, and press it with a hot iron.

Refinishing furniture

If, when refinishing furniture, you find that there are some places difficult to reach with a sanding block, use an emery board. It works beautifully! Makes it easy to reach into those hard-to-get places and saves fingernails from the abuse of sandpaper.

Furniture touch ups

Save old mascara tubes for temporary touch-ups of black or dark brown painted surfaces such as furniture, shelving, and anything else till painting or repair times come due.

A brown crayon is useful for touching up nicks on most furniture. Just apply and rub in.

Nuts to scratches

Scratches on light-toned furniture can easily be repaired. Break the meat of a pecan or walnut in half and rub the broken edge over the scratch. The oil from the nut seeps into the raw wood, darkening it just enough to hide the defect. Rub the whole area with a soft clean cloth to blend the oil with the original finish.

Protecting your furniture

When buying upholstered furniture that does not come with arm covers, ask the salesman to order an extra yard of fabric and make your own. This saves on wear, lets you take them off for company, and gives you repair fabric if the upholstery is burned or torn.

Preserving wicker

Use your plant mister to moisten wicker items, especially furniture. This will keep the wicker from drying out and splitting.

Easy glue removal

To remove glue, especially from furniture, rub the article with a soft cloth dampened in white vinegar. For large amounts of glue, use an eyedropper and let the vinegar stand for about an hour.

Moving furniture

When moving furniture on good hardwood floors, slip a heavy wool sock over each leg. Your furniture will slide easily, and it won't scratch the floor.

Easy repair

To mend a slit in an upholstered chair or sofa, slip a strip of adhesive tape that is longer than the break under the tear. Gently pull the two sides together, then hold a warm iron against the mended spot until the fabric and tape adhere. Tiny slits or punctures in vinyl furniture can be repaired with self-adhesive rubber appliqués (the ones designed for bathtubs).

Removing rust stains

To remove stubborn rust spots from chrome chair and table legs, dampen a piece of rolled-up aluminum foil with water and rub over stains.

Pretty candle holders

Clay flowerpot saucers—especially the smaller ones—make great inexpensive candle holders.

Odds and ends

A good use for odds and ends of candles is to melt them down over low heat and add spices, such as a few whole cloves. Then pour into attractive molds with wicks and you have scented candles to use as air fresheners.

Making your own candles

Rather than buying special coloring agents for candle making, use old crayons. Just stir the crayon in with the melting wax until well mixed. You can also make your own wicks by braiding cotton string tightly, knotting the ends, and dipping it into your melted wax. Hang until cool and then snip into desired lengths.

Longer-burning candles

Candles will burn more slowly and evenly, with a minimum of wax drippings, if you place them in the freezer for several hours before using.

Protective coating

A coat of self-polishing wax on workshop tools will keep them free from rust and protect the cutting edges.

Handy work center

Need a workshop in a city apartment? Create one by converting a small utility closet into a handy work center. Racks on the inside of the door hold tools. Stack and label cans of paint on the floor, place containers of nails, screws, and other hardware and supplies on shelves. A light fixture provides the outlet for small power tools.

Handy tool kit

Don't throw away that old handbag with shoulder straps! Use it as a tool kit for a spare hammer, pliers, screwdriver, tape, and small jars of assorted nails and screws. The handy bag is great for quick repairs around the house and saves time and trips to the workbench hunting for tools.

Help for the handyman

When you or your husband buy new tools, put all the instruction booklets and guarantee certificates in a three-ring binder and keep it near the workbench. The instructions will come in handy when you run into difficulty or need some expert advice.

ENERGY SAVERS

Ceiling fans to save energy

Old-fashioned ceiling fans can be both decorative and nostalgic, but, most of all, they help save energy. In the winter they circulate the warm air that collects at ceiling level; in the summer they stir the air and provide a cooling breeze.

Setting the mood

Spend an occasional cold evening by the soft light of a kerosene lamp. With a quilt tucked cozily about the knees to keep you warm and a bowl of popcorn or juicy apples set out, the mood seems just right for storytelling. Very often television-age children can outdo grown-ups in the yarn-spinning department.

Heat saver

Bronze or aluminum paint may reduce the heat output of your radiators. Oil paint has no effect. Dark colors are the best heat emitters; light paint the poorest.

Keep warm and save energy

Keeping your house colder than usual will often bring moans of anguish when it is time to go to bed in the winter.(Bedrooms are often colder than any other place in the house.) Here is a solution that makes winter nights more comfortable, even in the face of fuel conservation. In the fall, put flannel sheets on the beds—at first, just the bottom sheet, then both top and bottom as the weather grows colder. And in the dead of winter, have a special flannel top sheet with flannel additions stitched onto the sides so that they hang down 18″ on either side of the bed. The extra length seals in body heat and converts the bed into a nice warm spot.

"Energy Chief"

Teach your children to take turns as "Energy Chief." The responsibility of the Energy Chief is to turn off all the lights in the house and garage that are not in use. During the cold months he or she makes certain all the windows and outside doors are closed, and at sundown, draws all the drapes and curtains. Children enjoy the honorable title and do a good job helping to conserve energy.

Turn off the lights

In an effort to cut down on ever-rising electric bills, find an incentive to make your children participate. Charge them 10¢ for the first time they leave the lights on and 25¢ for each time thereafter. It's amazing how quickly they learn. Compare each month's bill to the previous one and split the difference evenly between them as a dividend.

Double duty

During the winter put your boiler room heat to some additional use. Purchase a portable wooden clothes rack for little money and hang all wash in the boiler room to dry. Adding extra fabric softener helps to give clothing the softness needed. The money and time saved are great!

Keeping cool

Here is a brief run-down on ways to keep your cool and remain comfortable through the hot summer months.

1. Air conditioners

If possible, place air conditioners in windows where the sun does not shine on them. They will use less electricity to cool off a room. Also, turn off air conditioners when leaving your house or apartment for a long time. Set a timer for it to go back on 15 minutes before you return home.

2. Awnings

Covering windows with a western exposure can reduce heat gain up to 77%. Awnings that perform best are those with side panels. They can add a pleasant decorative look to the exterior of your house! A summer bonus: windows protected by awnings require less-frequent washing.

3. Patio protection

This is a smart move for sliding glass or French doors, which usually connect indoor rooms to a patio, terrace or deck. If the glass faces any direction but north, solar heat gain is a problem made greater by the size of the glass opening. Some form of cover for the patio will not only intercept the sun's hot rays, but produce a comfortable, enjoyable outdoor space. A patio cover will divert as much solar heat as an awning will.

4. Solar screening

Here's the perfect way to combine the bug-stopping function of a window screen with a heat blockade. The horizontal strands of the screen are angled to face the summer sun. About 75% of the solar heat is reflected from the window. This screening is sold framed and ready to hang, or as rolled mesh and unassembled frames.

5. Operating shutters

One style is an exterior rolldown metal shutter (really a cross between a shutter and an awning) that retracts into the wall when you don't need it. Slits in the metal panels allow some air and slim shafts of daylight to pass through. Aside from its sun-reflecting duties, this shutter makes a fairly decent security cover. Venetian blinds are also helpful—diverting heat-bearing sun rays back through window.

6. Solar film

This nifty product is easy to use, has the consistency of plastic wrap, and stops up to 75% of the sun's heat. It is sold by the square foot, and is tinted in shades of yellow or bronze. Some film is removable in winter to permit as much natural heat as possible.

7. Deciduous trees

Trees that lose their leaves every year are nature's near-perfect way of controlling heat from the sun. As the leaves fall in colder weather, more direct sunlight begins to stream through windows to complement your home's heat.

8. Low-energy aid

Whole-house attic fans are, for many families, a logical and inexpensive alternative to central air-conditioning. The concept is simple: during the heat of the day, keep windows closed and shades drawn on the sunny side of the house; during the cool of the evening and all night, keep windows open and the fan on. Hot air in the house is flushed out while you sleep; replaced by cool (or at least cooler) night air.

Handy nightlight

Since most trips to the bathroom at night are quick in-and-outs, why not turn on the nightlight and save the overhead for when it's really needed? You are bound to save on energy since there is quite a difference between the 7-watt bulb in the nightlight and the 150-watt bulb in the regular overhead fixture.

Keeping out drafts

Use masking tape to seal a drafty window during the winter. You can buy tape in a color to match your paint. It won't leave sticky marks on your woodwork when you peel it off later.

Turn-off

A dab of bright red nail polish applied to the off switch of an outdoor light can show you whether or not it is still burning in the daylight.

For quick shopping trips

Use your bike for short trips to the grocery store to save on fuel. Purchase two large lightweight plastic letter file boxes and attach one to each side of the rear fender carrier. Not only are they large enough to accommodate a bag of groceries, but they also have lids and locks so that nothing spills out when you hit a bump or make a sharp turn.

Water conservation

In an effort to limit showering time and thereby conserve water, start keeping a kitchen timer in the bathroom, set to ring after anywhere from 5 to 7 minutes. Children especially enjoy the challenge of getting in and out of the shower within the allotted time.

Leftover heat

After a roast is done, use the leftover heat in your turned-off oven to warm plates, serving bowls, and platters.

Money-saving get-together

Conserve energy by giving TV-watching parties at your house. Invite several friends and neighbors to watch major events, like the World

Series, Academy Awards, Presidential Inauguration, a special movie. Serve simple snacks. For sports events, each guest is provided with a scorecard. For award shows, each fills out a ballot upon arrival, and a door prize is given to the one who had the most accurate guesses. TV parties can be a special neighborhood event—especially if you rotate houses.

Be a smart shopper

Give gifts with year-round benefits. If you have appliances on your gift list, select long-lasting models that use the least amount of energy.

Here are some simple energy-saving tips to follow at laundry time:

1. Wash garments in the water temperature recommended by the clothing manufacturer. When you have a choice of two water temperatures, choose the cooler water setting and save on water-heating costs.

2. Wash only full laundry loads. Several small loads of laundry use more water and electricity than one big load.

3. Sort clothes according to amount and kind of soil, colorfastness, and type of fabric. A regular laundry load will need a full 10-minute wash cycle; lightly soiled items can be cleaned by a shorter wash cycle.

4. Pretreat extra-dirty spots on clothes with a commercial spot and soil remover. Spray it on extra-tough spots and stains, let set for 1 minute, and launder the item normally with the rest of the wash.

5. Use an all-temperature detergent.

6. Don't overdry laundry. Besides wasting electricity, over-drying wrinkles clothes.

7. Take full advantage of clear, warm days and hang your wet laundry outdoors to be air-dried.

8. Save on ironing, by folding clothes while they're still warm from the dryer. This is the time to "press" wrinkles out by hand.

Save when drying clothes

1. Remove clothes that will need ironing from the dryer while still damp. There's no point wasting energy to dry them thoroughly if they only have to be dampened again.

2. Keep the lint screen in the dryer clean. Remove lint after each load. Lint impedes the flow of air in the dryer and requires the machine to use more energy.

3. Keep the outside exhaust of your clothes dryer clean. Check it regularly. A clogged exhaust lengthens the drying time and increases the amount of energy used.

4. If your dryer has an automatic dry cycle, use it. Overdrying merely wastes energy.

5. Dry your clothes in consecutive loads. Stop-and-start drying uses more energy because a lot goes into warming the dryer up to the desired temperature each time you begin.

6. If possible, use a clothesline in warm weather to save energy. It's also great for rugs and other items that should not be in the dryer. And what a good excuse to be out on a nice day!

7. Separate drying loads into heavy and lightweight items. Since the lighter ones take less drying time, the dryer doesn't have to be on as long for these loads.

8. If drying the family wash takes more than one load, leave small, lightweight items until last. You may be able to dry them, with only the heat retained by the machine from earlier loads.

Save time and money

If your dishwasher does not have a "no dry" cycle, set a minute timer and turn it off when it comes to the dry cycle, since most energy is used during the heating cycle.

Cut down on water and energy

It is not necessary to use as much water for the wash cycle of a lightly soiled load of clothes as it is for the rinse cycle. During the wash cycle, set your machine for a lower water level than that of the rinse cycle, since thorough rinsing is very important. This not only helps to cut down on the amount of water used for each load, it also helps to cut down on the amount of detergent and energy used!

Kitchen energy savers

1. Use cold water rather than hot to operate your food disposer. This saves the energy needed to heat the water, is recommended for the appliance, and aids in getting rid of grease. Grease solidifies in cold water and can be ground up and washed away.

2. Install an aerator in your kitchen sink faucet. By reducing the amount of water in the flow, you use less hot water and save the energy that would have been required to heat it. The lower flow pressure is hardly noticeable.

3. If you need to purchase a gas oven or range, look for one with an automatic ignition system instead of a pilot light. You'll save an average of up to a third of your gas use.

4. If you have a gas stove, make sure the pilot light is burning efficiently—with a blue flame. A yellowish flame indicates an adjustment is needed.

5. Never boil water in an open pan. Water will come to a boil faster and take less energy in a kettle or covered pan.

6. Keep range-top burners and reflectors clean. They will reflect the heat better, and you will save energy.

7. Match the size of the pan to the heating element. More heat will get to the pan; less will be lost to surrounding air.

8. If you cook with electricity, get in the habit of turning off the burners several minutes before the allotted cooking time is up. The heating element will stay hot long enough to finish the cooking for you without using more electricity. The same principle applies to oven cooking.

9. When using the oven, make the most of the heat. Cook as many foods as you can at one time. Prepare dishes that can be stored or frozen for later use or make all oven-cooked meals.

10. Watch the clock or use a timer; don't keep opening the oven door to check food. Every time you open the door, heat escapes and your cooking takes more energy.

11. Use small electric pans or ovens for small meals rather than the kitchen range or oven. They use less energy.

12. Use pressure cookers and microwave ovens if you have them. They can save energy by reducing cooking time.

13. When cooking with a gas range-top burner, use moderate flame settings to conserve gas.

14. When you have a choice, use the range top rather than the oven.

Dishwashing energy savers

The average dishwasher uses 14 gallons of hot water per load. Use it energy-efficiently.

1. Be sure your dishwasher is full, but not overloaded, when you turn it on.

2. When buying a dishwasher, look for a model with air-power and/or overnight dry settings. These features automatically turn off the dishwasher after the rinse cycle. This can save you up to 10 % of your total dishwashing energy costs.

3. Don't use the "rinse hold" on your machine. It uses 3–7 gallons of hot water each time you use it.

4. Scrape dishes before loading them into the dishwasher so you won't have to rinse them. If they need rinsing, use cold water.

Refrigerator/freezer energy savers

1. Don't keep your refrigerator or freezer too cold. Recommended temperatures: 38°F–40°F for the fresh food compartment of the refrigerator; 5°F for the freezer section. (If you have a separate freezer for long-term storage, it should be kept at 0°F, however.)

2. When buying a refrigerator, it's energy economical to buy one with a power-saver switch. Most refrigerators have heating elements in their walls or doors to prevent "sweating" on the outside. In most climates, the heating element does not need to be working all the time.

3. Bigger isn't necessarily better. Don't buy a larger or more powerful piece of equipment than you need. Whether it's a furnace, air conditioner, or water heater, make sure its size and power are right for your home. Ask your dealer, a trade association, or a consumer-interest group for assistance in judging this factor.

4. Comparison shop when buying appliances. Compare energy use information and operating costs of similar models by the same company and different manufacturers.

HAND-ME-DOWNS

Hand-me-down logic

Seasons in and seasons out, the confusion of "hand-me-down" logistics is enough to keep mothers in a flurry. It would be helpful if children could grow in a more orderly fashion and not skip sizes, leaving gaps for you to fill in! Try these hand-me-down hints to solve some problems:

1. Certain seasonal garments, such as coats and snowsuits, corduroy outfits, and woolen sweaters, should be saved for the next child. These basic wardrobe components are usually worth keeping; thoroughly clean at the end of each season and store for the next go-round.

2. Proper laundering can be an important wardrobe saver, even of kids' everyday play clothes.

3. Turn old T-shirts into useful rags. Other garments in better shape can be given to charities that collect usable clothing.

Easy mark

Mark the clothes of the older child with a dot, those of the younger one with two dots. When clothes are handed down, you need only add another dot—no changing of name tapes or initials.

A "swap" party

With the price of clothing out of sight these days, you can save a bundle by organizing swap parties with friends about the same size as yourself. For example, that dress you seldom wear because it's the wrong color may look terrific on another woman; her too-small cashmere sweater may be just right for you, and so on. Set up some full-length mirrors (these can be borrowed), put on some records for "atmosphere," and serve some light snacks. You'll find these parties are not only a fun way to shop, but serve a useful purpose.

MONEY SAVERS

Money-saving idea

To reduce the high cost of gift wrap for birthdays and other occasions, cut the glossy gift wrap ribbon in half. Buy a roll which measures 24′x ¾″, and it only takes a few minutes to cut through it lengthwise. Besides making the ribbon go twice as far, the narrower ribbon can be more attractive, particularly for bows.

Thinking big saves $

Children love to eat raisins from the little boxes. Buy a large economy-size box and keep filling theirs from the big one. This makes quite a saving.

Free patterns

If you like to knit or crochet, save money by using your local library as a source of patterns. All libraries have hardcover how-to books which contain dozens of patterns. Find one you like, and copy it.

Free quilt squares

Looking for an inexpensive source of quilting materials? Discontinued wallpaper books often contain swatches of matching fabrics. Not only are these materials sturdy, but they offer a wide variety of patterns and colors. As an extra bonus, the edges are cut with pinking shears so there is no raveling. If you're a quilter, start checking your local paint and wallpaper stores for free discontinued books. Use your imagination to create a beautiful one-of-a-kind quilt.

Family snapshots on a shoestring

If your family, like many others, is spread out all over the country and you write each other frequently, sending snapshots of the latest grandchild, a daughter's prom date, or the new puppy can be expensive. Here is a simple and inexpensive way to solve the problem. When you get photos you like to share, take them to a copying center and run them off, one per page, and use the pages for writing letters. The cost of printing is less than photo reprints, and you have attractive, personalized stationery which is cheaper than notepaper.

Old into new

Instead of paying quite a bit of money for the latest look in shirts with lace trim on collar and cuffs, make your own! Lace trim can often be found in thrift shops or at garage sales. A few dollars' worth will go a long way!

Inexpensive car repairs

Next time you're in need of an auto mechanic, give your vocational high school a call. Students in eleventh- and twelfth-grade car repair classes are closely supervised and welcome cars to practice on to learn their trade. The cost of an honest repair on your car will be very low.

Saving tip

Scouring powder is often wasted because some containers have too many or too large holes. Cover half of the openings with a piece of adhesive tape, and you will find yourself using less powder at a time.

Saving for a rainy day

Saving for a rainy day does not come easy right now—but here is one small solution. Each time you use a cents-off coupon at the supermarket, put the amount saved in a piggy bank.

Have a free dinner

Save all the money refunded from coupons, and when the amount is large enough, take the whole family out to dinner. You'd be surprised at how fast the money adds up.

Correct return addresses

Whenever you send away for something, drop one of your address labels into the envelope. The company can stick it on the outside of the package, thus assuring that it will arrive at your address.

Saving for a winter's day

During the summer, when you are too busy canning from the garden to enjoy knitting, collect a great assortment of yarn at garage sales. You can sometimes get unused skeins for little money. When winter comes and evenings are free, it is fun to dig into the box of multicolored yarns and knit or crochet afghans and numerous other things at little cost.

"Entertainment fund"

If you are on a limited budget, try to set up an "entertainment fund." With it, pick up a few party "extras," when doing your regular weekly shopping. When you find recipes that use these extras, tape them on the boxes or containers. This way, when unexpected company arrives, you can easily whip up a snack.

Ways to help you set up a budget

1. To be aware of your financial pitfalls, you need to know how your money is being spent. To do this, for at least one week (one month would be better) keep a careful record of every cent your family spends, and you will get a pretty good idea of everyone's spending habits.

2. Determine how much you have to spend by totaling up your monthly take-home income. Figure it on a four-week basis. Extra income, like tax refunds, overtime pay, and the like, should not be included.

3. Determine your current fixed expenses for mortgage, rent, utilities, insurance payments, groceries, and so on.

4. Subtract these expenses from your income figure to find out how much you have left over for credit payments and cash purchases.

5. Keep careful records—simple, but accurate and complete. The secret to a good budget is to keep strict records since they enable you to find out how much you owe. It also helps in anticipating future expenses.

6. Use credit carefully! Do not use it for daily expenditures!

RECYCLING

Instant bookcase

Before discarding medium-sized bureaus, remove the drawers and paint and nail them together. They make two wonderful bookcases. No one can tell what they were originally!

Hang on to your drawers

Salvage sturdy drawers from desks or bureaus that are beyond repair. They can be used for under-the-bed storage, as children's toy or drawing supply boxes, or as an unusual kitchen counter rack for cookbooks. Paint or self-adhesive paper will transform the drawers into room brighteners, or the natural wood can simply be varnished for protection.

An old basket

Make an attractive magazine holder from a large, old-fashioned, metal egg basket. Spray-paint it to match your decor and stand rolled-up magazines in it.

Spare seating

Don't discard those loose cushions with your old sofa. Recovered, they make comforable floor pillows. They also provide firm back support while sitting up in bed reading or watching TV, and they store easily under the bed.

Recycling an old peppermill

When the grinding mechanism of your peppermill wears out, remove the top and use the mill as a candleholder. Tall mills with short fat candles can be set on the floor as decorative accents. Shorter mills, holding traditional tall candles, are appropriate for table use.

Old place mats

Recycle old place mats that are no longer presentable. You can use them to kneel on while you work in the flower garden, or as clean seat covers for a dirty picnic bench in the park.

Recycled coloring books

Cover pages of coloring and puzzle books with clear plastic adhesive, and let the children use water-base felt pens or grease pencils to color them. Just wipe the plastic, and the pictures and puzzles can be used over and over.

Second use

Don't throw away that old ironing board cover. Sew a pretty piece of material over one side and use as an insulated table runner to put hot dishes on.

Useful old wipers

Next time you have the windshield wipers on your car changed, save one of the old ones. It'll be handy for wiping away the condensation inside car windows.

Good use for a single glove

Keep single mittens and gloves after they've lost their mates handy in your car to use at self-service gas pumps. They keep your hand warm and odor-free. Also, keep an old apron in the trunk to use while pumping to prevent accidental gas spills or oil smudges.

Don't throw away old dress gloves. They make excellent gardening gloves—soft but protective.

Make good use of old magazines

Never throw away magazines after you have read them and clipped handy coupons, recipes, and ideas. Roll and stuff them into boots to help keep their shape in storage. Rolled magazines, secured with an elastic, are handy weights to use for exercises. Give magazines you have read to a local hospital or nursing home. Patients never have enough to read and really appreciate them.

Recycling plastic flowers

When you tire of that bouquet of plastic flowers, cut their stems and use the flowers to trim packages.

Quick reminder

If you have tried reusing fabric softener sheets in the clothes dryer but could never remember how many times you had used a particular sheet, here is an idea: Tear off a small corner each time you put the sheet in the dryer. Now you can tell at a glance how often it has been used.

Recycled stationery

Moving again, just after ordering 500 sheets of stationery imprinted with your name and address? Don't despair: recycle it! If you've purchased standard 8½″ x 11″ sheets, cut them in half cross-wise, using the bottom half (without the printing) for note paper. Cut the tops in half again and stack near the telephone for recording messages. Or send the uncut pages to school with your college student for typing first drafts of term papers. Small children can use up stacks for rainy-day drawing or folding projects.

Second use

Recycle empty potato chip cans into holders for 5-ounce paper cups for picnics. Once the plastic cover is on, the cups remain clean and uncrushed.

Unusual jam glasses

Before jam season arrives each year, begin to check thrift stores and garage and yard sales for unusual glasses, cups, goblets, or whatever. They are mostly one of a kind and reasonably priced, and they make great gifts.

Interesting dinner napkins

At the next "white sale," purchase fingertip towels and use them as napkins. For easy identification, buy each family member a different color. They're easy to launder and look pretty stored in a wicker basket.

Different planters

Don't throw away cups with cracks and chips. They make nice planters for small plants and look good on a kitchen windowsill.

Recycling the Sunday comics

Try using the Sunday comics for wrapping children's gifts. They make bright, colorful packages tied with any ribbon or leftover yarn. And when the gifts are opened, the paper doesn't get ripped up and thrown on the floor because the kids love reading the wrappings!

Salvaging old games

Do your children have games they never play with because parts of them are missing? Encourage your youngsters to recycle them by combining pieces from various games and making up a new one of their own. They can give it a new name, write directions, and teach it to friends. The resulting "new" game will provide not only many hours of fun but also important practice in writing and following directions.

Painted pulls

Wooden spools, when painted and decorated, make attractive drawer pulls.

Inside out!

When your daughter's tights become nubby and consequently unsightly, turn them inside out. Instantly, you have a new pair of tights. This mode gives double your money because there isn't a noticeable difference in appearance.

A new look

A dingy fire screen can be made to look like new if you follow these simple steps: First vacuum off the dust and scrub the screen with a sponge and suds to remove the soot. Let the screen dry, then brush on a coat of self-polishing floor wax.

Homemade toys

Save all empty wooden thread spools and let the children decorate them with bright nontoxic paints. They'll have fun building things, stringing them with yarn, or creating anything they may dream up.

For the artist in the house

Don't discard the plastic foam trays meat and other foods come packaged in. Wash them in warm sudsy water, rinse, and use as paint palettes.

Saving buttons and zippers

Recycle buttons and zippers. Before discarding worn or out-of-style clothing, check garments for reusable buttons, zippers, and even trim. Remove and save for sewing. It's a great money saver!

Leftover lace

Don't throw away the leftover lace from your sewing projects. Save it to use as mending material for the tops and straps of bras and slips. Your garments will not appear mended but will look pretty and new.

New life for used yarn

To clean and prepare yarn for reuse, pull a wire coat hanger into a square shape and wind the yarn around it. Then hold over steam from a pan of boiling water for several minutes. Let dry, and the yarn will be like new!

Instant laundry bag

Cafe curtains that you no longer use make colorful bags for laundry or toy storage. Simply stitch them together along the sides and bottom, and run a cord through the rings or casing at the top to make a closure.

Magazine holder

A discarded wooden doll cradle makes a delightful magazine holder. Paint or stain to match decor.

An old filing cabinet

Coats of high-gloss enamel paint will make an old metal filing cabinet pretty enough for any room in the house. The deep drawers are perfect for storing towels, bulky cleaning supplies, cookbooks, recipe clippings, or fabrics for future sewing projects.

Unique shelving

Large wooden apple crates purchased cheaply at a fruit and vegetable market make unique shelving for a child's room. They are sturdy, weathered, and they stack beautifully in any arrangement.

An old pipe rack

A discarded pipe rack makes an attractive, functional toothbrush holder. Since most of them have six or more receptacle holes, they're especially convenient for larger families. Also, you can paint the rack to match your decor.

Paper recycling

After you have read those slick gift catalogs, remove the staples and keep the pages near the sink for wrapping vegetable parings and other small items of garbage.

Old newspapers

Tying up old newspapers for recycling always was an awkward chore. Slip them into regular-size grocery bags. When they are filled, it is easy to tie a string around them and make neat bundles for pickups.

Many uses for worn-out panty hose

Don't discard old panty hose. They make strong ties for bundling up newspapers for recycling, for tying up twigs and branches, for securing tomato plants to stakes, and for closing up garbage bags when tie-tapes are lost. You can also save them for donation to a senior citizens' group or nursing home to be used for crafts projects.

New face for old Parsons table

One way to revamp an old Parsons table is to cover it with bright cotton material, using a good porous household glue. The material sticks to the plastic easily, and the whole project, including measuring the material needed, takes little time.

Use for old lampshades

Old, small lampshades make perfect hat stands in your clothes closet. Just refresh them with a coat of cheerful paint.

Don't throw away your soiled lampshades. Buy a package of foreign stamps or pictures of cars from a hobby store and paste them all over the shades. The children will love them.

31

Instant mailer

Save empty waxed-paper tubes to use as mailers for hard-to-wrap papers, pictures, and magazines.

Cover your seat

Discarded shower caps make rainy-day covers for bicycle seats.

Blackboard eraser

An old powder puff makes an excellent eraser for a child's blackboard. It works like a charm and is easily washed when soiled.

Small squeeze bottles

Lemon-shaped plastic squeeze containers are handy for so many things. Pry open the top and fill it with shampoo for your children to wash their hair in the shower; with vinegar and oil (in separate ones, of course) for salads; with hand lotion from larger-size economy bottles to keep by the kitchen sink; and with hair-setting lotion for easier application.

Pretty book covers

Remnants of cotton fabric from sewing projects make attractive covers for schoolbooks. They can be washed, starched, and ironed.

Handy container

Use a clear plastic toothbrush container to hold a pencil and ball point pen in your handbag. It's easy to find and will protect the lining from marks.

On rainy days...

The long narrow plastic bags that newspapers are delivered in are ideal for storing wet umbrellas while shopping or visiting. Just slip the umbrella into the bag and secure the top with a tie. No more worries about getting your clothes wet!

Renewing worn erasers

If pencil erasers have become too smooth to do their job, file them with an emery board and they'll be just like new.

Use for old shower curtains

Don't discard that old shower curtain. Use it to cover the outdoor furniture or grill when the weather is bad.

Another use for pie plates

Save empty disposable pie plates for the upcoming summer days. Use them at picnics, barbecues, or poolside. Less dishes to wash and more time to enjoy yourself. When finished, just toss them in the trash.

New use for old socks

Save old worn socks and use them to shine shoes or polish silver and jewelry. They will keep your hands clean and do a good job.

Cut the unworn section of a soft, old, cotton or wool sock to use as a replacement for the lambswool on a manual floor-wax applicator. After use, the sock can be discarded and replaced by its mate. No more dry, caked wax, and the replacements are free!

Good for a second use

Do not discard those clear-top blouse and sweater boxes. They make excellent containers for sending bakery goods to school or someone's house. The best part is you do not have to retrieve a pan or cake carrier after the doings.

Recycling film canisters

Empty 35mm film canisters make excellent containers for fishing or camping trips. They are waterproof and airtight so they will even float if accidentally dropped in water. Salt, sugar, oil, mustard, and other condiments will travel safely in them with no danger of leakage.

SELLING, BUYING, EXCHANGING

Great finds

A great and often overlooked source of unusual items for gifts or for the house are sales at local arts and crafts centers, and university art departments. Call to find out when sales are held, since there usually isn't much publicity. Most of the works, including pottery, weavings, copper enamelings, and paintings, are done by amateurs, which means you can find one-of-a-kind items at very low prices.

Fashions with a past

To help combat the inflated cost of clothing and still be individual and stylish, collect vintage clothing, starting from Victorian times through the 1950s. To find them, haunt estate sales, garage sales, and thrift shops. Moreover, "antique" clothes can be combined with today's fashion for a unique, high-fashion look.

Tips for garage sales

When planning a garage sale, make sure you include cool drinks and easy-to-make snacks (like popcorn) among the items for sale. Customers will appreciate a quick refreshment at a low price, and you'll increase your profits.

Spring means "out with the old and in with the new!" Dress up your garage sale! Make signs and suggest new ways an item might be utilized. For example: fabric and yarn remnants for crafts, broken appliances for hobbies. Coordinate clothing and spruce up with accessories. Merchandise that looks good and explains itself also sells itself!

To save time arranging a garage sale, try to organize it throughout the year. As the children outgrow clothes, toys, and other items, price each article immediately and put it in a large plastic storage bag. When it's time for the sale, everything is ready to be placed on tables.

Be a barterer

The ancient custom of bartering may be on its way back as an inflation fighter. Try to trade space in your freezer for fresh produce from a neighbor's garden, or two hours of yard work by a young person in exchange for some mending and a batch of homemade granola. The possibilities are endless, and no cash need ever change hands.

With so many successful yard and garage sales going on, why not have a "barter bargain." You and your neighbors can get together and exchange outgrown baby clothing, strollers, and high chairs for tricycles, wagons, and clothing, for older children. Or, you can confine your barter to kitchen supplies, clothing or furniture. You may even be able to acquire some of those houseplants from your "green thumb" friends.

Give them your best

When you are expected to give something to be auctioned or sold for fund raising, why not give a service instead of some expensive item? You could offer baby-sitting services for an entire weekend, baked goods of the buyer's choice, mending or yard clean-up for a month. Donate something you enjoy doing and do well. Perhaps you have an interesting hobby and could give some basic instruction to the highest bidder—flying lessons, for instance, or a class in poodle grooming, macramé, or horseback riding.

Really showing it off

Look for "going out of business" or "moving to new quarters" sales to snap up bargains on display cases, especially those from older "mom and pop" stores. These sturdy and well-made glass cases make ideal havens for collections, such as shells, dolls, and old trains.

Book exchange

With the high cost of paperback books these days, keep those you have read in a basket and urge friends to help themselves. Net result: Everyone makes an extra effort to reciprocate, which increases your reading supply, at no extra cost.

Book and record swap

To save money, hold a record and paperback swap in your neighborhood. Everyone trades books and albums they are through reading or listening to. Presto—a new selection for everyone without spending a penny!

AND 36 MORE WAYS TO SAVE

Thrifty wrap

For an inexpensive gift wrap, use plain tissue paper decorated with sewing odds and ends or appropriate pictures cut from magazines. For a child's gift, for example, make a clown face with buttons and rick rack.

Double-duty gift wrap

When wrapping a large gift for an infant, use yards of flannel with an attractive and cute design. Later, the young mother can use the material to sew clothes for the new baby.

Rubber glove saver

A little cotton stuffed into rubber glove fingertips will prevent long fingernails from puncturing them.

Preserving your handbags

Apply colorless nail polish to the metal trimmings of your purse. It will keep them from tarnishing.

Saving shoelaces

When shoelace ends get frayed and hard to lace, try this: Twist the ends tightly (you may dampen them a bit), dip them into clear nail polish, and let dry. Your laces will be like new again.

Many uses for wallpaper

Rolls of discontinued wallpaper make excellent shelf paper. The plastic coating is easy to wipe clean, and the heavy quality provides long-term use. Use pretty patterns in linen closets and bathroom vanities and leftover scraps for covering wastebaskets and flowerpots.

For gifts—it makes unusual and inexpensive wrapping paper, and the prepasted kind can be used to brighten up and change the look of window shades. As coloring books—choose several black-and-white patterns to satisfy the most ambitious child's coloring urge.

Free bulletin board

Free and attractive bulletin boards can be made from one or several carpet samples tacked or nailed to the wall. Most come in a 2′ x 2′ size and are bonded on the edges. The size is just right for notes, bills, and phone messages.

Many uses for carpet tiles

Stick-on carpet tiles can be used in several ways. Cover a kitchen door with them, making it into a handy bulletin board. On the wall near the sewing machine, one tile makes a great pin cushion. Or use several together and you have a place for tacking up patterns, swatches, and notions.

Using every bit of it

Party paper tablecloths too long for your table? Trim off the extended piece and cut it up into matching placemats, or use it as a cover for a small table. Or, give it to a child for cutting or playing.

Magazine storage

Spray or paint a sturdy beer or liquor carton that has cardboard dividers. Use as a receptacle for rolled up magazines or newspapers.

Protecting a dictionary

Put a piece of adhesive tape over the letter tabs of a dictionary. This will protect the print and reinforce the thin tabs.

Small gifts

Save the trinkets from cereal boxes. Also send for any free toys offered for box tops and proof-of-purchase labels. They make excellent stocking stuffers for Christmas or small prizes at birthday parties.

Emergency vaporizer

If you need a vaporizer but don't have one, use your electric skillet. Fill it with water, set the temperature at "low" (250°), and place on the floor near the patient's bed. Refill with water about every 8 hours.

No more sticky tops

When opening a bottle of glue, rub a little cooking oil over the grooves. It keeps the top from sticking.

File for magazines

Referring back to an article in a favorite magazine is simplified if you remove the contents page and file it in a loose-leaf notebook tabbed for the different types of magazines.

Banish odors

Make your own home deodorizer to rid rooms of stale tobacco smoke. Mix a little diluted ammonia in a bowl of fresh water and let stand overnight in the offending room. Try this in your closets as well.

A key for your toothpaste

An old-fashioned slip-on clothespin or a giant cotter pin makes an ideal "key" for rolling up a tube of toothpaste. Nothing fancy about the idea... but it sure helps you squeeze every bit of paste out of the tube.

Easy identification

When shopping at a large department store, affix a self-stick name and address label to each package. If you lose something, it can easily be identified and, one hopes, returned.

No waste

A lot of paste shoe polish is wasted because it gets into the corners or dries out. Consolidate the old bits of the same color into one container. Place in a pan and heat slowly. The pieces will melt together, and you can use almost every bit.

An old pen

Sometimes ball point pens clog at the tip. Before throwing them away, try heating the tip for a few seconds. This often restores the flow of the ink.

Saving on soap

Save used-up bars of soap for the athletes in your house. Let each piece dry out and cover it with plastic wrap. Anyone who needs soap for public showers can grab one of these. If they get left behind—no great loss!

Storing unwrapped bath soap on shelves in your linen and clothes closets will not only make clothes and linens smell good but will add to the life of the soap by drying it out.

When hand soap becomes too small to use comfortably, save the pieces until you have accumulated a dozen or so. Center them between two colorful washcloths and stitch around all four outside edges. Without much effort, you have a "soapcloth" that will not slip out of children's hands, lathers easily, and is fun to use. Or: Tie them up in a piece of nylon net and make an inexpensive "loofah" body sponge.

Keep a plastic squeeze bottle half filled with water in the bathroom. When small pieces of soap are dropped into the bottle from time to time, the resulting soap jelly makes a pleasant hand soap.

Or: Place a pint jar with ½ cup of water in the bathroom and put all scraps of bath and hand soap in it. When the jar is full, run the contents through the food processor for 30 seconds, pour the resulting "cream" into a pump-type plastic bottle, and have a constant supply of "free" hand soap. A thorough rinsing in hot water removes all traces of soap from the processor.

Liquid soap is nice to use but too costly when you have several little pairs of hands that need washing every half-hour or so. Take an empty plastic hand lotion container (with a pump on top), fill it ¼ full with liquid dishwashing detergent and the rest of the way with water. The kids love using their "liquid soap," and it costs just pennies to make.

Keeping track

When you order items through the mail, write the address on the back of the check before sending. You will have the canceled check and the address in case you do not receive the merchandise or are dissatisfied with it. Certainly saves confusion later on.

Income tax

Whenever you write a check that eventually will be used in filing your income tax, mark with a red "T." When the check is returned from the bank, it will be easier to spot and can be filed separately.

Valuable protection

If you are a working couple, you should catalog all of your household items for insurance purposes. To save time on the project, make a cassette recording listing the items in your home, the date purchased, and their value. Keep the recording at work to prevent its being destroyed or misplaced at home. If the information is ever needed, you can transcribe it.

Speedy replacement

Did you ever have to replace lost or stolen credit cards, bank books, driver's license, and the like? Where do you start? A good solution to this problem is to make copies of them. Many neighborhood drug stores and most libraries have coin-operated copying machines. Jot down the address or phone number of each card company on the back of the copy in case you need to notify them.

Handy reference file

Keep a file of the instruction booklets that come with your appliances, including major ones like your refrigerator and minor ones such as your hand mixer. The day will come when the inevitable breakdown occurs. A few extra moments when you make the purchase may save you hours when service is necessary. Write the following information in the manual: date of purchase, store name, service data, check number, and amount paid. If a problem arises, it takes only a minute to determine whether or not the item is still under warranty and where to call for service.

Time checks

If you conduct a lot of business by mail—like paying bills, sending for free offers, or ordering merchandise, enter each transaction on a large wall calendar in the kitchen and check it periodically. This is especially helpful in verifying a payment that may have gotten lost, or if too much time has elapsed since placing an order.

Savings trick

When finished paying off a loan, keep on making payments—to your savings account.

Health book

Keep a health book for each member of your family with each illness, accident, and doctor's visit and the date, treatment, medication, and doctor's instructions. Clip a 3″ x 5″ card to the cover to each booklet with important information, such as allergies to medication and date of last tetanus shot. A quick glance at the book will make you well prepared when you pay a visit to the doctor.

Important documents

When a child leaves home for college or a job or to get married, give him a list of all his vaccinations, X rays, childhood illnesses, and the like. This information can come in very handy if medical attention is ever needed.

Two

272 Ideas For and About Kids

CHILDREN AND PLAY,
KEEPING BOREDOM AT BAY

I'm bored, Mom

To chase away those rainy-day blues, put together an ideas notebook. Collect simple projects and recipes found in magazines and newspapers. Then when you hear, "I'm bored, Mom," bring out the notebook and help your child pick a project: sandpaper prints, homemade play dough or fingerpaints, a salt garden, no-bake cookies.

Children need not be bored on rainy days if they have a "little city." Make the little city from every kind of cardboard box you can find, from cereal to shoe to ring boxes, painting them to look like different buildings. The children have hours of fun as they set them up, rearrange them, drive toy cars through the "streets." When the day is over the boxes get stacked inside each other and put away in a closet for the next rainy day.

On rainy days keep children busy filling jars with rainwater, which can be stored in the garage. The pure water is a most welcome treat for houseplants!

Next time your curious children find themselves at loose ends indoors, suggest making a book. Have them cut out pictures from old magazines of people, pets, flowers, houses, or whatever strikes their imaginations. Paste cut-outs on plain paper, staple them together to form a book, and have the children make up a story to fit the illustrations.

Children's mini garage sale

Children fascinated by community yard sales can have their own. Under guidance, the children set up their own sale. For days ahead they can busy themselves selecting salable but no longer used items, putting on price tags, and arranging everything on tables and benches. The sale is great fun, and they even gain experience at bargaining, deciding whether to accept a lower offer or stick to their original asking price. As they tally their receipts they may well chorus: "May we have another one next year?"

44

Children's flea market

During the summer, hold a flea market where children of all ages can sell and buy old toys and books. It's a great way to get rid of toys they have outgrown and at the same time get some new ones for a fraction of what they would cost new.

To earn extra money, have your children collect old newspapers from neighbors and take them to the local paper-recycling plant. Teaches them responsibility as well as giving them a little money incentive.

A "dress-up center" for your child

Save some of your old clothes and give them to your children for a "dress-up center." Dressing up and putting on either dramatic or comic plays will give them a chance to express themselves. Take time out to listen to the conversations that take place as your children assume different roles.

Keeping baby busy

Keeping a toddler busy while you prepare food in the kitchen can be tricky. To let the child explore the kitchen, store your unbreakable kitchenware in a low cupboard you leave open. Fasten the cupboards holding more delicate items and relax as your child happily plays while you cook.

8 ways to keep kids cool

1. Dress children in light colors. Cool cotton breathes and will keep them cooler than synthetics.

2. Allow kids to go barefoot. Contrary to popular wisdom, it will not hurt developing feet. When going barefoot is not appropriate or safe, canvas shoes or sandals should be worn with cotton socks.

3. Balance rest time with play time to keep kids from getting cranky. A quiet period of half an hour spent resting, reading, coloring, or listening to music can be very relaxing.

4. Encourage children to drink fluids in hot weather. They can be taken as fruit juice, plain water, or even ice cubes (often considered a great treat by children).

5. Use powder or cornstarch to avoid chafing or rashes.

6. Periodic sponge baths can be a treat if scented with mint leaves.

7. Playing with plastic water pistols can cool off a summer sizzle.

8. Hire the kids to defrost the refrigerator, wash the dog or car, or water the lawn. They'll get a little wet, but clothes can easily be changed.

Tape a tale

Does your preschooler have some favorite books he likes to have read to him again and again? Record them on tape cassettes, ringing a little bell to signal the turn of a page. Then, no matter how busy Mom is, he can listen to a story. This would also make a nice surprise for a child when Mom has a hospital stay or is going on a trip and cannot be there in person.

Bowling set for little ones

Small, empty juice cans or 8-ounce plastic bottles make great bowling pins for little ones. Paint each can a different color and have the children use a soft rubber ball as a bowling ball. Or use empty potato chip cylinders as bowling pins for an impromptu indoor game. Use a tennis ball as a bowling ball.

Make good use of spare time

With spare time hard to come by for most women, put the time spent at the laundromat to good use by reading storybooks to children. It surely helps the time pass more quickly for everyone.

Precious weekend sleep

Sleeping a little longer on weekends and holidays is a treat often disturbed by children's early awakening. To keep a two-year-old in bed and content a little longer in the mornings, try placing favorite books at the foot of the sleeping child's bed. In the morning he will spend quite some time "reading" while you get that much-appreciated extra sleep.

Ballet bar for children

A tension rod fitted properly into a doorway is a neat ballet bar for children to practice on. It can be fitted to a child's height and can also be easily removed.

For young artists

When young children begin using crayons, make an indestructible magic carpet by bringing out an old fringed vinyl tablecloth, spreading it on the floor, and letting them do their drawing and coloring on it. Before too long they will understand that anything messy—paste, paint, color—is done on the "magic carpet." The cloth is easily washed.

Chalkboards can be a great help when children are young and love to draw on walls. They can be made simply and cheaply to any size. Take a piece of wood, rough it up a little with sandpaper, and paint it with chalkboard paint.

A window shade makes an excellent floor cover when children are playing on a carpet. It keeps small puzzle pieces, beads, crayons, and the like from getting lost in the shag, as well as keeping the rug from getting soiled. When not in use, it can be rolled up and stored in a corner or under a bed.

Children love lots of room to draw on. Create a "scribble wall" by attaching a sheet of plastic to a wall in their room. Buy them a set of water-soluble markers—they are nontoxic and wipe off easily with a damp cloth.

Let young children draw on and decorate empty grocery bags destined to be used as garbage bags. It gives them a lot of paper to scribble on as well as the satisfying feeling that they're making something pretty that Mommy can use.

Mail for the little ones

Everyone loves to receive mail—and children are no exception. Recycle unwanted "junk" mail by giving the letters to preschoolers. They are delighted with what is a nuisance to parents, and after they are through scribbling on it and tearing it into pieces, this free toy goes right into the trash—until the mailman replaces it the next day.

Timing their visits

When your children's friends come to visit, set your kitchen timer, just in case you get busy and forget to send them on their way. When the buzzer sounds they know that playtime is over, and home they go. This helps to cut down protests and keeps other mothers happy.

TV game

To make TV watching time a little more educational, make it a game. Make up a list of categories such as food, sports, and songs, and set a time limit. Also have the children look for examples from each category in the show they watch. At the end of the time, the child with the most examples wins.

Protect your furniture

Little boys playing with toy trucks and cars often can't avoid running them into furniture and scarring it. You can easily prevent this by gluing strips of soft sponge across the toys' bumpers.

Baby sitter's cornucopia

Garage sales are a great place to find inexpensive toys or junk jewelry to create a "baby-sitting box." When you baby-sit bring found treasures—the children will love them! It also makes the job more fun.

Establish rules

Establish rules for indoor play and cleaning up before friends go home. A sitter should know the rules and reinforce them by stepping in and saying, "Okay, kids, it's almost time for Joey to go home, so better start cleaning up now."

Simple bed tables

Children confined to bed need tables to play on. A simple method for making one is to take a cardboard box, remove the flaps, and cut semicircles from the open edge in, to fit over the child's legs. Paint or cover it with brightly colored paper, if desired.

Another even simpler method for slightly older children is to use a jelly roll pan with its small rim. The edge will keep things like crayons from falling off.

Easy reminder for children

Instead of changing your children's curfew to suit lengthening and waning hours of sunlight throughout the year, simply tell them to come home when the street lights go on. Even those too young to tell time can handle this, and as streets are lit at dusk, they can be safely home before it's really dark.

In and out on their own

To make it easier for your toddler to get back into the house from the yard, put an extra handle on your screen door—down low where it's easy to reach. An extra kitchen cupboard handle works well, as does a large wooden thread spool.

Keeping the yard tidy

To keep the yard tidy each summer while the children are home on vacation, paint bright-colored flowers on two old 5-gallon trash cans and place them at each corner of the yard. Have the kids use them for soda cans, candy wrappers, and other litter.

Use a plastic garbage can with snap-on lock lid as a waterproof toy container in the play yard.

Clean swimming pools

The water in children's wading pools easily fills with grass from their getting in and out. Take a small plastic bathtub they have outgrown, fill it with water, and have them step into it before entering the pool. This rinses their feet and keeps the pool much cleaner.

Children's picnic

Let your children invite their friends to a picnic in the backyard. Every youngster brings his own lunch and you supply the refreshments, blankets to sit on, and games to play.

Pails and buckets

Colorful pails and buckets can be made from empty bleach jugs and some bulky yarn. After slicing off the top of the jug with a razor blade, use a hole puncher to make holes around the rim, spaced about ½" apart. Crochet a 1" band around the rim on the first row, pulling the yarn through the holes to the outside. On the last two stitches of the band, continue crocheting until you have an 8" strip. Connect this to the other side for a handle.

An even simpler method is to cut the top off a gallon-size plastic bleach bottle, make two holes opposite each other near the top, and run a piece of plastic clothesline through them for a handle. Use nail polish to write the name of each child on his or her pail.

Extra garden boost

Every beach vacation seems to end with a bag of homeless and unexceptional shells. Instead of throwing them away, let the kids break them up and then add to the garden to enrich the soil.

Easy beanbags

A child of four can help make the all-important beanbag. Take an old sock and let the child pour in the filling through a funnel. By age four the child can probably sew a simple running stitch to close the top.

Children's beanbags are easier for youngsters to handle when rice is used for the filling instead of beans.

Corky people

Save all kinds of corks from bottles to make dolls. Paint on faces and clothes, if you wish. They make super "people" for children to play with.

Instant playhouse

A cheap and easy indoor playhouse can be made from a large cardboard box. Just turn the box upside down and cut out holes for doors and windows. If you really want to get fancy, paint it like a house. Perhaps the best part is that children can help make the house or handle most of the work themselves.

READING, WRITING, RESPONSIBILITY

Summer school

Realizing that during the summer children's academic skills often take a dive, you can hold your own summer school. Each weekday, set aside an hour and gather the children to do simple math computation or spelling in individual workbooks. Following that, storytime. Older children can take turns reading favorite stories out loud to younger ones. Each week give them a "report card" which reflects their effort and achievement.

Birthday book program

Here is an idea for a "birthday book program." This is a voluntary activity whereby the child *gives* a book to the library for his or her birthday. It is an excellent way for a school to add to its collection and also encourages children's interest in the library. If parents wish to donate a book as well, the librarian can make a list of title suggestions. A special bookplate can also be put in the front of the book with the child's name and birth date.

Good reading on a shoestring

The prices of children's books can be prohibitively high if your children love to read. One way to combat it while still providing a thrill is to reserve special books at the library. Check the card catalog, make out the required postal cards, and watch your child's face light up when a postcard arrives in the mail for her or him alone.

Fun practice

Need a fun way for your children to practice reading or spelling, or reviewing math at home? Purchase some magnet-backed plastic letters and numbers, which are available at most variety stores. Place them on a refrigerator door where children can work with the pieces while you are busy in the kitchen. The letters are large and easy to read, so a parent can keep track of most activities and glance across the room to give the needed correction or praise.

Encouraging your child to read

One way to encourage children to enjoy reading is to couple it with a privilege such as staying up a little later. You can tell them that at bedtime they can leave the lights on an extra amount of time and read in bed. If they don't want to read, fine, but lights go out at the usual time.

Improving reading habits

Many schools participate in book clubs which encourage children to read. However, some children have a zeal for buying books which outweighs their desire to read them. One policy that works well to encourage reading but combats indiscriminate buying is to require children to buy the books from savings or allowance, and then you buy the book back at cost once it is read. This requires children to select purchases carefully as well as to think through all purchases to see if money is being spent wisely. Don't be surprised if your child reads more!

Bedtime stories

Who said bedtime stories had to be the same old book? Adventurous children might enjoy having magazines read to them. Some young children even enjoy mail order catalogs.

Another way to vary children's learning or bedtime stories is to let them help out with the story. Begin by thinly veiling their own identities and begin a story that leads them into telling you their own day's activities or imaginative lives.

Next bedtime, try using an atlas to tell stories. You can either make up characters who move from city to city and country to country, or use stories the children already know, or you can simply talk about history and geography.

Working parents who get home late in the evening sometimes have difficulty getting young children into bed at a reasonable hour without a fight. If you've done almost everything imaginable, try using a small cassette player in the room and let it "play" them to sleep. Make tapes of some of their favorite songs and nursery rhymes and some with Mommy and Daddy reading bedtime stories. Within the 15 minutes it takes to play one side of the tape, the children will probably be sound asleep without frustration on anyone's part.

A family approach to better writing

Here is an idea for a big family project: Start a newspaper. Assign the children as reporters while parents act as editor and production manager. Also, designate one child salesman and another staff artist. Set aside specific times at regular intervals to write short news paragraphs. Youngsters can report on foreign, domestic, and local events as well as adding an occasional crossword puzzle or poem. Take the copy-ready paper to a quick-copy shop for printing. Mail copies to relatives or deliver to neighborhood subscribers.

Now you tell me your story!

Parents who make up bedtime stories with their children might like to keep a record. Over the years, write down some of the choicest yarns—when the children are older they will enjoy rereading their early creative efforts. These tales may never win any prizes, but they may get youngsters interested in creative writing—and you'll always cherish that very special time spent together.

Daddy's world

Children eagerly await Daddy's evening arrival. Here's a good way to help make them feel involved in Dad's other world. Have Daddy take one of the children's toys to work one day. When he arrives home he can tell the tale of the toy's visit to the office.

When parents travel

Young children often don't understand that a parent who goes away on a trip will come back. To help them feel secure, get out road maps and atlases well ahead of your departure and show them exactly where you will be and how you will get there. Mark the route on a map and hang it up for them to see where you are when you're gone.

Another way to make them feel secure is to leave them something of yours to take care of while you're away. Choose something your child particularly likes.

Pictures of the baby

To help an older sibling adjust to a new baby, present brother or sister with a set of pictures of the baby all his own.

Bridging the gap

Is your child upset about a playmate's moving away? An inexpensive "pen pal" kit composed of pretty stationery or self-addressed, stamped postcards can bridge the gap. Your child learns about a new place through his friend's eyes. In addition, both children sharpen their writing skills and learn that distance needn't mean the end of a friendship.

Children's correspondence

To encourage children to write letters and thank-you notes, have some return address labels printed with their names, and give them each several stamps and a box of inexpensive stationery. It works, and it's good practice in grammar and etiquette.

Making shopping a game

Grocery shopping with an active four-year-old can be a harrowing experience. When a child is playing catch with the fruit and knocking over the displays, even the most patient mother finishes her shopping with a sigh of relief after realizing that she doesn't have to pay for half of the store. Try accepting this traditional childish reaction to the supermarket as a challenge by making shopping a game for an inquisitive child. As you enter the store, carefully give him one coupon at a time and guide him in the direction of the proper aisle. This allows Mom to shop more freely and makes him feel part of the whole trip.

Helping your child to grow

Teaching a child how to use the telephone properly is a very good way to help him or her gain self-confidence and independence. Beginning in their preteen years, let children make their own medical and personal appointments by phone. Visits to the doctor or dentist become easier, too, when the child has made some of the decisions, such as time and day of the appointment.

Teaching your children neatness

One way to teach children neatness is to appeal to their monetary sense. Each day as you pick up after them, keep the items recovered. Don't return anything for a specified time, say a month, unless they pay a penny apiece for the items in hock. Sometimes the article is hardly missed, but if it is a left tennis shoe, it will be worth the penny.

Time instead of money

Rather than use money as a reward to persuade children to help with the housework, tell them that if the work is done promptly, the whole family will have time to play games. The children learn to work together on household tasks, and everyone enjoys each other's company afterward.

Cleaner playground

If your apartment house playground is repeatedly littered with wrappers and soda cans, gather tenants' youngsters for an old-fashioned cleanup. The child who collects the most receives a prize—such as a bag of homemade popcorn. The children have a lot of fun, and it is a good lesson in not littering.

Children's garden

The planning and planting of a backyard vegetable garden is a project for the entire family. However, a three-year-old or a four-year-old can often be more nuisance than help in the actual planting. To solve this predicament, give smaller children a plot of their own and all the leftover seeds in each packet. They plant as you plant, and the wild abandon of their garden as it grows is often the most surprising and beautiful part of the project.

Preserving wild flowers

During the summer, have a "wild flower day" with your children. Let them gather small flowers, ferns, and other small plants, then press them in heavy books. During the winter they will have a supply for making Christmas cards (ferns make fine evergreen trees), candles, and other crafts projects.

The kids can do it

Here is a family project for the adventurous with teenage children. Turn the finances for the next family vacation over to the kids. Let the whole family decide where to go and what to do. Then give the kids the budgeted amount of money for the entire trip. Their job is to run the vacation within the budget.

Business cards for teenagers

If you have a teenager looking for neighborhood jobs, try having business cards printed. Cards listing services can really bring responses.

---

10 ways to help make your home safe for children

1. Check to make sure slats in baby's crib are no more than 2½″ apart.

2. Do not use plastic sheeting on baby padding.

3. Make sure all toys are too big to fit in an infant's mouth.

4. Install folding gates at the top and bottom of each staircase.

5. Seal off unused electrical outlets with safety guards secured with tape.

6. Guard all space heaters, fireplaces, woodstoves, and furnaces with safety barriers.

7. Keep all cleaning products and medications out of reach of young children.

8. Install safety catches on medicine and kitchen cabinets.

9. Take off the doors of large appliances when discarding them.

10. Do not use power tools or equipment near young children.

Emergency telephone numbers

Make sure children know all the emergency telephone numbers. Hang a chart near the phone with the numbers listed and a picture representing each: a fire engine next to the one for the fire department, grandparents' picture next to theirs, and so on.

A "What if" list

Often a child does not know what to do in an emergency. Type up a list of emergencies that could possibly arise and paste it inside your child's school bag. The list of "what ifs" includes telephone numbers which the child may know but might forget at the time, instructions not to give your address to strangers, only to tell them to call parents at the office. Should the emergency take place while parents cannot be reached, include instructions for calling Grandma or someone who may be a homemaker and could help out.

Safety whistle

When camping, put a dime-store whistle on a string around the neck of every child in the group. They can blow them if they run into difficulty or if they get separated from the group.

Child's ice pack

Here is an idea for child-size ice packs: wet and freeze cut up sponges. Having their own size packs takes some of the hurt out of minor bumps and bruises, and they save on messy cleanup, too.

Safety swings

Tack a rubber stair tread to the seat of your children's outdoor swing. The tread protects the youngsters from splinters, shields the board from rain, and will help prevent children accidentally sliding off and hurting themselves.

Another way to keep children from sliding off a swing seat is to affix rubber flower decals to the seat.

Easing the pain

When your small child gets a cut or bruise, draw a funny design on the adhesive bandage with a brightly colored felt marker. It will quickly help turn tears into smiles.

11-point checklist when calling your pediatrician

Before you call, note on paper:

1. Your child's temperature.

2. Your child's symptoms and how long the child has had them.

3. What and how much medication or first aid you have already given your child.

4. If your child has been exposed to contagious illnesses in the last few days.

5. The name and phone number of the pharmacy you use.

When you call:

6. If the doctor is not in, leave a brief but clear message.

7. Take down the doctor's instructions and read them back.

8. Ask if there are any other measures you should take.

9. Ask when you should call again or bring the child in to the office or hospital.

10. Ask what changes you should look for, and when.

11. Make sure you know where to pick up a prescription if the doctor prescribes one.

KIDS IN THE KITCHEN

Children planning meals

Try this idea for teaching responsibility and basic cooking skills: Cook for a Day. During their summer vacation, each child is assigned one day each week when he or she plans and prepares the noonday or evening meal for the whole family. Give guidance in selecting something from each of the four basic food groups and help in using electric appliances. It's a way of learning the basics of nutrition and simple cooking methods and enjoying the benefits of a job well done and the appreciation of other family members. The children are also eager helpers when Mom or Dad prepares meals.

Want to teach teenage children about family meal planning and food budgeting? One week of each month, for a few months, give them the grocery allotment with the understanding that they have to plan, purchase, and prepare the meals. Include the usual snacks, and give them anything left in the grocery money "pot" to spend as they please.

Busy moms with children from age 9 on might like to consider portioning responsibility for evening meals. Let the children choose which nights they would like to cook and let them go. Make sure they serve nutritionally balanced meals but let them make what they like. Special family meals may well become more elaborate as the proud cooks gain experience.

Wholesome snacks

Here is a way to get teenagers to eat more wholesome after-school snacks. Keep a variety of their favorite dried fruits, nuts, and granola mixture in matching clear glass jars on the kitchen counter. Place a bowl of fresh fruit in season nearby. Occasionally set out a special treat like a bowl of fresh strawberries or kiwi fruit. The display will be so tempting to young palates that kids will never go near the refrigerator—and dinner preparations are safe.

Summer treats

For a nutritious summertime treat, make popsicles from favorite pure fruit juices. For economy, dilute the juice with a little water. You can purchase popsicle molds at most grocery and variety stores during the summer. But make them during the winter months, too, for they are a great way to give important liquids to your children when they have colds or flu.

Toddler's treat

Try this as a hot weather refresher for a small child: Top a small scoop of ice cream with junior food apricots, pears, pineapple, or prunes.

Snowcones

Snow in the summer is one of the most exciting things for kids. Plan ahead if you have a large freezer with extra room by saving some of winter's fresh snow lightly packed in an empty milk carton. Come summer, you can make snowballs or snowcones by dribbling a little syrup over individual portions.

For fussy eaters

To stimulate a two-year-old's appetite, use cookie cutters to make fancy shapes out of cold cuts and cheeses. Children love eating "bologna clowns" or "cheese hearts." The scraps can be combined for other decorations.

"Small fry" hamburgers

Hamburgers are a real favorite with kids. But, with the buns just too big for toddlers to handle, parents throw away half-eaten meals. Solve this problem by using a round cookie cutter and making "child-size" hamburger buns out of the heels of a regular loaf of bread. The children can handle these smaller hamburgers easily, and it cuts down on waste.

Safety Rules for Kids Who Cook

1. Supervise cooking. Never leave the room while the stove or oven is lit. Always light the oven or stove yourself.

2. Avoid using any recipes which could easily cause a bad burn. Stay away from those that use hot grease or boiling syrups.

3. Back a sturdy chair up to the stove so your small child can stand high enough yet still have something to hold on to for balance.

4. Make sure neither you nor your children have dangling hair or articles of clothing which might catch fire or get caught in appliances.

5. Make sure children hold pot handles while stirring to keep both their balance and the pot's.

6. Keep pot handles turned toward the back of the stove while not being stirred to avoid anyone catching them accidentally.

7. Have children stir hot dishes with wooden or insulated tools.

Milk goblet

If you have a child who won't drink milk and have tried fancy straws and cups and flavoring the milk, try appealing to the child's sophistication: Pour milk into a wineglass like Mom's and Dad's.

Sugar shaker

To avoid spills and waste, fill a large kitchen salt shaker with sugar (label it!) and let the children use it to sweeten their cereal.

Jelly squeeze

Fill a plastic squeeze bottle with jelly, snipping the bottle's spout to make the hole larger. Children can fix their own jelly sandwiches without getting the table and themselves sticky.

Easier summer for Mom

Summer can be a hectic time for mothers. Older children may have jobs, younger ones may sleep late. One dawdles over breakfast while another is ready for lunch. The kitchen is a perpetual mess, and Mom yearns for a little routine. Solve the summer noontime hassle by making bag lunches early in the morning, tagging them for each child, and storing them in the refrigerator with pitchers of lemonade and milk. Children eat lunch whenever and wherever they please. The kitchen is more orderly, and everyone gets back together for a family dinner in the evening.

Clean or dirty?

One idea for helping children remember whether the dishwasher contains clean or dirty dishes is to put a magnetic marker on it when the dishes are dirty. When they are clean, take it off and put it on the refrigerator. Saves time and bother.

Everyone can pitch in

Train kids to clean up after snacks. Little children can carry dirty dishes to the sink; older kids can stow dirty plates in the dishwasher.

A special treat

After a holiday most stores reduce the price of paper plates, cups, and napkins. Purchase several sets and put them away for a preschooler's special lunch with friends, or as a treat when the children need cheering up. Somehow the food always seems to taste better and disappear more quickly from a "special plate."

Having a special picnic for your child? Surprise him or her by using a frisbee as a holder for the paper plate. It's useful during the meal and fun afterward. This is also a great idea for a child's birthday party. The guests will be delighted when they finish their food to find frisbees for party favors!

Lunch box addition

Insert a colorful washcloth into your youngster's lunch box. It cushions the thermos, makes a great placemat, and quickly helps wipe up any spills.

Tray for sick children

When children are ill, serve their meals in a muffin tin. The cups hold assorted foods, even a small glass of milk, and you won't have to worry about sliding and spilling.

Children's placemats

Children can have fun making their own placemats from jigsaw puzzles. After they have assembled each puzzle, cover the top and bottom with clear self-adhesive paper. The placemat can be easily wiped off, and the children will enjoy eating on their own work of art.

Small terry-cloth hand towels make fine placemats for children learning to eat. The towels come in attractive colors, are absorbent and easy to wash, and need no ironing.

Do your dinner guests often include small children? Smooth a piece of transparent plastic film over the tablecloth at each child's place. This protects the tablecloth yet doesn't spoil the table's appearance.

Make a table-setting diagram on an old plastic table mat for kids to follow when they set the table. Saves time and many questions.

ON THE GO

Airplane trips and small children

Traveling with an active two-year-old can be a strain on everyone, particularly if you travel by plane, train, or bus. Plan ahead by buying several small books and wrapping each one in brightly colored paper, tied with a ribbon. Hide the packages and when the child becomes fidgety, present a gift. The fascination of a wrapped gift and a new book will probably keep him happy—and seated—for the remainder of the trip.

Easing the boredom of car travel

To help youngsters enjoy car trips, give each a small suitcase. Fill it with their favorite toys and tuck in a few surprises. They will enjoy packing and repacking their "luggage," and it avoids car clutter.

A covered cake pan is ideal for holding crayons, pencils, paper, and trinkets while traveling by car with small children. When closed, the pan makes a good drawing board.

When planning a long automobile trip, pack a "lap desk" for children— a jelly-roll pan or a cookie sheet with sides. The sides prevent crayons and pencils from rolling off.

Attach a shoe bag to the back of the front seat of the car. The bag can hold children's toys, pencils, paper, magazines, and snacks to nibble on.

Or, fill a small bag with a colorful assortment of sponges to be used as building blocks. Easy to pack and fun to play with!

During those long and tiring car trips, let the children take turns being the front seat passenger. Looking forward to a change of place adds interest to the trip. Providing an extra set of road maps for the back-seat crew helps relieve the monotony of a long trip, too.

Less tedious waiting

Carry small notebooks and pens in your purse. Whenever children are bored waiting in doctors' offices or traveling in the car, they have their special "busy books" in which to draw or play word games.

Summer safety

When going to a crowded beach or play area it is a good idea to take along a colorful standard made from an old broom handle tied with colored balloons or streamers. Push it into the ground by your spot and rest easily, knowing your children will only have to spot the balloons or streamers to find you.

Versatile plastic bags

Take along several plastic dry-cleaning bags when you visit a beach with public benches. When you and the children come out of the water to rest or eat lunch, spread the bags over the benches to keep them dry for nonbathers. The bags can be used to hold wet towels later. They also come in handy for collections of shells and rocks.

Moving time

Moving from one place to another can be very hectic and confusing. For youngsters it can be particularly traumatic. It helps to make them part of the moving program. Let kids pack their own toys, collectibles, and the like. Save the Sunday comics for them to use as wrappings so they are able to identify their belongings when unpacking and feel they are part of the team.

Instant travel kit

Throughout the year, buy inexpensive trial sizes of shampoo, hand cream, toothpaste, and the like; store them in a shoe box. Add similar items which arrive in the mail as free samples. When one of your children spends the night with a friend or is packing for a vacation, these items fit easily into an overnight bag.

SPECIAL OCCASIONS

A thoughtful idea

Children love to act like grown-ups, and here's an idea to instill good habits toward hostesses. If your child dines with a friend frequently, send along a simple gift such as a bottle of soda or juice. You can even wrap it or tie on a ribbon.

Child's "happy box"

Hospitalized children are often limited in the number of toys they can have—there isn't much space. People often want to bring gifts and would like some guidance. One especially good idea is to take a lunch box and fill it with small, individually wrapped presents. Each day the child can open one present, thus having something to look forward to every day.

Gift from home

When sending homemade cookies to children at college, use your local newspaper (neatly folded) as packing to fill out the corners in the carton. The children will enjoy the news from home, plus the cookies.

Grandma's surprise box

Keep a "surprise box" for grandchildren on a lower shelf of a closet where they can reach it. Keep pretty things in it you know they will enjoy: tokens from cereal boxes, shells and stones, pictures, and, occasionally, a treat for a sweet tooth. The box can be a real source of joy for grandchildren—and for Grandma and Grandpa as well.

A warm welcome for the children

Children are often eager for a hug and some talk when they arrive home from school. When you can't make it home on time, leave something that shows you're thinking about them. It may be a special note, or a treat to eat, with their own initials from a magnetic alphabet board propped by each one's portion.

Pieces of memory

Start collecting pieces of fabric from children's worn-out or outgrown clothing. Once you have enough good combinations, plan a quilt for each child that will contain pieces of especially memorable clothing— John's favorite plaid shirt, Heather's Easter dress, Jimmy's striped bathing suit. In later years the quilts may stir pleasant memories.

Don't forget the older ones

It is customary to take a new baby a little gift. A moment's consideration for an older sibling can be greatly appreciated. When you wrap the baby's present, also wrap up a little trinket or gift for the older child, who might not understand why all the attention is being paid to the baby and none to him.

Trip and treat

Many parents like to bring a little treat for children when they return from a trip. It doesn't have to be fancy or expensive if you think of the things in your hotel room and the airplane. Small bars of soap with the wrapper and hotel name, small stationery pads, a plastic airline tray, or a drink stirrer are tailor-made miniatures and delight youngsters.

Double party bonus

Keeping active youngsters happily out of the way while parents entertain dinner guests can be a hassle. Here is an idea for providing them with a party of their own. When you prepare the grown-ups' refreshments, fill paper lunch bags with finger-food samples of the evening's menu. When the guests arrive, the kids take their goody bags upstairs and enjoy the unusual hors d'oeuvres, nuts, and other treats while playing or watching TV.

Fun birthday party

A fun idea for a girl's birthday party is a "doll fashion sew." Ask each guest to bring a doll. You provide material scraps, lace, needles, thread, and the like. Let the girls design their own outfits, and then have a fashion show, each doll modeling a new creation.

Don't miss that party

To keep children from getting lost looking for the birthday party, mark your house with a bouquet of balloons or a big colorful sign fixed to your front door, window, or mailbox.

Spur-of-the-moment birthday

Children love birthday parties, and sometimes a spontaneous one can really perk up a slightly saddened child. Just lower the lights, light a candle, sing "Happy Birthday," and figure out someone whose birthday it might be. Sounds silly, but it works.

Bonus gift

The perfect ribbon wrap for a child's birthday present is a new jump rope tied around it and made into a big bow. Children will love the extra little "bonus" gift.

A birthday candle

A large candle that can be lit each year is a nice gift for a baby. Mark a large pastel-colored candle with the numerals 1 through 21 in acrylic paint and add other decorations if you like. On each birthday, burn down the candle to the year mark. Commercially made candles of this type can be expensive, so try making your own—it costs less and is fun.

Birthday collage

Throwing away old birthday cards can be hard for a child. This year make a collage out of them, to give your child a year-long remembrance of the birthday celebration.

Waiting for Christmas

When the wait until Christmas becomes unbearable for children, give them last year's Christmas cards to cut up. Besides keeping busy, they enjoy creating unusual shapes, and you end up with lovely gift tags.

To keep children happy until tree-trimming time, put up one decoration somewhere around the house, *each* day. It doesn't matter whether it is a candle, mistletoe, or a door decoration. The fun of seeing who can spot the new decoration each day allays the children's impatience and also helps Mom decorate without hustle and bustle! End result—a happy, relaxed time for all.

The night before Christmas can be almost unbearable for children. Here is an idea which is fun for the whole family and helps the kids get through the waiting: a Christmas Eve potluck buffet. A week or so before Christmas, each family member plans a dish to serve (even the youngest child can manage something simple). A day or two before the buffet, everyone prepares his contribution. On Christmas Eve set the meal out on snack tables near the tree and sing carols or tell stories until bedtime.

The spirit of Christmas

During the Christmas season, parents want children to enjoy the spirit of giving as well as receiving. Take them to a toy store and let each select one item within certain price limits previously set. Each child then gift-wraps the chosen toy and gives it to a less fortunate child. This can be a very enjoyable and rewarding experience for the entire family.

Glitter and glue

Making pinecone ornaments is a very inexpensive Christmas project for children. Even preschoolers can participate. Have them gather the cones themselves; then with a little glue, glitter, and yarn they can make very pretty ornaments. The cost is minimal, and children love to create pretty things, especially at Christmas time.

Practical presents

If your children have difficulty choosing Christmas gifts for other family members, suggest they offer to take over some of Mom's, Dad's, or a sibling's duties—like washing dishes, trash duty, or mowing the lawn—for a few days. This gift can be given in the form of a cute note offering the child's services.

Safe holidays

If toddlers keep *un*decorating the Christmas tree, put it inside a playpen. It's also a handy way to keep gifts out of reach. You will save the ornaments, your patience, and most of all, your little ones from being hurt! It also keeps your pet dog away.

Decorating windows

If your children like to decorate windows for Christmas, give them a bottle of white shoe polish and its applicator. They can write with it and easily draw snowflakes, snow figures, and Christmas wreaths. Mistakes wipe off with a damp sponge. After the holiday season is over, just use clear water to wash the drawings off the windows.

Holiday placemats children can make

Have your children make Christmas placemats without much fuss or bother. Cut felt or any other fairly sturdy material that won't ravel to the proper size. Let the kids decorate the mats with Christmas motifs—holly leaves, stars, pine branches, and the like. They can use either paints, stick-ons, or whatever comes to their creative minds.

Safe Halloween!

Instead of candy at Halloween, try "trick or toy." Halloweeners who knock at the door can be treated to balloons, rubbery spiders, whistles, or other inexpensive toys available at novelty and carnival supply houses. These please most children—and mothers—more than candy, of which they get enough.

Jack-o'-lantern

Make a safe jack-o'-lantern for your children on Halloween. Use a flashlight instead of a candle to light up the features. Simply cut a hole in the bottom of the pumpkin to insert the flashlight. The children can light their own pumpkin safely this way.

KIDS AND THINGS, NEAT AND CLEAN

Morning organizer

To end the battle of getting young children up each morning in time to catch the school bus, give them alarm clocks of their own. They give them a sense of pride and responsibility, as well as saving everyone from a hectic, irritating morning.

No more tears

For children who scream each time their hair is washed, try making it playtime by letting them wear an underwater face mask. It keeps the soap out of tender eyes and is great fun.

Another way to keep shampoo out of children's eyes is to apply a little petroleum jelly on the forehead just under the hairline.

Another way to avoid shampoo tears with very young children is to rub their hair with a lathered washcloth. Rinse with the washed out cloth.

Toys in the tub

Many children love playing in the bath. For an added treat, try adding a few drops of food coloring to a bubble bath. The colored bubbles will delight the kids.

Here is a neat way to reuse old wine corks. Glue them together and give them to your toddler at bath time. The corks become a fascinating flotilla to imaginative young children.

To make a bathtub fountain toy, punch small holes in a plastic bottle. When filled, it sprinkles water out in dainty streams.

Styrofoam meat trays make good bath toys. They float and can be used as flat boats, barges, or trays.

Styrofoam egg cartons are also good bath toys. Filling the separate compartments can provide endless entertainment.

Store children's bathtub toys in a net vegetable bag hung over the bathtub. Toys dry quickly, are out of the way, and keep tidily in one place, ready for the next bath. The bags are also easily replaced.

Teaching youngsters to dress

Putting on boots can be a frustrating experience for a small child. One way to help him out is to place a piece of wax paper or plastic in the back of the boot, allowing the shoe to slip in.

Teaching children to lace shoes is time consuming. To help a child understand the process of criss-crossing the laces properly, dip half of a white shoe lace in nontoxic vegetable dye. It will then be much easier to see when a shoe is laced properly and why, when it is not.

Another good way to teach a child right from left is to color-code a foot with its corresponding shoe. Paint toenails of the right foot a distinctive color with permanent ink or a felt-tipped marker. Paste a big spot of the same color in the inside of a right shoe. By the time the ink wears off, in a few days, the child will most likely know right from left.

Easy tip

Sometimes the zipper tag on coats is to small for children to easily grasp. To solve this, save free key chains from banks, gas stations, and the like. Attach one to each zipper tag to make an easy pull.

Lost and found

Children seem to have a talent for misplacing belongings. One way to cut down on "Hey, Mom, do you know where my pens (or notebooks or marbles) are?" is to have a lost and found drawer.

Attach notebook rings to the zipper tabs on your children's boots. Small fingers can easily grip the rings, and they can be used to hook the boots together at school or when the children go visiting!

Print your child's name on a spring-type clothespin and keep it in his raincoat pocket. When he visits a friend or goes to school, he can use the clothespin to clip together his boots or rubbers.

To cut the loss of children's mittens or gloves, sew a button on each the same size as the buttonhole of the child's coat. Then teach him to button the handwarmers to the coat when taking them off.

Bag 'em

Carry a shopping bag with you when taking small children to any group gathering. Stow caps, mittens, and scarves in the bag as wraps are removed. When it's time to leave, there will be no frantic last-minute search for missing belongings.

Hang it up

Here is an idea for organizing children's outdoor accessories right when they come in. String plastic clip-type clothespins on picture wire and fasten to the back of the door to the play yard. Above the wire install a hat and scarf rack. When the children come in from playing, they clip their mittens and gloves to the wire and leave hats and scarves hanging. Damp things dry quickly, and everything is easily found.

Tack a large spring clip or clipboard to the inside of the door of the closet where the children keep their outdoor clothes. Clip report cards, papers, and notes they must take to school, so they won't forget them.

To keep mittens sorted and in one place, clip them to a multiple skirt hanger on the hall closet door.

No more lost mittens

To keep your children from loosing their mittens, sew a button to each glove's cuff to fit the buttonhole on their coats. Then, when they take off their mittens, the kids can simply button them to the coat.

Keeping track of winter caps and mittens for young children can be frustrating. To solve this problem purchase inexpensive stackable vegetable bins, tape their names on each, and store on the floor of the coat closet.

73

Paper covers

Opaque white freezer paper makes durable covers for children's schoolbooks. After shaping the cover, seal the edges with a moderately hot iron instead of gluing them.

Saving children's shoes

Want to save on children's shoes? Teach them to use a shoehorn! It will keep the children from breaking the stitches in the back of the heel of the shoe, so they'll last longer!

Cleaning and polishing

If you can't find shoe polish the color of your daughter's party shoes, buy white liquid polish and tint it with food dye.

Polishing children's boots and rubbers with petroleum jelly is an easy way to help waterproof them.

Use a cotton-tipped stick dipped into polish to clean the hard-to-do space between the uppers and the soles.

Apply colorless fingernail polish to your child's shoe tips after polishing to cut down on scuffs.

Use a moistened soapy scouring pad to clean the white rubber on children's sneakers. For extra-heavy soil or tar marks, use a scouring cleanser.

Preventing stains

Slip your child's frozen ice cream bar stick through a small paper plate or piece of cardboard and save his clothes from drips and stains.

Stretching clothes

Sew bands of plaid flannel wide enough to form cuffs on your youngster's outgrown blue jeans. It will add another few months' wear.

Last year's slacks may well be too short for a growing girl. Cut them below the knee, make a hem casing, and insert elastic. Voila, stylish new knickers!

Insulated underwear doubles nicely as warm, durable pajamas for children. Flower and cartoon prints are often available in hard-to-find 100% cotton.

One-of-a-kind

A perfect use for a colorful, single pillowcase no longer needed is to make it a sleeping bag carrier. A child can easily spot his bag in a crowd. Bulky sleeping bags also fit more easily into pillowcases, which are roomier than the stuff bags sold specifically for sleeping bags.

Bringing home papers

Save the cardboard tubes from waxed paper, foil, and paper toweling. Let the children use the tubes for carrying school homework, such as drawings or maps, that they don't want to fold. Once home, write the name and date on the outside and use the tubes for storing the papers.

Youngsters who often come home from school with beautiful, original works of "art" can display them in an inexpensive scrapbook. Children delight in taping in the pictures and at a moment's notice can produce their own art work. Also, books can be shared with everyone in the years to come.

A great deal of devotion goes into those "works of art" children so proudly bring home two or three times a week—too much devotion not to have the work proudly displayed. But where? The refrigerator door is an ideal spot. Small, inexpensive kitchen magnets are perfect for holding the papers and make replacements easy. A lot of family togetherness takes place in the kitchen, so your children will be reminded that you care.

One way to preserve children's art work is to dip the papers in a shallow pan filled with skimmed milk. Dip quickly and hang to dry.

Recycling children's art

A novel way to share children's art work and school progress is to use their papers as stationery when writing to an interested friend or relative. Write letters on the back of the papers, thereby saving paper and making the children proud for having their work treated so specially.

For the young musician

A magazine rack beside the piano gives children a handy place to put their music books without cluttering the piano.

"Paintbrushes" for youngsters

Cotton-tipped swabs make perfect paintbrushes for young children. They are easy to handle enabling youngsters to be creative making all kinds of paintings and designs without too much of a mess. Use one swab for each pot of paint, and throw them away at the end of the painting session.

No more lost brushes

To solve the problem of misplaced brushes when young children use "paint with water" books, cut two horizontal slits in the cover of the book. When the brush is not in use, it can be slipped through the slits and will always be there when children want to paint.

Neat ways to sharpen pencils

Tape a small pencil sharpener to the inside rim of a wastebasket in the children's playroom. This eliminates searching for the sharpener, and the shavings fall into the basket.

Toy box on wheels

An about-to-be-discarded bassinet on casters can be used as a toy cart for children to push from room to room.

Orderly books

Keep children's small books neatly arranged by slipping them into one of the rubber plate racks you can buy in housewares departments.

Easy reminder

After a trip to the library with younger children, remove the cards from the books and put them in a safe place. This not only protects the cards, it serves as a reminder of how many books have to rounded up to return on time.

Keeping toys at hand

Your toddler will have fun putting toys into a shoe bag hung on the side of his playpen, and the bag is a convenient storage place for the toys when they are not in use.

If you have a small child, keep a box of special toys in the laundry room for him to play with. Then you can keep an eye on him and do the laundry at the same time.

Clear identification

After marking school items or toys with your child's name, cover it with a coat of clear nail polish for a lasting, nonsmear, washable finish.

To prevent squabbles over toys in the neighborhood playground, attach name tags to your children's toys. Color-code the tags for children who are too small to read their names.

Children always enjoy "fixing" their toys with Dad's tools, which they often lose in the grass or misplace somewhere, causing endless searching. Painting the tool handles with luminous paint will help solve this problem. They're easy to spot—even if partially covered with mud or grease.

Storing game pieces

Wash out and save some of those plastic containers in which sour cream, ready-to-eat salads, cottage cheese, and the like are sold. The containers are wonderful for storing parts of games and odds and ends that children collect. Label the containers and keep them neatly on a toy shelf.

Preserving toys

Wax children's wagons, strollers, and bicycles with paste wax. It will keep them looking like new and protect the paint and metal if they are accidentally left out in the rain.

Coat children's metal toys or any new painted toys with clear varnish or shellac. It prevents rust and keeps the colors bright. They will survive the outdoors much better, and it will prevent paint marks on woodwork.

Give the children's cardboard game boards a coat of shellac or plastic varnish before they are used. They can be wiped off easily and will last longer.

Clean the blades and metal fastenings on shoe skates with paste wax before storing them. It prevents rust.

Vacuum children's stuffed toys using the upholstery brush. This keeps them clean longer, and they stay fluffy.

Wrapped in aluminum foil, children's modeling clay or play dough will stay moist and pliable indefinitely.

To keep a doll house dust free, make a plastic cover—like a giant toaster cover.

Easy cleanup

Pick up those small toys and building blocks with a dustpan and brush. It's a quick and easy way to carry them to your youngster's toy box.

BABY BUSINESS

Changing time

Some babies really like changing time, and as most mothers know, it's a good time for playing, but it is also a good time for exercises such as stretching and pumping legs.

Next time the disposable diaper tape won't stick, is torn off, or is just missing, try using a piece of masking tape.

To avoid a middle-of-the-night hassle, make baby's bed with two sets of sheets separated with a waterproof pad. That way, when you have to change the bed in the middle of the night, you can just take off the top set and the bed is made.

On chilly days, just before bathing the baby, put his receiving blanket, bath towel, and fresh clothes into your clothes dryer. Tumble a few minutes, then wrap in a warm towel. When the bath is finished, baby's clothes will be waiting, warm, and cozy.

Wear a cotton glove on the hand you use to hold the baby when you bathe him. This will help prevent his slipping or wriggling out of your hands.

Useful old sock

If a baby's glass bottle is too slippery for tiny hands to hold, or a plastic one too cold or too hot, slip a child's sock over it—a good way to make an orphaned sock useful.

Quick cleanups

A neat and easy way to keep the tray of a wooden high chair clean and unscratched is to cut a placemat to fit the inside of the tray. It adds color, which baby enjoys, and for Mom it's easy to clean by just lifting the mat out and washing it off.

Mount a regular paper towel holder to the back of your baby's crib for quick cleanups. One single roll takes up little space and can be a great help.

Another simple way to make meal times easier is to attach a rod to the back of baby's high chair to use as a towel rack. A washcloth and towel placed on it during meal times makes cleanups a lot easier.

Mattress cover

Covering a baby carriage mattress with a pillowcase instead of carriage sheets will ensure a smoother surface.

Keeping feeding time easy

Make sure that you consider feeding time a happy time. Even young babies can sense tension or unpleasantness.

Choose a quiet place to feed the baby. Allow enough time so that feedings are not rushed, or you will probably find yourself wasting time coping with a distressed baby.

Make sure baby is secured in the highchair with a safety strap. If the chair doesn't have one, use a strip of soft strong cloth, or a belt.

Wash the entire feeding area before each meal. This includes the highchair seat, tray, armrests, and the hands of everyone who helps.

Keep cleanup equipment handy so that spills won't interrupt the process.

Spoon out baby's portion into a serving dish. Do not feed directly from a jar since the germs from baby's mouth will go right back into the jar and can multiply if stored.

CHILDREN'S ROOMS

Baby's room decor

Here is a way to furnish a baby's room functionally and decoratively at a very low cost. For a changing table, use an old two-drawer, two-door buffet, stripped of its finish and painted a bright, light color; it's just the right height. Near the changing table hang a pretty shoe bag to hold the necessary powders, diaper pins, and the like. Above the table hang a piece of felt as wide as the buffet and ceiling high, suspended from a brass curtain rod. This "bulletin board" serves as a gallery area on which to hang posters, pictures, numbers, or anything else that is colorful and enjoyable. For a toy box, cover a large cardboard storage box with colorful self-adhesive paper and glue a parade of brightly colored animals around it—cut from a roll of children's gift wrap paper. All of these things not only help to furnish a baby's room inexpensively but can stimulate a child's interest in his environment.

Create cheerful, inexpensive nursery decorations with animal-shaped plastic placemats. Simply glue colored burlap to a piece of plywood and attach placemats to the burlap. The "picture" can be framed or left as it is. These decorations are not only inexpensive, they're practical, too—since the placemats can easily be wiped clean, they can be hung low enough on the walls for small children to enjoy.

Hang up the toys

Tie ribbons around children's stuffed toys and hang them on hooks. They stay clean when not being played with and are a whimsical decoration for the room.

Sew tape loops on children's stuffed animals and hang them on a pegboard in the children's room. This keeps the animals off the floor and makes an attractive display when not in use.

Keeping order

Get bins, boxes, and/or shelves so your children will have places for things. Use ordinary plastic laundry baskets, cardboard grocery cartons (the kids can decorate them), or old bookcases. With adequate storage, many a chronically messy children's room improves dramatically. (Of course, the children must understand that picking up and putting away is *their* job.)

Play proof bedspread

Use a large, gaily colored beach towel as a bedspread on a boy's bed. Perfect for an active boy—it's wrinkle-proof and washes easily.

Stars on the ceiling

Is your youngster afraid of the dark? Does he or she insist on having a light left on in the room all night, energy crisis or no? Here is a happy solution to the problem. Buy a packet of fluorescent stars sold in variety stores and paste them in a random pattern on the ceiling to resemble the night sky. When the light goes out, children no longer fuss about sleeping in a dark room, because they're fascinated by the glow of the stars.

Simple bed making

Simplify bed making so that children can do it themselves. If they can't maneuver a top sheet and several blankets, eliminate them and get a warm and easily washable quilt or comforter instead. The kids can smooth the bottom sheet and comforter into place.

With nylon fishing thread, baste together the blankets on each child's bed. This keeps the blankets together at night and makes it simpler for the youngsters to make their own beds. (The thread is easy to pull out before washing the blankets.)

Pillow pockets

Stitch a small pocket on one corner of each of your child's pillowcases to hold a handkerchief or tissues.

Making closets work for kids

If two children share the same closet, paint half of the closet one color and the other half a harmonizing color. Then paint hangers to match each side. The children will find it easier to keep their closet in order.

Have closet rods lowered so your small children can reach their clothes more easily. It's certainly a time saver for Mom in the morning.

Fasten a swinging, three-rod, kitchen towel holder in your little boy's closet at a height low enough for him to use as a trousers hanger.

Make a shoe bag with extra-deep pockets and hang it behind a door in a child's room. Such a bag can hold dolls and other hard-to-store toys.

Attractive storage

Bright-color denim, burlap, or felt that harmonizes with the color scheme of a child's room can be used to slipcover an unused trunk or foot locker for storing the youngster's out-of-season clothes or sports equipment.

Bookworm bag

Here is an idea for children who sleep in bunk beds. If the child on the top bunk accidentally wakes up the child below when getting down to get a book or toy, hang a cloth bag on one of the bedposts. Favorite books or small toys can be stashed within easy reach.

Bank bookends for children

Use colorful piggy banks as bookends in your child's room (fill them a little to weight them down). The banks serve a dual purpose: as an inspiration to save money and to keep books in order.

Bucket baskets

The gaily colored plastic buckets available in housewares departments make wonderful wastebaskets for children's rooms. Youngsters like to carry them from project to project.

Less confusion

Colorful paint eliminates drawer confusion when several youngsters share a single dresser. Use different colors to help kids identify their own drawers.

Drawer organizers

Use the oblong plastic baskets that tomatoes are packed in as sock holders in children's drawers.

Neat storage places

Tape pictures of your children's toys to the appropriate spot on their toy shelves. They can tell at a glance where each item belongs. It will help keep the room and the storage area looking really tidy.

Mount a child's electric train tracks on a large sheet of plywood fitted with casters. When the child isn't playing with the trains, the layout can be rolled under the bed.

A old twin bed mattress makes a terrific extra bed for a child's sleep-over friends. Covered with a plastic mattress cover, it slides easily under a bed for storage and is hidden by a dust ruffle. When pulled out for use, it makes up almost instantly with sheets and a pillow. Incidentally, it also provides a great place for small children to bounce and tumble.

Unique picture gallery

An old window shade hung on hooks in the children's room is a good place to tape pictures, invitations, souvenirs, and the like. When filled, it can be rolled up and filed.

Instant blackboard for children

A window shade makes an inexpensive, convenient blackboard for a child's room. Paint one side with blackboard paint and mount with brackets to a strip of wood. Roll it up, and it's out of sight when not in use. Children will love it!

Clean sweep

Is your child's bedroom door covered with old stickers that will not come off? Next time, put a large sheet of clear plastic adhesive paper on the door first, and when it is time to "redecorate," everything will pull off with one sweep!

Three

247 THOUGHTFUL IDEAS FOR FAMILY AND FRIENDS

HOLIDAYS, GIFTS, AND GUESTS

"Cookie exchange"

One way to have a wide variety of treats at Christmas without spending weeks in the kitchen is to organize a "cookie exchange." Before Christmas, invite friends for coffee or lunch, asking each to bring a batch of their favorite cookies. Provide a large coffee can covered with Christmas wrap for each guest, if you like. The sweets are then divided and redistributed during the party.

A neighborhood cookie-tasting and recipe exchange is another good idea. Buy several small spiral notebooks and decorate them with either a cut-out from an old Christmas card or a Christmas sticker. Ask each person to bring a dozen cookies and the recipe written clearly so it can be easily copied into the notebooks. This gives neighbors a chance to share their baking talents and enjoy each other's company before the holidays.

Holiday gifts

At Christmas each year, try giving close friends gifts of food packed in decorative canisters with a copy of the recipe enclosed. The recipient can replenish the supply of goodies and will also have a convenient and pretty storage container.

Give calendar towels for inexpensive (stocking stuffer) gifts for Christmas. To add a personal touch embroider the family name in a festive color. The towels can be hung, and later used as decorative pillow tops, as well as dish towels.

Instead of exchanging the usual greeting cards and gifts with friends, exchange a handmade quilt square every Christmas. Each one is original, signed and dated by its maker. Some day the squares can be sewn together to give each of the participants an irreplaceable friendship quilt.

Christmas can be a simple but thoughtful and joyous time. Families can exchange cookies, other specially baked goods, and homemade presents. Those who have a garden can give packets of seeds for favorite plants and vegetables. Write a note with each packet, promising to plant and care for the plants until ready for harvesting.

At Christmas time it is nice to give guests a small gift. One way to do this is to make felt tree ornaments. As guests are leaving, they each pick one off the tree.The ornaments are inexpensive and can be made ahead of time to keep the tree filled.

Stage a Christmas play

This is a unique Christmas gift for grandparents. Stage a play following Christmas dinner. Preparations are minimal, usually starting the day before. Create costumes and props from what's on hand—Christmas wrapping paper and boxes, for example. It seems to work better to have a narrator and keep speaking parts to a minimum. Script material is easy to find—Christmas songs, poems, and stories are fine.

Useful gift

If you knit a gift for Christmas, enclose the label from the yarn and any leftover for mending. The label shows the yarn's content and often gives washing instructions.

Try wrapping the gifts with a generous amount of the leftover yarn. The result is not only attractive but practical.

The wish book

Begin each Christmas season with a wish book. Staple a few pages of paper together with a Christmas card on the front as decoration. Each person has a page on which to write things he would like. In the back, keep a list of everyone's sizes, color choices, and the like.

Holiday notebook

Holiday time always brings the problem of what to get for family members and friends. Throughout the year keep a little notebook in which to jot down suggestions mentioned at various times. Write down favorite colors and sizes. Before Christmas the family can consult the book for ideas.

Get a head start

Magazines are filled with articles of ideas around Christmas time. One way to save and organize them is to begin a "Christmas Book." Clip and paste each article, then put them into a looseleaf notebook that is sectioned into several categories such as "Christmas decorations," "gift ideas," "gifts to make," and "recipes."

Holiday decorations

It is more difficult to hang holiday arrangements or ornaments on a metal door. Try a large magnetic hook like the ones used on doors of kitchen appliances.

Decorative pinecones

Making crafts with pinecones is fun, but sometimes a few of the cones are shut tight and rather unattractive. Try using Mother Nature's technique of opening them—with heat. Set the oven at a low temperature, place the cones in a pan, and in about an hour they will have opened enough to use.

Plan ahead for Christmas: In the autumn collect acorns, pinecones, thistles, milkweed pods, twigs, and the like. Shortly before the holidays spray them with gold, silver, green, or red paint and use them for holiday tree ornaments and table centerpieces and on gift wrappings for Christmas packages.

Make pretty tree decorations by dipping pinecones in self-polishing wax. While they are still wet, spray cones with hair spray and sprinkle on silver or gold glitter. When dry, tie to the tree with red and green ribbons.

Instant ornament hangers

People always run out of Christmas ornament hangers before the last ones are hung. Paper clips can help finish trimming in no time. Bend out the large part of the clip so it fits snugly over the branch. Paper clip hangers are not only cheap and easy to make but also much sturdier than commercial ones.

Pipe cleaners are a wonderful help in trimming a Christmas tree—to attach lights and cords to branches, to fasten a reinforcing stick to a limp treetop or twig, to substitute for missing ornament hangers. Hobby shops and dime stores carry them in many colors.

Memorable Christmas decorations

Instead of discarding crib mobiles, save them and add the delicate figures to your collection of Christmas decorations. They bring back tender memories for all.

Everyone likes to bring back mementos from an enjoyable vacation or trip. Select one special small item that is typical of each area visited and hang it as an ornament on your Christmas tree. That tiny bell from the Swiss Alps or the miniature bear from Yellowstone will rekindle memories each Christmas at tree-trimming time. Or, if you prefer to enjoy your souvenirs year-round, fasten an attractively shaped tree branch to a wall and suspend your collection from it for a permanent decoration. Either way, you will have a unique remembrance of happy times past.

A good idea for grandmothers (or mothers): Every Christmas give each child a tree ornament to be placed on the family tree and eventually to become a part of that grandchild's own Christmas treasures when he or she leaves home. It is fun to watch the treasures accumulate over the years and to know how welcome the memories will be when those ornaments are placed on that first tree away from home.

Safety during the holidays

Having a toddler in the house makes parents worry about hanging ornaments with dangerous hooks on the tree. Instead of hooks, use red and green ribbons to tie the ornaments onto the tree. It both lessens the worry and adds a nice touch of color to the Christmas tree.

For feathered friends

If your dishwasher rinse agent comes in a white plastic basket, save the empty ones and fill with goodies like raisins, sunflower seeds, and popcorn for the wild birds on Christmas Eve. They look pretty hung on an evergreen—or even a bare tree branch.

Outdoor lights

Stringing outdoor Christmas lights and decorations to your house is easy when you screw cup hooks at intervals across the surfaces to be decorated. Then just slip the electric wiring through the hooks. (Be careful to use wiring suitable for outdoors.)

Use brightly colored plastic clothespins to fasten lights to outdoor Christmas trees. Neither wind nor ice will dislodge them, and during the day the bright bits of color are attractive against the green of the trees.

Create your own candlesticks

If you should need extra candleholders during the holiday season, make your own! Cover small squares of plywood or scrap lumber with strips of adhesive-backed shelf covering or wallpaper. Then drive a small nail through the underside of each square to hold the candle.

Saving tablecloths

To save your holiday tablecloths from candle wax stains, cut a hole in the center of a fluted paper baking cup and push the candle through the hole and then into your candlestick. By using matching or contrasting colored candles and cups you can make your table look especially festive.

"Family" cookbook

With budgets so stretched these days, it's often difficult to afford a wedding gift. One solution is to make a "family" cookbook—a unique gift that costs no more than a package of index cards. Ask relatives and friends of the bride and groom for their favorite recipes and handwrite them on large index cards with the name of the giver on each card. Organize them in a file box or have them bound as a book and then write a warm personal note on the first card.

Thoughtful gift

If your budget is tight, a thoughtful and inexpensive gift to take to a bridal shower is a nice notebook in which you have written your best homemaking tips. You can feel sure the bride-to-be will use your gift for a long time!

A really unusual and appreciated wedding shower gift is a laundry basket of useful items for the new homemaker. Include in it such things as paper towels, wax paper, plastic wrap, napkins, tissues, toothpicks, matches, scouring pads, silver polish—the list is endless and a lot of fun to give.

Golden anniversary gift

Make a fiftieth wedding anniversary even more special by giving the couple a "memory" scrapbook. Each page is decorated by a family member with poems, art work, or letters, telling in words or pictures of past times with the honored couple.

Shower favors

Planning a bridal or baby shower and wondering what to give as favors? Consider this: About two months before the shower, take cuttings from your houseplants and place them in water. In a month or less, the cuttings will root enough to be potted. Buy tiny peat pots from your local nursery, plant each cutting in an individual pot, and adorn it with ribbons or some other symbolic decorations. This inexpensive favor will delight your guests.

Practical baby gift

When giving a baby gift, enclose some cents-off coupons for disposable diapers, baby food, powder, lotions, and the like. Your gift will be doubly appreciated.

A gift money can't buy

If you'd like to do something very special for a mother-to-be, make an attractive booklet of "coupons" instead of a customary gift. One coupon could state that you will baby-sit, another that you'll run errands for her, and another that you'll drive or accompany her on the baby's first visit to the doctor. She'll very much appreciate your thoughtfulness.

Unique baby gift

Looking for a thoughtful and unusual baby present? How about a gift certificate from a local plant nursery? Every child needs a tree to climb.

Flash: arrived

An idea for daddies-to-be: When the eagerly awaited event arrives, no doubt you'll want to let everyone know. To quickly notify the neighbors, tie a pink or blue ribbon on the mailbox.

Birthday books

Instead of sending cards on children's birthdays, send small story books. The difference in cost is small, and the books are a little more special and enjoyed for a much longer time.

Easy reminder

Help your husband remember birthdays and anniversaries! Hang a calendar on the inside of his closet door and circle all the important dates with a red pencil.

Snack-a-luck

Here's an ideal way to have a party and still stay within your budget. Send out invitations to your friends asking them to bring their favorite snack. You'll end up with a smorgasbord of snacks to choose from. You provide the beverages, and everyone is set for an evening of fun.

A delicious birthday gift

Prepare a really useful birthday present for a working person who lives alone: a selection of frozen single-serving portions of dinners cooked for your own family. To "dress up" the present, include a small bottle of wine or beer to go with each dish. A couple of miniature loaves of homemade bread and individual dessert portions complete the package.

Birthday cake for the weight-conscious

Planning a birthday luncheon for a group of weight-conscious friends who never want to eat dessert can be a problem. What fun would the celebration be without a birthday cake? Solve the problem by making a molded salad in an angelcake pan and serve on a cake platter surrounded by colorful healthy garnishes!

Party aids

Save the little scoops that come in cans of soft-drink mixes. They make pretty nut and candy cups for almost any party. The scoops can be spray-painted or covered with colorful paper. Add a bow, a plastic flower, or a pipe-cleaner figure to fit the occasion.

Inexpensive party favors

Save your empty bathroom tissue rolls. When it's time for a children's party, fill the rolls with small treats, gum, and candy. Cut a piece of crepe paper about 4″ or 5″ longer than your tube. Wrap it around the roll, securing it with a rubber band or thin ribbon on each end. Then, when the party is over, hand the favors out at the door. Children will love them.

Birthday party idea

For a child's birthday party, cut squares of vinyl material to the size of the chair seats, staple ribbon or string ties on the corners, and affix each child's name on them. With 10 minutes of work, you protect your chairs, make place markers, and give the mothers a welcome take-home gift!

A special gift wrap

A road map makes an interestingly different gift wrap for a man's birthday or Father's Day.

To wrap an exceptionally large gift package, use a gaily decorated paper tablecloth.

To cut down on gift wrapping costs around Christmas time—or any other occasion—keep several skeins of colored yarn on hand—red and green for Christmas, yellow, pink, and blue for other occasions—to use in lieu of ribbon. The skeins are inexpensive and really last a long time. Instead of bows, make pom-poms. They look very pretty and add a homemade touch!

Different invitations

The next time you're having a party, give your invitations a novel look: Type them on blank telegram forms obtained from your local telegraph office. Then, have one of the kids on the block deliver them to each guest. You'll enjoy the reactions from this offbeat idea!

Getting to know you

When using place cards at a wedding reception or any other formal occasion, write the name on both sides. This way the cards can be read from either side of the table and will help guests remember the name of the person sitting across from them.

Evenings together

Instead of being restless and fidgety with an uninteresting television program, you can be doing something useful while spending valuable time with your husband or children. Make a desk out of a favorite chair by cutting a piece of plywood to fit over the chair arms and over your lap. Stain and varnish it to match the furniture, if you wish.

"Wish Box"

Here's a handy source for gift ideas: Keep a "Wish Box" covered with pretty paper and filled with a slot. Throughout the year you and your family write your wishes on paper and slip them in the box. Using the "Wish Box" for gift ideas helps eliminate guesswork.

Gift drawer

Whenever you run across an item on sale that would make a nice birthday gift or a small "thank you" for a friend, buy it and keep it in a special "gift drawer" of your dresser. Your collection will prove handy many times and help save money, too.

All-occasion gifts

Provide yourself with a cache of little gifts. Save empty baby-food jars and fill with homemade jam or homegrown dried herbs.

If you have ever picked up lovely feathers but not known what to do with them, here is a way to turn them into gifts. Thoroughly wash, dry, and brush them, then push an ordinary ball point pen refill into each hollow end. Secure them with a drop of glue, and behold, beautiful quill pens.

Unusual moving gift

When good friends move, find out the new address ahead of time and present them with a set of new address labels as a housewarming or departing gift.

Gift kits

Create your own original kits as gifts for children. Take empty cigar boxes and cover with gingham or colorful self-adhesive paper. Fill the boxes with such "discovery" items as a magnifying glass, pencils, tracing paper, and a kaleidoscope. A "dress-up" kit could contain old costume jewelry, a powder puff, a scarf, and perhaps a mirror. It is an inexpensive but thoughtful and creative gift.

Welcome basket

To help a houseguest feel at home, place a basket filled with fruit, tissues, a brochure or map of your city, a paperback novel, and the evening paper in the guestroom. Your thoughtfulness will be very much appreciated!

Easy directions

Try to place a map of your town close to the telephone. When out-of-town guests want to know how to get to your home, it will be much easier for you to direct them "from where they are to where you are." No street names will be forgotten since they will be right in front of you on the map as you talk on the phone.

No mix-ups

When expecting guests in snowy or rainy weather, clip clothespins around the top edge of a cardboard box and place it on the porch. Each guest clips his overshoes to the box. This saves mix-ups at the end of the party.

Last minute hints for a successful party

Don't send "regrets only" invitations. You'll only worry about who is really coming and who simply forgot to call in.

Dress for the kitchen as well as the party. Unless you have planned a totally self-service meal, do not wear an impractical dressy outfit to your own party.

Instead of piling coats on a bed, hang them on an improvised clothing rack made from a sturdy clothesline or broomstick hung between pipes in the basement. Or, if possible, rent or borrow a rack. Also make sure you have enough coat hangers and ashtrays to take care of a crowd.

Mark drinking glasses with guests' initials or numbers at a large party to avoid mix-ups when they are refilled. Use nail polish on glass, marking pens on paper or plastic cups. The polish can later be wiped clean from glass with remover.

Care package

Don't throw out those old shoe boxes! Instead, paint and decorate them, top with a lovely ribbon, and use as "care" packages. You can give one filled with paperbacks, candy, and the like for a lonely shut-in, or put crayons, paper, and small games for a sick child in another. Make these boxes in advance and always have them on hand to brighten someone's day.

A thoughtful gift

When giving a well-loved cookbook as a present, pencil stars in front of the recipes you have tried and like. Also make notes next to those that are improved by less spice, more cooking, or some other variation. The recipient will most surely be grateful for the comments.

Avoid the crowds

When shopping, always pick up a box for the article just purchased, even if you do not need it just then. At year's end you will have boxes of all shapes and sizes for Christmas gifts and will avoid the frustration of standing in line for them during the holiday rush.

Last-minute gifts

For a last-minute, thoughtful gift, give a cake mix along with the matching pan to bake it in. For extra fun, add a can or box of frosting, and a decorating tool.

When in need of a last-minute gift for a sick friend, wrap up a good novel you've already enjoyed, and write a heart-felt message on the inside flap.

Winning idea

To further the cause of economic ecology and neater closets, consider making a rule that prizes for bridge or other clubs must be either edible or otherwise disposable.

A different gift idea

If you have someone who is difficult to shop for, but has hobbies or interests that you know about, give him or her a course at the local community college or adult education program.

Pretty basket

A can of acrylic paint can give second life to a worn picnic basket. Add a fabric lining and you have a gift to rival the best crafts and gift shops.

A gift of your own time

In these days of inflation, gift giving can become a problem. Instead of a bought gift, donate time to help with major household chores, or offer to babysit your friend's children for an evening. It's a gift of value and deeply appreciated by most!

Seasonal giftwraps

For unique giftwrapping of small gifts, save scraps of material to make little bags using colors that go with the holidays or season. Try bright green with white felt shamrocks glued on, and tied with string for March; red bags with white fake fur cuffs and white ties for December. Let your imagination run wild!

OUTINGS AND GAMES

Refreshing cleanups

The evening before a summer picnic, put some wet, rolled-up face towels into a plastic bag and place them in the freezer. Pack them with your cold drinks and before the meal each person can refresh himself. It's especially delightful on a very hot, humid day.

A clean wading pool

Summertime wading pools have a tendency to get full of grass and other backyard debris. A cheap and easy way to clean it all out is to skim the water with a frying pan spatter guard.

Traveling colander

You can quickly make your own disposable colander by punching holes in an aluminum foil pan and bending it into the shape you need. Great idea for campers and vacationers.

A handy picnic apron

On camping trips, take along a mechanics tool apron. It is usually made from heavy canvas material, and has pockets in which you can put knives and forks, can opener and other camping needs. Fill the pockets, then roll up the apron for traveling. At the campsite, unroll and tie it around a nearby tree, and it's a handy kitchen cabinet.

Make it ahead

A good way to save space and weight on camping trips (especially backpacking trips) is to premix and preprepare much of the food. Instant coffee and powdered creamer can be mixed before leaving home. English muffins can be split, buttered, and then reassembled before wrapping. A package of gravy mix can be mixed with instant rice (dry). Then all you have to do is add boiling water for hearty rice and gravy.

Picnic box

An empty egg carton makes a wonderful nonsquash carrier for boiled or deviled eggs being taken to a picnic.

Keeping it cool

Planning a picnic? The day before, fill several small balloons with cold water, knot each opening, and place the balloons in the freezer overnight (filling them not too full, or they'll break). Come picnic morning, put the balloons into the picnic cooler and pack the food around them. They will hold the water as the ice in them melts, and the food remains cool and dry.

Useful containers

The styrofoam and cardboard containers that fruits, vegetables, and meats are sold in make excellent picnic plates or, when decorated, can be used for a child's birthday party.

Save on paper plates

When packing paper plates for a picnic, put a sheet of wax paper between each plate. Serve the main meal on the paper, and then discard it, leaving the plate clean for dessert.

Time savers for cookouts

When having a cookout you can save a lot of time by placing a piece of charcoal in each compartment of a cardboard egg carton. Close the top and light the carton. When it is burned down, your charcoal will already have started.

Those who love to cook out during the summer often find there is a lot of running back and forth to the house. To cut down on this, keep a picnic basket filled with paper plates, napkins, cups, plastic eating utensils, salt, pepper, and other condiments. The basket also serves as a great cleanup bin after the cookout. Before storing the basket, fill it again for the next time.

Cute idea for a picnic

When going on a picnic, use colorful bandanas as napkins. They can be inexpensively purchased at the dime store and are practical and festive.

No more fly-away tablecloth

Sew pockets on the underside corners of your picnic tablecloth. At the picnic site, place a few stones in each pocket. The cloth will always lie smooth and won't blow away.

Hanging tools

Hang drapery hooks (pointed end inside) over the edge of your outdoor barbecue. They're handy for holding cooking tools and mitts.

Protect your hands!

Buy welder's gloves for use around barbecue grills and stoves. They far surpass cloth mitts in both control and protection.

Foil scrubber

A ball of foil, used as a scrubber, works well for scouring pots on a campout.

Clean camping pans

To clean all-metal camping pans, put them into your self-cleaning oven ... and just look at them sparkle!

Pre-prep for campfires

Now is the time to collect small twigs and branches for those campfires this summer, as most camps are picked clean of tinder by other campers early on. Put the tinder in paper bags for easy carrying to your campsite.

Litter solution

Since camping with young people can result in quite a bit of littering, here is a solution to the problem. During outings, whether with friends or family, make wrappers, napkins, or other trash the "ticket" which must be shown before treats or privileges are given.

Easy picnic table

Instead of taking your old card table to the rummage sale, cut the legs down to make a perfect beach or picnic table. It's easy to transport in your car, too.

Time-saving transport

To save time and extra trips when you have many things to take to the beach—toys, picnic jug, beach blanket, towels—pack them in a shopping cart (small enough to fit in the back of the car) and wheel them from house to car and from car to beach.

Build a sandbox

A quick and inexpensive sandbox for your toddler can be made from a small, hard plastic wading pool. Just add sand, shovels, and pails, and your youngster is all set.

A sticky problem

With oil and tar becoming an increasing problem on beaches, people are sometimes faced with having to remove sticky substances from bodies and beach gear after an outing. Rubbing peanut butter (yes, peanut butter!) into the soiled areas will quickly dissolve the oil, and then the spots can be easily wiped off.

Recycling rocks

During an outing, collect rocks that you find interesting. Cover the bottoms of your favorite ones with felt to use as bookends or paperweights. They also make great last-minute gifts.

Hints for joggers

Before jogging or going for a long walk, slip a label with your address into a pocket. This serves as identification in case of an emergency.

If you do most of your jogging at night, put fluorescent tape on your shoes. This simple step is a real safety precaution, especially if running on a busy street or highway.

Using local school facilities

Call your local school for information about the use of their facilities when they are not scheduled for student use. Chances are good that you can exercise in the gym, use audio-visual equipment, read in the library, or work in the shop. Some community education programs schedule time and space for adults from 7 PM until late at night.

In case of emergency

If you bike alone quite frequently but dislike being encumbered by a pack or purse, keep a few dimes taped securely to the bottom of your bike seat. Ready and waiting, should the need arise, for a quick telephone call.

Exercise suit

Instead of throwing out that old bathing suit, use it as your daily exercise suit. It's easy to get into and out of, and it provides maximum freedom of movement.

For puzzle fans

If you like to assemble jigsaw puzzles but do not like to take up space that is usually needed for other more important things, purchase a large desk blotter. You can easily move the puzzle from one room to another without disturbing it or taking up valuable space.

Here is another simple idea for a portable puzzle board: a 28" x 32" piece of sanded plywood, varnished and edged with molding to prevent the pieces from falling off. It can be carried easily through doorways, from one table to another, or out onto the porch, or put down on the floor for the children.

Play money

Square plastic bag closures such as used on bread bags make great tokens for children's board games where pieces are missing or as lost "money."

ON THE GO

Hire a housesitter

During a vacation, hire a student for a nominal fee to stay overnight in your house to take in the mail, turn on the lights, and the like. You'll enjoy your holidays even more knowing someone is looking after your home.

Vacation memories

Vacation mementos often end up in boxes, packed away and forgotten—a jumble of postcards, menus, brochures, and other souvenirs. To prevent this, take along a large manila envelope for each day of the trip and put the day's accumulation of remembrances inside. Once home, it's an easy job to slip them into plastic-paged albums, along with any photographs taken.

When traveling, send picture postcards home to yourself with dates, times, and special happenings regarding the scene pictured. When home again, the postcards are helpful in jogging the memory and pinpointing the people, places, and things enjoyed.

When traveling, you may find it helpful to pack some plastic storage bags, preferably ones that zip shut. They're handy for packing mementos of your trip—postcards, the pretty rocks and shells you couldn't bear to leave behind—and any bathing suits or damp clothing that didn't quite dry the night before.

Taking the boredom out of travel

Make each long car trip a learning adventure by keeping a dictionary handy—a small paperback copy easily fits into your glove compartment. Children and adults alike can share the fun of learning new words as they zoom along the often monotonous stretches of superhighways. You also might enjoy keeping lists of new words learned during each trip.

Traveling in a car for long distances can be boring to all concerned. Radio shows are often a disappointment. A tape deck can really make a difference. Collect tapes several months in advance of the trip. At the local library you will find recordings of old radio shows such as "The Shadow" and "Ellery Queen." Copy them onto cassette tapes to take along on the trip. You can even rent books-on-tape from a company that puts out best sellers. The miles fly by as you let your imagination take hold and are off in another world.

Here's another way to cut down on boredom

Try improve your vocabulary while sitting at traffic lights or riding along. Dictate words that you want to make part of your everyday speech into a small tape recorder. Listen to the set of words for several days or weeks until you know them; then move on to a new set.

Quick reminder

Keep a spring-type clothespin on the visor of your car and clip it to the ignition key when you turn on your headlights in the daytime. It's a handy reminder to turn them off.

Helpful information

To remember when the car was last serviced, note the most recent service date on a 3″x5″ card and clip it to the sun visor for easy access.

First aid on the go

An unused metal lunch box makes an ideal first-aid kit. Keep it stocked with essentials and carry it along on outings.

Home for an orphaned sock

Most people keep a flashlight in the glove compartment of their cars. The noise it makes rattling around as the car moves is very annoying. Silence it by slipping it into a sock whose mate has been lost.

Neat and clean

When you travel by car, carry a large empty milk carton for use as a wastebasket. It won't leak and holds fruit peels and cores as well as paper. It's also a good way to teach children not to be litterbugs.

End seat-belt confusion

If your car has three sets of seat belts and shoulder straps, mark corresponding fastener ends with one, two, or three dots of bright-colored nail polish to eliminate confusion. You'll know at a quick glance which parts of the straps buckle together. Even small children will be able to fasten seat belts correctly.

For scribblers

Put a magnetic pad and pencil on the dashboard of your car. It will be handy for you and your kids to scribble notes on.

For a neater car

Use a child's play broom to clean out your car. The small broom reaches into corners, and the short handle makes it easier to use.

Floor mats for your car

During the messy winter months, plastic car mats do little to help keep the car clean. Replace them with a piece of carpeting, cut to size, in front of each seat. It will absorb the wet snow that clings to boots much better than the mats. Most carpet stores sell their discontinued samples for just pennies.

Are you having trouble finding floor mats to fit your new compact car? Check the housewares section of any department store for kitchen-sink mats. They fit well, and you can get them in many colors to match your car's interior.

Makeshift flares

Don't throw out all your cardboard milk cartons. Keep a few in the trunk of your car—they make good emergency flares because they burn slowly, but brightly.

An old window shade

Carry an old window shade in your car or camper. It's handy to lie on if you have to get under the car for repairs or to place beneath a sleeping bag.

Cold weather aid

Keep scraps of old carpet in the car during the cold weather. A piece placed in front of each back tire provides traction to pull the car out of icy situations.

Removing bumper stickers

Remove old bumper stickers by rubbing with nail polish remover.

End to misplaced road maps

You will never misplace road maps if you file them alphabetically, by state, in a record file (use the accordion-pleated type). No more last-minute hassle looking for a map before you start off on a trip.

I can see clearly now

Finding an unfamiliar address at night can be difficult, even with a map. It's even worse when you are driving alone with no one to help navigate. Here's a trick that prevents eyestrain—and wrong turns! Before leaving home, take a yellow wide-tipped felt pen and trace the planned route on the map. Then, with a flashlight kept on the seat, you can glance at the map and clearly see which roads and turns to take.

Keep a magnifying glass in your car's glove compartment. It comes in handy when you have to read road maps on a trip.

Easy travel

Next time you pick up a road map, get *two* copies. File one in the glove compartment for reference as needed. Cut the second copy into 8″ x 10″ sections and paste on pieces of cardboard. You'il find these much handier to use in the car than a large map that needs folding and unfolding.

When traveling by car, attach route directions to the inside of your car visor. When you need to refer to them, just flip the visor down.

Traveling tip

When traveling, keep a large safety pin attached to the underside of the lapel of your coat or to the lining of your handbag. If you slip your rings on the pin whenever and wherever you wash your hands, you won't risk leaving the jewelry behind.

Suitcase check

When packing a suitcase, make a list of the contents and tape it inside the lid. Check the list when packing to leave a hotel. This way you'll never leave anything behind.

Happy traveling

Traveling can be exciting, and what you take with you on a trip can influence your enjoyment. Before leaving on your next out-of-town jaunt, consult this packing checklist to help ensure you're heading for a happy time:

1. Expert travelers travel light. Take along coordinates and separates that can be interchanged for several looks, at least two pairs of comfortable shoes, and accessories to "dress-up" and "dress-down" outfits.

2. Laundry can be a bother on a trip. Bring along some mild detergent for hand washables.

3. Transfer the amounts of toiletry and cosmetic items you'll need into reusable plastic containers—this prevents accidental breakage or leakage of bottles in your suitcase and also cuts luggage weight.

4. Place shoes inside plastic bags to guard against soiling your clothes. Then put them and other heavy items against hinges of suitcase so they don't shift and crush things.

Cushion breakable items between layers of clothes or with small pieces of apparel such as socks, scarves.

Fold clothes in thirds along body lines and "weave" around other pieces, rather than stacking them, to prevent creasing.

Clothes and travel

Take several spring-type clothespins along on your next trip. Used with the wire hangers provided in most hotels and motels, they make instant skirt or pants hangers.

When only wire hangers are available in your hotel room, put two or three together to hold heavy coats or dresses. They won't bend or sag.

When traveling, tuck a couple of medium-size plastic garbage bags into your suitcases to hold soiled garments. This will keep your unworn garments fresh, and the bags can be emptied right into your washer upon return.

Try packing a few sheets of the anti-cling product usually tossed in the dryer. It's practically weightless, and when added to rinse water, tames hand washables.

Instead of packing clothespins to use while traveling, take along a collection of plastic bag closures. They work just as well on light items and take up far less room.

Solving a luggage problem

Purchase a denim laundry bag for each family member. Mark individually with each person's name in bright fabric. These washable, squashable bags fit in odd corners of the car and help conserve space. They also help identify children's belongings at summer camp, accompany them on overnight visits to friends, and can even go to college as a laundry bag.

Handy night light

Pack a night light for traveling. It makes trips to the bathroom less frightening for the little ones, and other family members' sleep won't be disturbed.

A sign on the right door

When staying at a hotel or motel with small children, tape a picture outside your door. This will make it much easier for a wandering child to find the right room.

MOVING RIGHT ALONG . . .

Planning to move?

If you are planning to move to another city, get acquainted beforehand with your new surroundings. Subscribe to one of the local newspapers and read up on various events. You will get a pretty good idea of your new town by the time you actually start packing.

Easy moving tips

Before moving from an old house to a new one, tape easy-to-remove labels on each piece of furniture—plus all the boxes—telling which rooms they go into. It keeps the moving men from constantly asking where to put things.

If you're moving to a new house, pack one box or suitcase with enough sheets, pillowcases, and towels to take care of your needs on the first night at your destination. Mark the container distinctively so that it's easy to find among the other luggage when you arrive.

Moving? Slip a paper plate between each dish. When unpacking, don't throw away the paper plates; use them at meals while you're getting settled in your new quarters.

When moving, wrap dishes and glasses in damp newspaper. As the paper dries, it forms a protective wrapping in the shape of the article.

Cardboard cartons with sectional dividers come in handy to carry bottles of foods such as catsup and sauces when you move. The bottles will remain upright, and you'll have no spillage.

THE THIRTY-DAY MOVING PLAN

Fifteen to thirty days before:

1. Eliminate everything you won't move.
2. Prepare inventory of goods.
3. Call moving companies for estimates.
4. Arrange method of payment.
5. Purchase full coverage on movables.
6. Arrange for packing cartons needed.
7. Notify post office of new address.
8. Fill out change-of-address cards.
9. Gather medical and dental records.
10. Check and clear tax assessments.
11. Notify schools, have transcripts forwarded.
12. Close local charge accounts.
13. Arrange pet shipment and immunization records.
14. Make travel plans.
15. Make hotel reservations if needed; confirm later.
16. Begin to use up the food in your freezer.

17. Decide what items of low value you are going to give to charity. Get a signed receipt for what you give away to use on your taxes.

Two weeks before:

1. Pack a little bit at a time. Don't wear yourself out.

2. Use your kitchen cart or server as a mobile packing table.

3. Collect clothing and items to clean or repair.

4. Return things borrowed, collect those loaned.

5. Have bank transfer accounts and release safe deposit box.

6. Arrange to disconnect utilities.

7. Arrange to connect utilities at new home.

8. Have farewell parties, visits.

9. Make arrangements to have heavy appliances serviced for move.

10. Have a garage sale to eliminate articles you don't want to move.

11. If driving, have car tuned-up for the trip. Check oil, water, battery, and tires.

One week before:

1. Dispose of all flammables.

2. Pack suitcases.

3. Plan travel games, activities.

4. Set things aside to pack in car.

5. If mover has not been asked to do so, take down curtains, rods, shelves, and TV antenna.

6. Get sitter for moving day.

7. Check with your phone company to see what phones you may take. This may entitle you to a credit.

8. Withdraw the contents of your safe deposit box.

9. If traveling with pets, get pet tranquilizers for the trip. Make sure vaccinations and papers are in order.

10. Assemble "survival kit," containing items needed to spend the last day or so in the old house and the first ones in your new house before unpacking.

11. Make up "do not move" cartons for articles to be taken in car.

Day before moving:

1. Empty and defrost refrigerator and freezer and let them air for 24 hours. Place charcoal, coffee, or baking soda in a sock to deodorize.

2. Clean and air your range.

3. Finish packing personal items.

4. In urban areas, call the police to request that "No Parking" signs be placed in front of your home so you'll be assured of a parking and unloading spot.

5. Get a good night's sleep.

Moving day:

1. Be there or have someone there to answer questions.

2. Accompany the van operator during inventory of things to be moved.

3. Make final check of appliances to be sure they've been ser viced.

4. Sign and save copy of bills of lading. Be sure delivery address and place you can be reached en route are included in mover's information.

5. Tell driver exactly how to get to new address, if you can.

6. Confirm delivery date and time.

7. Ask to be advised of final cost (determined after van is weighed). Then, make sure you'll have cash, money order or certified check to pay before van is unloaded at destination.

8. Strip beds, but leave fitted bottom sheets on mattresses.

9. Have your vacuum ready to clean bed rails, piano backs, and other hard-to-move items.

10. Load sweeper last, have it in new home first. Fast cleanups in both places really help.

11. Before leaving house, check each room and closet and make sure windows are down and lights out.

KEEPING IN TOUCH

Handy address labels

When attending events such as cooking school shows and sports shows, where you register for prizes, take along address labels. A quick lick and stick will allow more time for looking at the displays and exhibits. It's no guarantee of winning, but it does save time and is more legible than a quick scrawl.

Address files

If your address book has been looking messy from all the changing of addresses and telephone numbers of friends and relatives who have moved, here is an idea that works well and looks good. Take two wooden recipe boxes that match your kitchen decor. Designate one for recipes and the other for your address box. The addresses are written on separate cards, so that if someone moves, all you have to do is make a new card. Use the matching boxes for kitchen bookends on top of the refrigerator.

Also use them to note birthdays, anniversary dates, gift suggestions, clothing sizes, and any other information you want to preserve. When you receive a letter from a new friend or a change of address and are busy, simply drop the envelope in the file box in its alphabetical order. Later, transfer it to a card.

Answering letters

As you answer each letter, put the date on the envelope. You will never have to wonder who wrote last!

Remembering special days

In order not to forget birthdays and anniversaries, buy all your cards at one time. Then address the envelopes and index them according to the dates on which they should be mailed.

When you see an especially pretty and appropriate greeting card for a specific occasion, buy it, address the envelope, and paper-clip it to the correct calendar page. Too often, special days just slip by without being remembered.

Here is another suggestion for getting birthday and anniversary cards into the mail on time. On the first of each month—the easiest date to remember—address each card that needs to be sent during that month. In the upper right-hand corner, where the stamp will later hide it, write the date that the card needs to be mailed. As the month progresses, each greeting goes out on time.

Family news letter

If your family is scattered across the country, here is a great way to keep in touch. Once a month, type all general news and make a copy for each family member. Then personalize each copy with a handwritten note especially for that person.

News tape

One good way to keep in touch with family members far away is to use a cassette tape recorder. News can be related as often as wanted. When the tape is full, mail it off. For many, it is a much quicker system than writing, and they find they remember more news.

Constructive chatter

For those who feel they should be using telephone time constructively, try keeping a bag of chores that do not need full attention such as mending, small sewing projects, and coupons to be clipped near the telephone.

Mini art lesson

Each time you visit a museum, stop at its gift shop and purchase a stack of postcards imprinted with works of art. Use these as greeting and birthday cards. Add a short phrase, like "Happy Birthday" or "Congratulations," and both the receiver and sender learn a little more about art.

On the move

After a move, when it comes time to write friends back home, buy stationery and postcards picturing a local scene. Write a short note on the stationery and enclose the postcard with your new address. This way, friends receive the news of the move, the new address, and an idea of what the local scenery is like.

Useful gift

To encourage children to write, give them a box of note paper at birthdays, Christmas, or other major holidays.

Christmas notes

Many people correspond with certain friends and relatives only at Christmastime and keep a separate book with their addresses. Throughout the year, jot down bits of news or a funny incident that would interest each person. When it is time to send Christmas letters, simply refer to the notes kept throughout the year.

Vacation greetings

Because vacations always pass by so quickly, it's hard to spend precious time writing postcards. Addressing in advance on self-adhesive labels shortens the task considerably.

Sharing your vacation

To continue the pleasure of an enjoyable vacation and also share it with friends, cut up no longer needed travel brochures and paste the pictures on plain white writing paper. Presto, custom stationery. The stationery serves as a pleasant reminder of the trip and allows one to share thoughts too lengthy to fit on postcards.

Mailing packages

When mailing packages, cover the mailing address with transparent tape. Or, apply clear nail polish over the address. The ink won't smear if the parcel gets wet.

Make a collage of snapshots

How many really good snapshots have you taken throughout the years, then tucked away in a drawer or photo album? Buy a big picture frame, make a collage of your favorite photos, and hang it in the hallway where everyone can enjoy it. This also makes a nice gift for grandparents.

Identifying photographs

Take a couple of minutes to write names and dates on the backs of newly developed photographs. This will supply the answers to questions that invariably turn up later. Who hasn't looked at family pictures and wondered when they were taken and who some of the people were?

COMMUNITY ACTIVITIES

Beautification program

If you have a small, messy, and neglected area of city property near your home, try giving it some special care. Invite your neighbors to help fertilize the grass and plant trees and flowers. Soon what used to be an eyesore will become a beautiful addition to the neighborhood.

Community projects

Reach out to your community. The next time your organization or club needs a service such as a simple printing job done, press release written, or a mailing sent out, check with local schools and colleges to see if there are classes or individual students who would like to help.

Don't miss your favorite radio program

If you have missed hearing a favorite radio program because of a ringing phone or doorbell or the interruption of a chore needing attention in another room, try turning on a cassette recorder when the program begins and tape it for later listening, just in case. It gives greater freedom without the nuisance of missing something special.

Walk and talk

Here is an idea for a neighborhood to strengthen community togetherness. Once a year have a neighborhood "walk and talk" night. The objective is to go out into the street and meet and chat with neighbors. It can be a potluck picnic supper with organized games for the children, a barbecue, block-long flea market, and even dancing under the stars. The police will often cooperate by giving permission to seal off the street from traffic for a few hours that evening. It's fun to meet old and new neighbors while solidifying the feeling of a community within a large or small city.

For a safer neighborhood

The sound of bells and wind chimes resounding through a neighborhood whenever someone opens a door or gate, besides providing pretty tunes for all, makes it virtually impossible for a stranger to enter "sound-proofed" premises without being spotted by a neighbor.

Mother's helper

Mothers can help each other by forming a baby-sitting pool. One night a week, on a rotating basis, one woman takes care of all the children, leaving the other mothers free for the evening.

Another way to give mothers free time and children playtime is to form a play group that meets two mornings a week. The mothers take turns caring for the children, giving them a simple soup-and-sandwich lunch and returning them home for naps. This gives each mother free mornings to do as she likes, and the children look forward to playing away from home.

Just moved to a new town and need a reliable baby sitter quickly? Call the local senior citizens' center. They often have a list of women who would like to baby-sit. They are dependable, and their grandmotherly manner is often comforting to the child in a new environment.

The first apartment

For young people moving into their first apartments, give a "Secondhand Rose party." Friends and relatives can be invited with instructions to bring only secondhand items such as odd glasses, pans, and cleaning products. People enjoy giving and finding homes for old but useful goods, and it allows the young ones to set up housekeeping on limited budgets.

Unique housewarming gift

As a neighborly gesture to owners of a house under construction, snap pictures of the progress. After its completion, assemble the snapshots in a photo album and present it to the new homeowners as a housewarming gift.

Welcome new neighbors

Whenever a new family moves into your neighborhood, make them feel welcome by preparing a "welcome to the neighborhood" basket. List some of the neighborhood stores for them, emergency telephone numbers, local organizations, and the like. To give it a personal touch, add homemade cookies, together with the names, addresses, and phone numbers of the contributors. It's a great way to make new friends.

A thoughtful gift to welcome a newcomer to town is a personalized map of the city. Maps are available, for a small fee, at many service stations. In some cities you can also get one at the newspaper publishing company. Mark schools, churches, shopping malls, favorite supermarkets, and the like on the map.

Looking forward to spring

If you are planning to sell your house in the winter, consider providing the new owners with a complete sketch and possibly a few photos of the garden. This helps them visualize what spring will look like and also can save certain plants that might be mistaken for weeds.

Keeping track

If you have ever forgotten who has books and records you have lent, start a "lending chart." Whenever someone borrows one, keep track of its title, the date, and the borrower in a small notebook. This saves hurt feelings, frustration, and misunderstandings later. Every few months refer back to it, and make gentle reminders if they are in order.

When lending a book, give only the book and keep the dust jacket with a notation of the borrower and the date. The empty jacket will remind you of the missing book, and you will know whom to contact in case it is not returned.

Books lent to friends are more often returned when the last page is inscribed, "Please return to (name)."

Missing jars

Do you share your preserves with friends and family and then wonder where all your jars are the next season? This year, write your name on a piece of tape and attach it to the bottom of each jar that you give away. This should assure its swift return.

Laundry room library

Instead of discarding paperback books you'll never reread, start a laundry room library in your apartment building. Line up the books on an old bookshelf or table—your neighbors will catch on quickly and donate theirs. It will help pass the time while you're waiting for the wash to finish.

Magazine pass-alongs

To save money on magazines, books, and newspapers, start a reading-exchange with your neighbors. Certain people can buy certain magazines, and you can buy others, then swap when you're finished.

Jigsaw puzzle exchange

After conquering the challenge of a new puzzle, do you tire of redoing it? Try to organize a puzzle exchange at your local library. A conveniently located table can serve as a depository. Everyone may help themselves to puzzles, provided they are replaced with an equal number of used ones.

Good use for old toys

The perfect recipient for children's outgrown but still usable toys may be your pediatrician! Many are pleased with donations as the toys in their waiting rooms get above average wear and tear.

Four

333 Hints for In and Around the Kitchen

LUNCHES TO GO

Lunch-time sandwiches

When making sandwiches for lunch boxes, try spreading the catsup, mustard, or mayonnaise between the slices of cold cuts or cheese instead of on the bread. Less soggy sandwiches at lunch time!

Lunch-box meals

Here's a tip for lunch-box meals at work or school: When you heat soup for the vacuum bottle, heat one or two hot dogs also, then pack both soup and meat in the bottle. If you put buttered rolls in the box, your husband or children will have hot soup *and* a hot sandwich for lunch.

Lunch-time helpers

Save those small plastic pill containers with snap-on lids—they're perfect vessels for salad dressing, catsup, or mustard in brown bag lunches. With them you'll never have soggy sandwiches or droopy salads again.

Save the round plastic boxes notions are sold in to hold relish, mustard, jelly, or jam when packing a lunch box for the youngsters.

Old spice jars are perfect one-shot salad dressing containers to take along with a salad lunch. Pour your choice of dressing into the bottle and place in the container with the salad. No wilted lettuce or leakage!

Foil that foil

Don't frost homemade cupcakes on top! Split the cake and put frosting inside to hold halves together. This will prevent the frosting from sticking to the paper when packing a lunch.

Enjoy your lunch

Try packing a lunch for yourself in the morning when you prepare lunches for the family. If the weather is nice, take an impromptu excursion to the park or sit outside and enjoy the garden. If the weather is bad, invite yourself over to a friend's house for a quick lunch-time visit.

BAKING

Keep track when baking

When baking, put all ingredients needed to the left of the mixing bowl. As you add the various items, set each container to the right of the bowl. Should you be interrupted, you will know how far you have gone.

Sifting flour

Before sifting flour onto wax paper, always crease the paper down the center. This creates a handy pouring spout.

A quick rise

To make hot-roll mix or bread rise quickly, set the bowl of dough on a heating pad and turn the heat indicator to low. The dough rises in no time.

Try mixing dough for bread or rolls in a deep-well cooker, cover, and put it back on the range after heating the unit for a minute—just long enough to keep the temperature in the well at about 85°F. This protects the dough from drafts and keeps it out of the way.

Colorful reminder

When using a warm oven to make yogurt or croutons or to raise bread dough, put a colorful magnet on the door to remind you the oven is in use.

Testing a cake

Sometimes toothpicks are too short to test a cake for doneness, but a piece of uncooked spaghetti works just fine.

Baking hint

Notch your bread board in inches, so when you roll dough you'll know exactly when you have the size pastry you need. Also, machine-stitch circles on your pastry cloth to indicate crust sizes you most often need.

Rolling out the dough

Glue rubber fruit-jar rings under each corner of your pastry board so it won't slide around when you roll out biscuits or knead bread.

Put a rubber sink mat under the pastry board to prevent its slipping when you roll out pastry.

Anchor your pastry cloth, and it won't scoot away from you as you roll out piecrust or cookie dough. Just pull the cloth tightly over a cutting board and tuck the edges underneath. The board serves as a weight so the cloth will stay put and wrinkle free.

Foil-lined cookie sheets

Cut aluminum foil to fit cookie sheets, place cookies on the foil, then slide onto a cookie sheet and bake. When the cookies are done, slide the foil off and put on another sheet. This saves time because you can prepare all the cookies at once and hold them until there is oven space for them.

Solution to a sticky problem

When your holiday baking calls for chopped dates and other sticky fruits, spray the kitchen shears or chopping blade with a nonstick cooking spray. The chopping will be done in half the time, and cleanup will be a breeze.

Forming dough

If the cookie recipe suggests shaping the dough into balls, try using a melon ball scoop instead of rolling the dough in your hands.

When baking French bread, shape some into buns for individual submarine sandwiches. These are great for "brown baggers!"

Ideal kitchen tool

A pair of pinking shears makes an ideal cookie cutter or pastry trimmer to trim the edges of pies, to cut fancy sandwiches, and to cut cookies into odd shapes to delight the kiddies.

Burned cookies

When cookies turn out too dark, let them cool and scrape off the burned part with a vegetable peeler.

Frosting tips

To give frosting a hobnail pattern, press the tip of a spatula against the frosting and pull quickly outward. For best results, apply frosting thickly to the cake.

Colored icing goes on cookies in a hurry when painted on with a 1″ paintbrush.

Easy slicing

Try using a ham slicer to cut icebox cookies. With it you can make thin neat slices without flattening them.

Energy-saver bread crumbs

Make use of the "wasted" heat when the oven is cooling off after a baking session by putting several slices of bread in it. By the time the oven has cooled, the bread will be crisp and crunchy (but not brown). Crush the slices with a rolling pin, putting the coarse crumbs into a jar to be added to melted butter for casserole toppings. Add herbs to the finely crushed crumbs for breading fish, chicken, or chops.

For your holiday baking

Never throw away expensive leftover coffee. It makes a delicious flavoring when baking gingerbreads or spiced fruitcakes.

Sparkly cookies

Brush freshly baked cookies with corn syrup or frosting, then sprinkle on color with any flavored gelatin.

Tasty nutritious touches

Sprinkle your pastry board with 3–4 tablespoons of quick rolled oats before rolling out your dough to give the crust—for fruit pies, especially—a "nutty" flavor and extra nutrition.

When a recipe calls for the cake pan to be dusted with flour after greasing, use wheat germ instead. It keeps the cake from sticking and adds flavor and nutrition.

When preparing French toast, pour wheat germ on a separate dish and, after dipping the bread in the egg, also dip it in the wheat germ.

Gift trays

Save the foil trays frozen dinners are packaged in, wash them carefully, and use as gift trays. Fill with nuts, candy, and cookies; cover with a transparent wrap and tie with colorful ribbon.

Cookies galore

Make batches of basic cookie doughs (sugar, oatmeal, and peanut butter work best), divide them into individual margarine tubs with lids and baking instructions taped to the top, and store in the freezer. They keep for several weeks and are handy for quick after-school or late-night snacks. Also give them as small gifts to elderly neighbors or friends.

Be prepared!

Keep a large supply of cupcakes in the freezer. Then, when unexpected company arrives, take out as many as you need for a fresh treat without a lot of leftovers. Frost as needed.

Save on your grocery bill

Buy day-old bread and bakery items at reduced prices. Freeze, then use for toasting, grilled sandwiches, French toast, or stuffings.

Easy slicing

Slice English muffins in half before freezing. This saves you work later on, and they'll thaw more quickly as well.

To wrap a frosted cake

Before wrapping a freshly frosted cake with clear plastic, freeze it first—and the wrapping will not stick to the frosting.

SUBSTITUTES

No waste

Don't toss out that last half-inch of French, blue cheese, or Russian salad dressing that refuses to pour out of the bottle. Transform it into a new dressing. Add 2 teaspoons of vinegar or lemon juice (or one of each). Recap and shake vigorously. Gradually add ½ cup of mayonnaise or sour cream, shaking as you add. It's a delicious way to use up all those leftover dressings.

Other uses for candy

If another strawberry, mocha, or chocolate cream candy is more than you can stand, don't throw it out: Mash or chop it. Put aside and use in cake frostings. The bits of chocolate add texture to the frosting, and the various flavors can be heightened or toned down.

Spicy substitutes

If you don't have the fresh herbs a recipe calls for, simply substitute with dried ones. Three parts fresh equals one part dried. Be sure to crumble dried herbs to release their flavor.

Tasty breakfast

Like oatmeal that's really piping hot on cold mornings? Don't add cold milk. Instead, stir in ⅓ cup of instant dry milk per serving and a little extra water as you cook it. The result is a creamy, smooth cereal that stays hot to the last delicious spoonful—and costs less, too.

Thickening soups

Thicken soups and stews without adding calories by putting the onions and celery in the blender for a few seconds before adding. You not only thicken the soup but at the same time add flavor—and even disguise the vegetables your children may not like.

Every crumb counts

To dry bread for stuffing, place it in a colander. The holes allow air to circulate and reach the underside, which saves having to turn it.

Syrup for pancakes

If you happen to run out of syrup, add a bit of water and a dab of butter to fruit jelly and heat. It makes a delicious topping for pancakes.

Quick topping

Put the crumbs in your cookie jar to good use. Combined with brown sugar and a pinch of cinnamon they make a great topping for your favorite coffee cake.

USING GADGETS

Quick cracker crumbs

Use your onion chopper to make graham cracker crumbs. The crumbs won't scatter, and the chopping blade turns out finer crumbs than a rolling pin can.

Easy slicing and cutting

Save time by slicing bananas with a pastry blender.

Here's a safe and easy way to cut squash that has a tough rind: Use a meat saw.

An easy, quick way to cut pizza pies is with kitchen scissors.

The simple egg slicer can be a great labor-slicing device. Use it to make uniform slices of cooked or canned potatoes and beets or fresh mushrooms, peeled cucumber sections—anything firm, that will fit into the egg-sized mold.

When cutting bar cookies, use a pizza cutter. Makes nice, smooth squares in half the time.

Perfect meatballs

Use a melon-ball maker to form appetizer-sized meatballs. If grated onion is used in the recipe, dip the baller in cold water occasionally to keep the meatballs from sticking.

Versatile spoon

A grapefruit spoon with a serrated tip works very well to scoop out tomatoes in preparation for stuffing.

The easy way

An easy way to open the end of a box that instructs you to "Press here": Use a beverage can opener. It will save your fingernails.

Terrific shrimp deveiner

The pointed end of a beer-can opener is an excellent tool for deveining shrimp.

Easy spread

When butter or margarine is too firm to cut, use a potato peeler to cut thin slices from a stick. It will soften in minutes.

To pit cherries

Use the tip of a potato peeler to pit cherries. It's quick and efficient.

Versatile trays

The plastic-coated trays that hold meat, sweet rolls, and other items from the supermarket are ideal to drain fried bacon, sausages, fish, and other fried foods.

A simple trick

While your bread is toasting, place the cream cheese or butter dish next to the toaster. The emanating heat will warm and soften the spread without melting it.

Peeling and paring

Use a vegetable peeler to cut orange or lemon rind peels. They will come off without the white membrane.

Use a vegetable peeler to remove the strings from less tender stalks of celery. It's quick and efficient.

If you peel broccoli to remove the tough skin, put the stems under fairly warm water first. This makes the skin less brittle and allows it to come off easily. Just snap off the flowerettes, then peel from the bottom of the stem toward the top.

Slicing raw meat

The job of slicing or cubing raw meat is easier if the meat is partially frozen, but fingers usually become numb from the cold before the job is half finished. If you put a hot-pad mitt on your left hand and slip a plastic sandwich bag over it, you can hold onto the meat without freezing your fingers.

Cutting a pineapple

Get a good grip on a pineapple while cutting it—and save wear and tear on your hands, too—by wearing an oven mitt.

Pitless lemon juice

Need a little lemon juice? Instead of cutting a lemon, roll it on a hard surface to soften, then pierce twice with an ice pick near one end.

Soft brush

Rather than purchasing a costly gourmet "mushroom brush," try an inexpensive soft toothbrush.

An easy scrub

Scrub the vegetables you cook with the skins on with a nylon-wool scouring pad. This method is quicker than using a vegetable brush, and the pad actually does a better job.

Basket bonus

Instead of throwing away plastic baskets you get in supermarkets, use them as colanders to rinse mushrooms, radishes, and berries. Also stack several near the sink to hold soap and sponges.

Removing corn silk

The easiest and quickest way to remove corn silk from ears of fresh corn is to rub them with a vegetable brush under running water.

Handy squeeze bottle

A small plastic squeeze bottle is handy to use for putting small amounts of cooking oil in a pan or skillet. It is easier to squeeze just the right amount into the pan than it is to pour from a large bottle. Saves oil and messy bottles.

Clever cover-up

When you fill the coffee basket of your percolator, put a thimble over the stem. This prevents the grounds from getting down into the pot.

Baking cupcakes

When making cupcakes, use an ice cream scoop to fill the pans. The lever releases the batter neatly into the cups, keeping the pan clean and the cupcakes all the same size.

Easy fill

A soup ladle is fine for filling small molds or pastry shells with gelatin, custard, or other liquids.

Quick cake decoration

Press an animal-shaped cookie cutter into the center of an iced cake. Tint animal part with contrasting food colors.

No fuss—no mess

Serving tacos on everyday flat plates can be messy and frustrating since they do not stand up very well alone. To keep them from tumbling over and spilling out, save the plastic foam containers fast-food restaurants place hot dogs in. The containers are reusable if washed carefully in warm, sudsy water.

Useful dish

Individual corn-on-the-cob dishes also make useful holders for those messy chili dogs or plain hot dogs. They're especially good for small children.

Carbonation saver

Here is a new use for the snap-on lids from 9-ounce plastic glasses: They make excellent tops for most soft-drink cans. No more problems with flat leftovers when the kids can't finish what they start.

Smooth slide

Use a pancake turner to slide sandwiches into sandwich bags. This keeps sandwiches with soft fillings from falling apart.

Patience saver

Weary of juggling bowl misfits when you want to cool a gelatin mixture fast or whip a bavarian over ice and water? Call on your double boiler for help. Mix or cook in top, then place ice in the bottom, and put the two together. What a spill and patience saver!

Handy salad spinner

After washing raisins for use in baking, dry them in the salad spinner. They shed all the water and can be used at once.

Healthy and refreshing

One simple way to make a frozen fruit juice more interesting is to mix it in the blender. Just a minute of blending makes the juice frothy and light.

Easy cooking

You'll never have to "fish" in the kettle for ears of corn, if you first put them into a basket such as that used for French fried potatoes, then into the kettle of boiling water. Just lift out the basket when corn is done.

Prevent splattering

To prevent splattering when frying meat or fish, cover your frying pan with a metal colander. The steam will escape, the food will brown, and most of the fat will stay under cover.

Useful egg poacher

To heat food for the baby, use a four-unit egg poacher. Put meat in one cup, vegetable in another, fruit in a third, and remove the fourth cup for the bottle. The poacher makes a good warmer while feeding, too.

Want to reheat only a *few* muffins? Put them in an egg poacher.

Versatile electric fry pan

Speed the defrosting of frozen foods by using your electric frying pan. Set control on low (about 200°F), then place fruit (still in its container), meat (unwrapped), or vegetables (unwrapped) in the pan. Heat, keeping them covered, just until they separate.

Here is another method for using an electric frying pan to defrost frozen food: If your electric frying pan has a broiler lid, put the frozen block of unwrapped food on a glass pie plate and place it in the frying pan. Insert the heat control in the broiler lid and set the dial at "Warm." Heat about 10 minutes—and the frozen block can be broken apart easily.

Use your electric frying pan to make candy—especially fudge. The controlled heat produces a better confection.

To pop corn quickly and evenly, use your electric frying pan. Put popcorn in cold pan and set indicator at 350°F. When nearly popped or indicator light goes off, turn pan off and leave lid on until all corn is done.

A perfect cup

When brewing tea with an infuser, leaves seem to float around in the cups. Eliminate this problem by lining the infuser first with a coffee filter cut to size.

Canning tips

Remove pear cores with a melon-ball scoop when canning. This method is time saving, and makes the finished fruit look more attractive.

Sterilize your lids and rubber jar rings in the deep-fat fryer basket when you're canning. It's easy to lift them out of the boiling water.

Make a jelly bag of muslin or several thicknesses of cheesecloth, with the opening large enough to fit over a pair of embroidery hoops. With the hoops in place, the bag is easy to fill—and the hoops snap off when the bag needs to be washed.

Making jam and jelly

When making jam, cook the berries and sugar together in a fryer-cooker, with the control set at 300°F. The constant, even heat cooks without burning or sticking.

Mock powdered sugar

Next time you find yourself out of confectioners' sugar while in the midst of a recipe, substitute with granulated sugar that has been run through the blender.

Cubes and trays

Ice cubes will be clearer if you fill the trays with warm water. This prevents the formation of small air bubbles which, when trapped inside the cubes, give them a cloudy appearance.

A watering can with a small spout is fine for filling ice cube trays in the refrigerator. No water is spilled on the kitchen floor.

Freeze leftover tea or coffee in an ice cube tray. The next time you serve iced tea or iced coffee, use the cubes instead of plain ones, and your drink won't be diluted.

Instead of plain ice cubes in a punch, freeze fruit juice. The cubes look quite attractive, especially when you add some cherries or mint leaves before freezing, and the cubes do not dilute the punch.

Next time you find a sale on lemons or limes, stock up and preserve the juice by freezing it in ice cube trays. Garnish each compartment before freezing with a sliver or two of zest for added flavor.

Often beef roasts produce more pan juices than can be used for gravy. A good way to save some of it for later use is to put it in ice cube trays and freeze. When solid, wrap one or two cubes in foil, store in freezer, and you will have instant beef stock.

Use an aluminum ice cube tray when making fudge. After the fudge is cool, press the ice cube divider into the candy to make uniform squares.

A good way to preserve fresh herbs is to blend them with a little water and freeze them in ice cube trays. Transfer frozen cubes to plastic bags or freezer containers. Drop cubes into soups, spaghetti sauce, stews, and the like for the color and flavor of fresh herbs.

Protecting your cookbooks

Keep a small pane of glass with safe edges, or a square of clear plastic, on the shelf together with your cookbooks. When the recipe is found, place the pane over the open page. It will keep the book open and the page spatter-free!

Or: cover your cookbooks with transparent wrap to protect them from soiling during food preparation.

Or: give them a new lease on life by applying a decorative adhesive covering.

Cookbook shelf

To give a cookbook shelf a new look, cover each book with paper that fits your color scheme. You'll find it adds a nice note to your kitchen.

Dish for church supper

When preparing a covered dish for a church social dinner or picnic, line the dish with transparent wrap or aluminum foil and you can take it back home clean.

Company coasters

Small, handpainted tiles make attractive and inexpensive coasters for guests.

Neat apron

Put a safety pin in the waistband of your apron. Hang the apron by the pin and avoid tying the apron strings.

Unique placemats

For elegant and inexpensive placemats use large oval or rectangular antimacassars or doilies. No longer fashionable on furniture, they are often found at garage sales and thrift shops.

Melting chocolate

To melt chocolate for baking, place squares in a boilable plastic bag, tie, and dip into boiling water. When chocolate is melted, cut off one of the corners and squeeze. There's no mess to clean.

Sweet smells

Next time you make a meal that calls for fresh garlic and fresh ginger, try chopping the garlic first. The ginger, when chopped, will remove the strong garlic smell from fingers and chopping board.

The onion

To turn strong-tasting yellow onions into mild, sweet ones, slice them thinly into a bowl, pour boiling water over, drain, and chill. They will be crisp and almost as mild as the big, sweet Spanish onions.

When chopping onions, put the chopping board on the range top and turn on the exhaust fan in the hood. This helps eliminate odors—and tears.

Ways with foil

Try baking apples in cups shaped from aluminum foil and placed in a shallow pan. It's easy to slip the apples onto dessert dishes from these cups, and you'll have no sticky pan to wash.

It's easy to make a liner for a baking pan if you shape the foil over the outside of the inverted pan and then fit the foil inside.

When preparing that occasional meal of assorted leftovers, are you fed up with the number of pots and pans on the stove and in the dishpan when the meal is over? Next time, try putting each leftover into "bowls" shaped from aluminum foil. Put these bowls in a pan, add a little water, cover, and steam.

To help keep rolls hot and protect the roll basket from grease stains, place a piece of aluminum foil under the napkin in the basket.

If you have accidentally cracked an egg you can still soft- or hard-cook it if you wrap it in aluminum foil before immersing it in boiling water.

"Filter" tip

If grains of rice fall through your steamer while reheating, try placing a coffee filter on the bottom.

Easy beating

Before creaming cold shortening in an electric mixer, heat the beaters for a few minutes by placing them in hot water. This helps prevent the shortening from clogging and sticking to the blades.

Easy measuring

Before measuring syrup, honey, or molasses, grease the measuring cup or spoon thoroughly with either butter or oil to prevent clinging.

Quick strain

Strain used fat through coffee filter paper.

For school lunches

Save individual-size cereal boxes and use them to pack raisins, cookies, popcorn, or potato chips for school lunch boxes. Fastened with a rubber band, these make neat spill- and crush-resistant carriers.

To scale a fish

Use an office clipboard when scaling small fish. The clip holds the tail firmly while you scale, clean, and fillet.

Draining paper for fried foods

Cut clean brown paper bags into convenient sizes for draining bacon or other fried foods. It's both neat and economical, and the brown paper is remarkably absorbent.

Marinating magic

When meat needs marinating, put it into a plastic bag. It needs only half the usual amount of liquid to cover it. Tie tightly and turn every now and then.

Pretty centerpiece

For a pretty summer table centerpiece, place washed carrots, celery, green peppers, radishes, and cherry tomatoes in a large brandy snifter and sprinkle with crushed ice. The vegetables stay crisp and delicious.

Easy pour

Mix gelatin in a 2-cup glass measure. Pour in the gelatin, add hot water to the 1-cup level, then cold water to the 2-cup level. The spout makes it easy to pour the mixture into molds.

Crisp is easy

When you need crackers for mealtime and they're limp because of humid weather, save them with a quick heating in the toaster oven. It will make them crispy-fresh again.

Preventing soggy salads

To prevent salads from getting soggy, place an inverted saucer in the bottom of the salad bowl. The excess salad dressing will drain off under the saucer, leaving the salad crisp and fresh.

Salad wrap-up

Save minutes at mealtime with this make-ahead salad idea. Put the dressing in the bottom of the bowl, add the greens and vegetables, then cover with transparent wrap—and place in refrigerator to chill. The salad will stay crisp and fresh for an hour or two—then simply toss.

Opening jars easily

When a screw-top jar won't open, simply wrap a few rubber bands around the lid to make a firm grip.

No mix-up

When cooking sweet and hot sausages, insert a toothpick into the hot ones. This will help distinguish one from the other, and there is no need to break them to taste which is which.

Cabbage holder

A wooden pick or two inserted through a cabbage wedge will hold the leaves together during cooking.

Stop the drip

The perfect solution for a drippy milk pitcher! Put a dab of butter or margarine on the pour spout of the pitcher to eliminate milk drips (or other liquid drips).

Emergency coffee filters

Out of coffee filters? Fit an ordinary unscented facial tissue into the coffee basket. It will work just as well.

Keep it cool

Place two or three cans of frozen fruit juice wrapped in a cloth or paper towel in the center of your picnic basket. This keeps the food cool, and the fruit juice is ready to mix and serve.

MEAL PLANNING

Easier menu planning

Finding a desired tried-and-true recipe can be time consuming, especially if your cookbook collection is large. Simplify your search by making an index on cards. Using one card for each category, list the recipe name, cookbook, and page number. File in your recipe box. No more frustrating searches, and menu planning will be easier, too: Each card offers tested suggestions.

Save your menus and grocery lists, staple them together, and file. Make sure they are dated so that you do not repeat the same meal too often. Also, attach the tape showing cost of groceries for the week. That way you will be able to pick out a menu that fits your budget when you may be short of money.

To avoid repeating menus for the same dinner guests, keep a small dinner party notebook. In it record the date, menu, wine, and names of the guests. And if something turns out especially right—or especially wrong—note that, too. It's a real memory jogger.

Another way to avoid repeating party menus with certain guests is by using 3″ x 5″ cards to keep a record. Write each guest's name at the top of the card, the dates of their dinner visits, followed by the menu served. Also make notations such as "Does not like cucumbers" and "Prefers tea." It can be a great help, and guests are always impressed when their hostess remembers their preferences.

Stick 'em up

Self-stick photo albums—which can be used to organize a variety of household paperwork—make especially nice recipe scrapbooks. The clear plastic paper covers keep the recipes safe from cooking splatter, and recipes that don't work out can be quickly removed from the waxed page. Save any illustrations accompanying the recipes too, to make your homemade recipe book colorful as well as functional.

For the recipe collector

When preparing a recipe, nothing is quite so annoying as not finding necessary ingredients at hand. One way to combat this is to use a felt-tipped pen to highlight all those ingredients that you would probably not have on hand so that you can see at a glance what you need to buy without reading the entire recipe.

A quick reminder

Don't remember which magazine offered that great idea or recipe? Staple an index card to the cover of each magazine and, while looking through it, write down the page number and item of interest that you want to make note of. It's a quick and easy way to check a reference.

Time saver

Do you sometimes start dinner a little later than you intended, then thumb through your recipes hoping to find something you can prepare in the amount of time left? Choosing and preparing last-minute meals is much less of a hassle if you note at the top of each new recipe the amount of time it takes to prepare.

Meal variety

Many busy, budget-minded people miss the fun of eating out. Here is one idea to make dining at home festive. Set aside one evening a week to prepare a special meal. One week make it Mexican, another, Italian or Chinese. Set the table with a cloth or mats, napkins, and candles to suit each occasion.

Tip for working wives

Here is a good alternative to defrosting meat on the counter. Place the frozen food in an empty cooler. The meat will thaw more quickly than in the refrigerator, less quickly than out on the counter, and will be kept firm and cold.

Attach a copy of the week's menu to the refrigerator door with magnets. This way you know what to take out of the freezer before going off to work in the morning. It also helps weight- and nutrition-conscious teenage daughters plan their snacks during the day.

Equal shares

Have you ever found that the cookie jar is emptied before everyone gets his fair share? Try filling a separate container for each member of the family, plus one for company. Label each family member's jar with his or her name. This ensures even distribution and encourages children to learn to budget wisely.

SHOPPING

Grocery list

Write your grocery list on an envelope, and you will also have a handy pocket for your redeemable coupons, receipts, and notes.

More for your money

When buying cauliflower, broccoli, or lettuce that is sold by the piece instead of the pound, pick up several of the largest and weigh them to get the most for your money. Weigh pints of strawberries to get best value.

Smart shopper

When shopping, take along a magnifying glass on a cord or chain around your neck. The small-print information on products can be easily read and compared to other brands.

Shopping aid

When grocery shopping in hot weather, take along a lightweight plastic foam cooler in the car. Place freezer items in the chest to keep them from thawing before you get home.

More shopping tips

As an added precaution, keep an old plastic gallon milk container filled with water in the freezer, and you'll have a leak-proof cake of ice to pop into the cooler on especially hot days.

To avoid being caught unprepared, keep a plastic tablecloth in your shopping cart. Whenever it begins to rain, use the tablecloth to cover the groceries in the cart. In an emergency use the cloth, folded into a triangle, as a rain cape.

Place the top of a cardboard shoe box in the bottom of your shopping bag. It keeps the bag open and the bottom dry when you carry frozen or moist foods.

MAKING SPACE

Instant cookie jar

Don't throw out empty potato chip cylinders. Decorate them and use as gift boxes for cookies or candy, or as individual cookie jars at home.

Do you have an ice bucket that you rarely use for ice? Why not store your cookies or nibbles in it? They'll stay fresh and crisp since the lids on most ice buckets are pretty airtight.

Recycling vitamin bottles

Save your empty vitamin bottles to use as spice containers and purchase some attractive labels to identify the contents.

Disposable cutting boards

To keep a cutting board odor free, save the plastic foam trays from produce and meat packages. After they are washed, rinsed, and dried, use them as cutting boards for onions, garlic, and other strong-smelling vegetables. They stack in very little space, and after several uses can just be discarded.

Storing paper bags

An ordinary trousers hanger makes a handy bag holder for large supermarket paper bags used to line trash containers. Just fold the bags in half, snap the pants hanger over them, and hang in a convenient place.

An old dish rack is a convenient holder for folded grocery sacks. Kept under the kitchen sink, they stay neat and are easy to reach.

Spare trays

Spare ice cube trays can be convenient organizers and storage containers for small odds and ends cluttering kitchen, desk, or workbench drawers.

Instant trash container

Empty milk cartons make great garbage containers for wet trash like cooking grease and coffee grounds—they prevent messy items from going down the sink or into the garbage can. They are also convenient as garbage collectors when on a trip or a picnic.

Extra storage areas

Try using "in" and "out" wire office baskets in the kitchen for a high-tech look. Air will circulate freely around fruits and vegetables placed in them to ripen, or you can use them to organize stray jars and bottles.

Baked goods storage

Try using an unused refrigerator freezing compartment as a storage place for baked goods. With the control off, it makes a handy bread box.

At your fingertips

Affix self-adhesive cork squares to the inside of one of your kitchen cabinet doors. It's a handy spot for tacking up recipe cards or shopping lists.

Recipes on 3″ x 5″ cards can be kept away from food-preparation spatters if you make this simple holder for them: Glue a spring-type clothespin to a 5″ x 5″ piece of plywood. Paint or stain the wood and the pin to match your kitchen cabinets. Then affix it at eye level above your mixing center.

Easy access

A rotating necktie rack screwed to the underside of a wall cabinet in the kitchen can hang measuring spoons, measuring cups, and odds and ends that clutter kitchen drawers.

Or, keep a set of measuring spoons hanging on a cup hook in your spice cabinet.

No more lost jewelry

Affix a cup hook under a cabinet or windowsill near the kitchen sink to hang rings and watches for safekeeping while you're doing the dishes.

Easy reach

Hang a pair of kitchen tongs in a convenient place and use them to reach boxes or cans on high kitchen shelves.

Additional counter space

Kitchen counter too small? Using hinges, add a shelf that can be raised when needed and lowered when not in use. This will provide extra space or even a breakfast counter without sacrificing room required for a more permanent arrangement.

A portable bar makes an excellent island for a kitchen. Besides liquor, it holds cookbooks and placemats and gives extra counter space. When company comes, it's a perfect buffet table.

When extra counter space is needed for baking or serving, pull out a cabinet drawer and place a pastry board or tray across it.

Spare table

If you're short of dining space, use your adjustable ironing board—set to the proper height—as a table for the children.

Handy rack

An old bicycle basket attached next to a back door makes a handy rack for holding bundles or grocery bags while you're unlocking the door.

Quick drying

Attach a spring-type clothespin in a convenient spot over the sink to hold plastic bags and bowl covers after they have been washed.

Storing placemats

If you don't have a big enough drawer or shelf to store placemats, buy a clipboard. Attach mats and hang in a closet or cupboard.

Saving steps

To make table utensils convenient, fill a small vase, crock, or jar with an assortment of flatware and place it on the dining table.

Stacking ease

When stacking nonstick pots and pans, place a paper plate in the bottom of each to cushion and protect it from scratches.

To prevent scratches on plates when stacking, use milk filter disks between them. The disks are available in various sizes and can be reused.

Instead of discarding plastic foam trays from meat packages, wash them in warm sudsy water, rinse, and dry well. Then cut to shape and use as cushions when stacking your good china.

Order in the drawer

Are your skewers always scattered among the kitchen tools in a too-full drawer? Store them in plastic toothbrush containers.

Line the storage drawers in your range with blotters. They absorb any moisture left on the pans and lessen the clatter when pans are put away.

Handy reference

Keeping appliance instruction books on the same shelf with cookbooks gives you a handy reference library that eliminates a lot of guesswork when using the appliances.

Storing cords

When storing your electric appliances, loop the cords and fasten with a rubber band or a pipe cleaner twisted around them.

Empty cardboard bathroom tissue rolls make useful sleeves for keeping loose electrical appliance cords organized. They may be decorated with adhesive-backed paper and labeled with stick-on vinyl letters.

Hang it up

Sew a small plastic curtain ring to the top of your mixer cover and hang it up while using the mixer.

Keep it clean

Store your flour sifter in a plastic bag. It keeps the kitchen shelf clean and the sifter free from dust when it is not in use.

The plastic lid from a coffee or shortening can may just fit the bottom of your flour sifter, keeping the mess off the cabinet when you use it.

For stamp savers

Keep an empty boutique-size tissue box on the kitchen counter to place trading stamps in until ready to put them in the saver book. A second box also serves as a handy temporary bin for coupons.

STORING FOOD

Keeping cake fresh

Keep a delicious cake from drying out too quickly by putting half an apple in the cake box. The cake will keep moist very nicely.

Neat place for instructions

Glass cork-topped canisters are attractive for holding frequently used items such as pasta and rice. To remember cooking times, tape or glue the directions to the inside of each cork top.

Another way to keep track of directions is to cut them out and tape them to the outside of canisters. Add date of purchase to ensure freshness.

Storing bread crumbs

Save your next empty salt box to store homemade bread crumbs. Fill it through a funnel and shake out of the spout as needed.

To store cheese

In these times of high prices, storage of food is especially important. To make cheese last longer, wrap it in moistened cheesecloth first.

Neat milk cartons

To prevent a milk carton from leaking onto other foods in the refrigerator or leaving a coating of wax on the shelves, place the carton in a plastic container.

Saving wrappers

Save the papers in which quarter-pound sticks of margarine or butter are wrapped. Put them in a small plastic bag and store in the refrigerator. When baking cookies or cakes, use them to grease the pan or cookie sheet.

Cover-up

Small-size plastic bowl covers are fine for covering the cut end of most sausages.

A quick dusting

Buy an inexpensive powder puff and store it in your flour container. When flour's needed, there will be no spills, no mess!

Storing garlic

Since most recipes only require a small amount of garlic, it is difficult to store unused cloves and still have them remain fresh. Here is a way that is easy and convenient and keeps them from drying out: First peel the cloves, then place in a small jar filled with cooking oil. Cover and refrigerate. This is a sure and simple way to have your garlic stay fresh and ready for use. And the garlic-scented oil is a nice ingredient for salad dressings.

Tips on spices

To keep spices fresher longer, store them in the refrigerator.

Spices kept too long on the shelf lose much of their good seasoning value. Cut small pieces of masking tape, adhere them to the bottom of each newly purchased spice jar, and note the purchase date on it. No more worry about freshness!

Spice racks in disarray are a common problem. One easy way to solve it is to arrange the various herbs and spices in alphabetical order.

Don't throw away prescription drug bottles. Wash them and use to carry small amounts of spices for outings and traveling.

Here's another solution to the problem of storing spices and herbs: Attach the lids of screw-on baby-food jars to the underside of kitchen wall cabinets, arranging the lids in a neat row. Using black paint, label the jars, fill them, and screw in place. They're easy to reach, and there's no dusting problem.

A handsome and unusual spice rack can be made from an old medicine chest. Bought cheaply at tag sales, auctions, or antiques fairs, they can be cleaned and either stained or painted to match any kitchen decor.

Easy storage

Store those clutter-making envelopes of soup, sauce, and salad-dressing mixes in a paper napkin holder to help keep your cupboards neat.

Or: tack a small square plastic freezer container to the inside of a kitchen cupboard door.

Sealing tip

Keep a package of pipe cleaners handy in the kitchen. Use them to close opened plastic bags of foods such as marshmallows, coconut, and beans. Spring-type clothespins also do a good job.

Freezing techniques

To freeze liquids such as soup, use a plastic bag inserted into a coffee can that comes with a plastic lid. After filling, close the bag, snap on the lid, and freeze. When frozen, remove the bag from the can, replace in freezer, and reuse the can.

Freezing soup stock? Pour it into loaf pans, freeze, then remove it from the pans and wrap in freezer paper. The blocks are easy to store and take up a minimum of freezer space.

When rewrapping prepackaged meat for freezing, cut the label from the original wrapping and tape it to the new package. This keeps a record of the cut of meat, its weight, and date of purchase.

Want to manage your frozen-food storage better? Keep a date stamp and pad with your freezer-packaging materials. Stamp each package as you prepare it, as well as each box of commercially packaged frozen food.

To avoid getting caught short or leaving food in the freezer too long, attach a list of the items showing the amounts and purchase dates to the door. Update it as you use the food.

Before stacking packages of the same kind of food in your freezer, number them. Then place in the freezer, with no. 1 on the bottom. Whenever you remove one of the packages, you'll know exactly how many others are left.

Save the compartmented aluminum plates from frozen dinners. When you have leftovers from meals, freeze them in the trays for future ready-made dinners.

Save plastic margarine containers. When there is an ice cream sale, take advantage of it, fill the containers three-quarters full of ice cream, add different toppings, and store in the freezer for quick, inexpensive desserts.

Tops of cottage cheese or margarine containers are useful for freezing hamburger patties. Divide the meat, press into the tops and wrap patties in aluminum foil or freezer wrap. Tops are easy to wipe clean for reuse.

Intersperse waxed paper sandwich bags between hamburger patties when packaging them for the freezer. This eliminates the chore of separating, and the double thickness prevents sticking.

Shelling Brazil nuts is simple when they've been frozen. The shells are brittle, and the meats will come out whole.

When freezing green peppers, remove the seeds, blanch peppers in hot water, and freeze whole, fitting them inside each other. This saves space in the freezer, and they can later be used for stuffed peppers or cut up for various dishes.

When onions are cheap and plentiful, buy a large quantity to peel, slice, and store in ½-cup amounts in sandwich bags in the freezer.

All bits of leftovers (sliced meats, cold shrimp, and the like) can be made useful if they are foil-wrapped and tossed into a "smorgasbord pot" in the freezer. When the dish is full, dinner will be a colorful array of open-faced sandwiches made from the contents on cocktail-size rye or pumpernickel bread and garnished with greens from the salad bin. Labeling is unnecessary since surprises add to the fun!

If you have too much fruit to process for jelly at one time, cook the fruit, strain the juice, pour it into freezer containers, and freeze until you have time to make the jelly.

Handy food storage chart

Meat	Refrigerate	Freeze
beef steaks	1 to 2 days	6 to 12 months
beef roasts	1 to 2 days	6 to 12 months
pork chops	1 to 2 days	3 to 4 months
pork roasts	1 to 2 days	4 to 8 months
fresh pork sausages	1 to 2 days	1 to 2 months
veal cutlets	1 to 2 days	6 to 9 months
veal steaks	1 to 2 days	6 to 12 months
lamb chops, steaks	1 to 2 days	6 to 9 months
lamb roasts	1 to 2 days	6 to 9 months
stew meat (any type)	1 to 2 days	3 to 4 months
ground beef, veal, lamb	1 to 2 days	3 to 4 months
ground pork	1 to 2 days	1 to 3 months
variety meats (liver, kidney, brains)	1 to 2 days	3 to 4 months

Meat keeps best in the refrigerator if it's loosely wrapped in plastic wrap or wax paper. To freeze it, wrap in moisture/ vapor-proof wrapping, such as heavy plastic wrap.
Always remember to label and date your meat.

Poultry	Refrigerate	Freeze	
whole chickens	1 to 2 days	12	months
cut-up chickens	1 to 2 days	9	months
chicken giblets	1 to 2 days	3	months
whole turkeys	1 to 2 days	6	months
cut-up turkeys	1 to 2 days	6	months
whole ducks or geese	1 to 2 days	6	months

In the refrigerator, remove giblets and wrap and store them separately. Store poultry loosely wrapped in the coldest part of the refrigerator. To freeze, wrap in a moisture/vapor-proof wrap. Label and date it. Caution: Never freeze poultry with the stuffing inside. Stuffing may be frozen separately.

Cooked meats & leftovers	Refrigerate	Freeze	
fried chicken	1 to 2 days	4	months
leftover beef roast	3 to 4 days	2 to 3	months
leftover beef stew	3 to 4 days	2 to 3	months
leftover canned/cured ham	4 to 5 days	1	month
leftover fresh ham or pork	3 to 4 days	2 to 3	months
gravy and meat broth	1 to 2 days	2 to 3	months
meat sauce (spaghetti sauce)	3 to 4 days	6 to 8	months
meat loaf	2 to 3 days	3	months
cooked pork or lamb	3 to 4 days	2 to 3	months
cooked chicken slices or pieces, covered with broth or gravy	1 to 2 days	6	months
cooked chicken, not covered with broth or gravy	1 to 2 days	1	month
chicken salad or tuna salad	1 to 2 days	do not freeze	
leftover fish	2 to 3 days	1	month
chicken and turkey pies	1 to 2 days	2 to 3	months

Always chill leftovers and cooked meats quickly. Keep covered in the refrigerator. Separate leftover poultry meat from the stuffing when refrigerating. To freeze, package and freeze quickly. Meat stuffing should always be frozen separately.

Cured meats	Refrigerate	Freeze
ham, whole	1 week	1 to 2 months
ham, half	3 to 5 days	1 to 2 months
frankfurters	1 week	1 month
bacon	1 week	2 to 4 months
canned ham	1 year, if unopened	not recommended
ham slices	3 days	1 to 2 months
corned beef	7 days	2 weeks
luncheon meat	3 to 5 days	not recommended
sausage, smoked	7 days	not recommended

Keep meat loosely covered in refrigerator. To freeze, wrap it tightly in moisture/vapor-proof wrapping, pressing out as much air as possible. When freezing smoked meat, wrap extra well so its odors won't permeate other foods. Cured meats don't keep their high quality for long when frozen, because the seasonings that are added in the curing process speed rancidity.

Fish	Refrigerate	Freeze
fresh fish	1 to 2 days	6 to 9 months
shrimp	1 to 2 days	2 months
lobster, crabs	1 to 2 days	1 to 2 months
oysters, clams, scallops	1 to 2 days	3 to 6 months

Before refrigerating, first rinse fish thoroughly in cold water. Pat dry with paper towels and cover loosely with wax paper. Store in the coldest part of the refrigerator. To freeze fillets, wrap them well in moisture/vapor-proof wrapping. Shrimp keep best if frozen uncooked. To freeze crab or lobster, cook first without any salt, cool in refrigerator and remove meat from shell before freezing. To freeze oysters, clams or scallops, shell them first and pack in own liquid. Don't forget to label and date your fish!

Dairy products	Refrigerate	Freeze
butter	2 weeks	6 months, unsalted 3 months, salted
eggs, whole	2 to 3 weeks	6 to 8 months
eggs, whites	1 week	6 to 8 months
eggs, yolks	2 to 3 days	6 to 8 months
milk, cream	1 week	1 month
cheese spreads	1 to 2 weeks, when opened	1 to 2 months
hard cheeses	2 to 3 months, when wrapped	6 months
soft cheeses like Camembert	2 weeks	2 months
cottage cheese	5 to 7 days	1 to 2 weeks
cream cheese	2 weeks	2 weeks

In refrigerator, store eggs in their own carton. To freeze, eggs must be removed from their shell first. For whole eggs, stir in 2 tablespoons sugar or 1 tablespoon salt for each pint of lightly beaten eggs. Pack in freezer containers, leaving half an inch for headspace. Label and date. Refrigerate cheese in its original wrapping, if possible; or cover cut surface tightly with plastic wrap or foil. To freeze cheese, wrap in moisture/vapor-proof wrap or store in the original wrap with a foil overwrap. Do not freeze in amounts larger than 1 pound.

CLEANING

Kitchen surfaces

If everything in the kitchen were made out of the same material, it would probably be the easiest room in the house to clean. But since this isn't the case, it's useful to know how to treat various kitchen surfaces. For example:

Butcher blocks. These popular wooden work surfaces can take a lot of rough treatment, but you must avoid saturating them with water, which causes warping. To clean a butcher block, wipe it quickly with lukewarm water or mild suds and dry. Reseason when necessary by pouring boiled linseed oil over wood surfaces and rubbing it in with fine steel wool.

Formica countertops are attractive, but they scratch, so don't use them as cutting surfaces. Avoid using abrasives such as steel wool when cleaning. Steel wool leaves scratches on some kitchen surfaces, which can catch dirt and become the breeding ground for germs.

Sink faucets which have been chromium or nickel plated should not be washed with scouring powders, which can wear off the plating. To keep faucets sparkling, clean them with nonabrasive spray cleaner.

Of pots and pans

Pots and pans come in a variety of materials, and as a result, they cook food differently and require different care, too. But it really isn't necessary to consult a cookware directory every time you cook. Try these basic rules to keep your pots and pans in good condition:

1. Do not run cold water into a hot pan. Cold water can warp a metal pan and crack glass and earthenware.

2. To remove greasy residue, don't use harsh abrasives and metal scrapers, which can scratch some pans. Just add a grease-cutting liquid to your dishwater to make cleaning easier.

3. If a pot must be scoured, use a plastic pad—metal scouring pads can scratch some pots.

4. Do not let gas flames lick up the sides of pots and pans—it could cause heat stains.

5. Do not use metal or enameled cookware to store food as they may be damaged by salt and acids.

6. Remove stuck-on food by pouring cold water into the pan and letting it stand until the food is soft.

7. Remove burned-on food by boiling water in the pan.

8. Dry cast iron cookware immediately after washing to lessen the chance of rusting.

To make inexpensive pot scrubbers, take the net bags that onions and other produce come in, cut them into suitable lengths, and tie together in a pom-pom fashion. They are ideal for scrubbing and will not scratch your pots and pans.

Clean pots, pans, and dishes as you cook so you won't have a sky-high pile after each meal.

For shining porcelain enamel on your pots and pans, treat them as you would glass. When food sticks or is burned, soak the utensil in hot suds until it's loosened. To remove stubborn spots, use a nylon scrubber. Avoid using metal scouring products—they may leave dark marks on the surface.

Always clean sponges

To clean sponges and small dish mops easily and regularly, place them on the top shelf of the dishwasher, and let the machine wash them with the dishes.

Scouring pads

One place to store a scouring pad when not in use is in a small, covered, plastic refrigerator dish. It keeps it rust free and neat looking.

Cleaning up after dinner for a large family means lots of pots and pans. To reduce expenses, cut soap-filled scouring pads in two. Large kitchen shears work very well, and half a pad is adequate. Also, no more scouring pads left rusting on the sink!

Protect your sink

To protect your porcelain enamel sink from the dark marks aluminum pans make when you scrub them, place a sheet or two of paper toweling under the pans.

Drying dishes

You can do a much better and quicker job of drying dishes if you hold a dish towel in each hand. Makes the dishes skid-proof, too.

A quick shine

An inexpensive way to remove streaks and spots from chrome and glass is to wipe the surfaces with a soft cloth dampened with rubbing alcohol.

The care of pewter

Polish your pewter occasionally, using a soft cloth and regular pewter polish. Always rub in the direction of the shape of the article. Remember that pewter is a soft metal and is easily scratched, so never use an abrasive on it. Keep it away from heat, and don't let pieces touch one another, for contact causes dark burn marks. *Never polish antique pewter*. To keep it looking presentable, just wash occasionally in hot suds and dry with a soft cloth.

Easy polishing

Worn powder puffs, especially the bath size, make excellent cleaners for silver, copper, and the like. Use one side of the powder puff to apply the polish and the other side to buff.

Make your own silver bags

Silver cloth, the tarnish-retardant flannel, is available by the yard in fabric and department stores. Silver bags are very simple to make and cost far less than store-bought ones.

Good catch

A dampened sponge placed on a kitchen range makes a good spoon holder. The sponge catches drips and is available instantly to wipe up spilled food.

Simple swish

To clean your blender, put soap or detergent and a small amount of hot water into the jar. Blend for a minute, then drain, rinse, and dry.

"Working gloves"

Rubber work gloves stay in good condition when sprinkled, inside and out, with cornstarch after each use.

Versatile brushes

Use a curved vegetable brush for easy cleaning of the inside of your food chopper. The brush won't catch on the blades.

A vegetable brush works well to clean muffin pans.

A toothbrush makes a great kitchen utensil for cleaning hard to reach places and hard to scrub vegetables.

Cleaning hint

Since cleaning a grater is always a task, especially after grating cheese, try spraying it with a nonstick vegetable spray. Nothing sticks, and cleanup is a breeze. Also spray a grease-spatter screen before use.

Kitchen canisters

A blow dryer works well to thoroughly dry washed canisters, preventing rust as well as keeping food dry and fresh.

Shine like new!

To make your kitchen appliances shine like new, apply car wax and polish. The result is unbelievable.

333 HINTS FOR IN AND AROUND THE KITCHEN

Useful pipe cleaners

To remove grease or drippings from the little holes in the burners on a gas range, use a pipe cleaner.

Clean the hard-to-scrub parts of a wall can opener with a pipe cleaner. Just insert the tip between the gears and the cutting blade and brush off accumulated dust or grease. Dip the cleaner in suds and brush again for a thorough job.

Clean the tip of a cake-decorating tube by using a pipe cleaner as a brush. Dip the cleaner in suds and insert into the crevice.

Use a fresh pipe cleaner to clean the glass sippers you use for tall summer beverages.

Cleaning the toaster

Use a percolator brush to rid your electric toaster of crumbs. The brush will clean the sides without touching the elements.

Cleaning placemats

Clean your woven placemats that hold spills and spots by dipping them in clean sudsy water just before doing the dishes. Rinse with warm water and roll each mat in a small hand towel to dry.

Applying paste wax to linen-like plastic table mats makes them easy to wipe off and keep clean.

In and around the refrigerator

Clean up spills immediately in the refrigerator as well as on floors and countertops. An untended spill may dry hard or become a stain.

At least twice a year, move both your refrigerator and freezer away from the wall, disconnect the plugs, and carefully vacuum the coils and compressor to remove all energy-wasting dust.

Cleaning your refrigerator? Try washing the removable shelves, racks, and glass in your dishwasher (but be careful not to include any plastic parts).

There are a few easy rules to follow if you want to keep a new porcelain enamel range, sink, or refrigerator gleaming. Most important is that you use hot water and suds for regular cleaning and never use a harsh abrasive cleaner on it. Abrasives will scratch the surface and dull it. Promptly wipe up spilled juices and acids such as vinegar. Immediately wipe up spills on your oven or range top, but don't do that thorough cleaning while either is still hot. Wait until the surface cools. Use a rubber or plastic mat to protect the bottom of your sink, and you'll keep it shining, too.

Use your baster to speed the job of defrosting the refrigerator. Fill the baster with hot water, then squirt the water over the walls of the freezer compartment. Repeat several times, and the frost will melt rapidly.

To prevent ice cube trays and food packages from sticking and to keep the freezer clean, cover the bottom with aluminum foil or wax paper.

Line the bottom of your hydrator with paper towels. They help keep it clean by absorbing any excess moisture that may drip from fruits or vegetables.

Clean the rubber gasket on your refrigerator door with the cleaner used for white sidewall automobile tires.

After defrosting a chest-type freezer, use a sponge mop to soak up the water in the bottom. This saves stooping and collects the water that's in the corners.

On refrigerators with the air intake in the front below the door, the grill can usually be removed and the coils cleaned by hand or with a vacuum cleaner. To cut down on this chore, line the back of the grill with cheesecloth or nylon net. Either can be easily removed and rinsed or replaced.

Oven cleanup

Your oven will always be clean and shining if you use proper cooking methods, clean up as you cook, and occasionally do a thorough scrubbing job, using effective cleaning products. The old-fashioned roasting method of high-temperature searing usually spatters fat on oven walls and racks (and, incidentally, shrinks your roast), so why not avoid this by using the low-temperature method of roasting? As soon as the oven is cool, clean it by wiping the lining with hot suds. Use a mild abrasive, if necessary. When broiling, trim steaks and chops of as much fat as possible, place meat 4″–5″ from the element or burner, and broil meat from a cold start. Be sure to wash the broiler pan after each use. An oven is hard to clean after grease has been burned on, and this can't happen if you clean it every time it's used. If it *is* crusted with burned-on fat, apply a caustic oven cleaner that chemically softens or loosens charred food and fat. When you use these products, however, be *sure* to follow the manufacturer's directions carefully and do not let cleaner touch aluminum, linoleum, wood, or painted surfaces.

To make short work of oven cleaning, place a cup filled with ammonia inside the oven at night. Next day, grease and burned-on food will be easier to wipe away.

Since the grease from frying foods tends to spatter all over, try placing extra lids or pie pans over the other stove burners so they won't become soiled. They're a lot easier to clean than the burners.

Exhaust fan cleanup

A good meal isn't all you whip up in your kitchen. Take, for instance, the cooking odors, smoke, excess heat, and grease that you concoct right along with your gourmet treats!

In combating home pollution, your stove's vent hood and exhaust fan gets some pretty heavy use. To maintain top performance, this essential piece of kitchen equipment should be cleaned regularly. Here are a few easy steps to follow:

1. Read carefully the manufacturer's instructions regarding cleaning.

2. Turn the exhaust fan to the "off" position and allow it to cool before cleaning.

3. Soak all removable parts for 10 minutes in warm, sudsy water. Rinse and let dry.

4. With a wet sponge or cloth degreaser, wipe the fan blades, hood, and all those hard-to-get-at places. Rinse with a clean sponge and polish with a soft clean cloth. Be certain to keep all liquids away from all electrical wires.

5. To keep your fan from becoming sluggish, use a drop or two of machine oil in the motor once a year.

Clearing a drain

A slow kitchen drain slows *your* work as well. Speed up a sluggish drain by pouring in ½ cup baking soda followed by ½ cup vinegar, let it fizz, then flush with plenty of hot water.

Almost like new

Are your rubber sink mats and drainboard or range mats discolored? Try bleaching them. Close the drain in your sink, run in about 2 quarts of warm water, and add ½ cup of chlorine bleach. Soak mats in this solution for 15 minutes, rinse and dry. They'll come out looking like new.

The drainboard

Coat a rubber drainboard tray with a light film of polishing wax to prevent rapid staining and to make the tray easier to clean.

Neat cabinets

When you must clean and straighten kitchen cabinets, divide them into five sections and clean one section each day of the week. By the end of the week the cabinets are finished, and you are not too worn out.

Cutting shelf paper

Put a roll of shelf paper in an empty waxed or transparent paper box and use the metal cutter to cut the shelf paper. It makes neat, evenly cut sheets.

Catch those drips

Plastic lids make good saucers under drippy bottles (oil, syrup, and the like) in cupboards and refrigerator.

Freshly painted surfaces

When the fresh paint on your cupboard shelves is thoroughly dry, put a coat of cleaner-polisher wax on them. This preserves the paint and keeps china from sticking to it. Whenever you want to repaint the shelves, just wash the wax off with sudsy water.

Stainless steel counter

Use club soda to wipe your stainless steel counter, range, and hood top. It dries to a gleam without streaks or spots.

Taking care of cutting boards

Attractive cutting boards of wood parquet will often split and separate at the joints when washed regularly in soapy water to keep them sanitary. The wood can be kept from drying out by oiling it after each cleaning with any cooking oil.

Discolored bread and meat boards can be whitened and made free of smells: Rub the boards with lemon rinds turned inside out and then wash in warm water.

Stop the invasion!

To stop a nasty ant invasion in your kitchen, before you spray with unpleasant-smelling sprays, try washing countertops, cabinets, and floors with equal parts of vinegar and water.

Fun door

Is the inside of your pantry door cracked and dingy looking? One way to liven it up without wasting time scrubbing and painting is to turn it into a collage! Over several months save the labels from favorite canned and baked foods and glue them neatly to the inside of the door in an attractive pattern. Not only is it fun, but it provides a neat record of family eating patterns.

Hide the cord

Is the cord on your kitchen wall clock conspicuous because you haven't a special wall-clock outlet? Cover the cord with a plastic telephone-wire cover that is the same color as your wall. The cord won't be nearly so noticeable.

Easy floor cleaning hints

Use a long-handle windshield brush to clean between the kitchen range and adjacent base cabinets. The brush is especially handy in removing small particles of food that may have lodged in the narrow openings.

Remove dust from under a refrigerator and narrow places with a long-handle duster made by pulling an old sock or stocking over a yardstick.

If you wax your kitchen floor every week, reconsider. Wax adds shine but also leads to an unsightly, hard-to-remove wax build-up. Sweep and damp-mop between monthly waxings.

Before scrubbing your kitchen floor, use a plastic windshield ice scraper to pry loose any dried-on food. The scraper is easy to work with and won't mar flooring.

Since the kitchen is often the center of traffic for children, after mopping the floor put several thicknesses of paper toweling under the sponge mop and run it over the damp floor to speed drying and prevent footprints from impatient feet.

Easy reach

Use your long-handle sponge floor mop to clean the kitchen ceiling easily and effectively.

165

SAFETY

Freezer safety

Home freezer failure needn't mean food spoilage. If the failure is mechanical, call your serviceman immediately. If it is a power failure, check your local utility company for the time needed to make the necessary repairs. Then act! Keep the freezer closed as much as possible. If it is fully loaded, the food will stay frozen about two days, even without power. But if the freezer is less than half full, food will last only a day. If you think it will take longer than a day to get the freezer working, consider one of these alternatives:

1. Move the food to a local locker plant.

2. Drop dry ice into the freezer. (Fifty pounds of dry ice will keep an average-size freezer at 15° F. for about two days.)

3. Can the food.

Whatever you do, *never refreeze thawed meat, poultry, vegetables, shellfish, or cooked foods*. To do so may be dangerous.

Prevent bacteria spread

To prevent spread of bacteria, clean the wheel of your can opener often with a sponge dipped in a solution of hot water and baking soda.

Safe reminder

Tie a piece of colored ribbon on the door of your refrigerator when you advance the freezing control. This will remind you that it must be reset.

Versatile mitts

Oven mitts can double easily as freezer mitts. They protect hands effectively when you rearrange frozen foods.

Wear a pair of clean cotton gloves when removing the frost in your freezer or rearranging frozen-food packages. The packages are easier to handle, and the gloves keep your hands warm.

Safe handling

Some recipes require that you finish cooking a dish by placing the skillet in the oven. To prevent the nonmetal part of the handle from burning, wrap it in aluminum foil.

Don't discard your old long-handle two-tine fork. Bend its prongs to form hooks and use it to pull hot pans to the front of the oven.

Save your fingers

When cutting and preparing fruits and vegetables for canning, wrap a piece of adhesive tape around your thumb and forefinger to prevent nasty cuts and blisters.

Cut down on cuts and nicks by slipping a rubber index finger (the kind used in offices) over your thumb when you pare fruit or vegetables.

Want to keep your fingers from getting jabbed when you are looking for a thumbtack in a drawer? Simply keep tacks in a cork. It makes them easier to find, too. The larger the cork, the more tacks it will hold.

EMERGENCY NUMBERS TO KEEP
NEAR THE KITCHEN PHONE:

Ambulance Service_____

Address_____
Phone_____

Family Doctor_____

Address_____
Office Phone_____
Home Phone_____

Family Doctor_____

Address_____
Office Phone_____
Home Phone_____

Nearest Hospital_____

Address_____
Phone_____

Police Department_____

Phone_____

Fire Department_____

Phone_____

Gas & Electric Company_____

Phone_____

Five

337 Tips to care for Clothes and Laundry

WASHING AND DRYING

Cloth-covered buttons

If cloth-covered buttons on garments don't come out clean, give them an extra going over with a soft toothbrush and liquid detergent.

Washing pillows

If you've been wondering how to wash high-quality dacron-fiber-filled pillows, you'll be delighted to know that they can be easily laundered and will retain their soft fluffiness after many cleanings. The secret lies in hand washing them in lukewarm water to which has been added a light-duty soap or detergent (preferably a nonsudsing detergent to make rinsing easier). Create a flow of water through the pillow by compressing it repeatedly, but never twist or tear the filling by agitating it either by hand or in your washing machine. Soiled spots on the ticking can be scrubbed with a soft brush, if necessary. Rinse thoroughly in clear water and squeeze to remove excess water. Dry in the air or in a tumbler-type dryer.

Keep it soft

After laundering a plastic shower curtain, keep it soft and pliable longer by coating it with baby oil. Leave the oil on for a few minutes and wipe off. Smells good, too!

How to care for curtains and drapes

If your curtains are white cotton, they can go into the washer along with a white load. If they are pastel, use warm water. When washing bright-color or dark curtains, use cold water and a light-duty detergent. Wash these often to prevent heavy soiling.

If they are made of dacron, polyester, nylon, or other man-made fibers, tumble them in your dryer, using the air-fluff or cold-air drying cycle, before laundering. This will remove much of the dust and surface soil. Then wash them in cold water, using a generous amount of detergent. If they are excessively soiled, agitate for 5 minutes, then stop the machine and soak for 10 minutes. Restart the washer and allow it to complete the cycle. Use a final rinse conditioner to eliminate static electricity and give the curtains a soft feel. Tumble dry, using the "warm" or (if your dryer has it) the "wash-and-wear" setting.

Glazed chintz curtains will retain their finish longer if they are washed in cold water with a light-duty detergent. Glass-fiber curtains and draperies should also be washed in cold water. Fill the washer with cold water, add detergent, and agitate 1 minute. Then add three or four panels (depending upon their length) and soak 10 to 15 minutes. Do not agitate. Spin out the water if you have a "gentle" setting on the machine, then remove the curtains, shake out excess water, and rehang. If your machine has no "gentle" setting, remove the curtains and hang them in a place where they can drip-dry.

If your ruffled nylon curtains are wilted looking, wash and dry them, then dip into a starch solution made with 1 tablespoon cold-water starch to 1 quart cold water. To drip-dry quickly, use spring-type clothespins to clip the hemmed edge of each curtain to a clothesline.

To ensure proper rehanging of draperies after removing them for cleaning, take an indelible laundry marking pen and draw a dot where the tip of the drapery hook is being removed. After the draperies have been washed and dried, you will know exactly where to reinsert the hook. This will save time and frustration.

If your sheer curtains don't hang straight after they have been laundered, slip a curtain rod through the bottom hem of each and let them hang for several days. When the rods are removed, you'll find that the curtains will fall as they should.

Draperies and slipcovers can stay fresh and clean at a fraction of what it used to cost: By dry-cleaning them often in a local coin-operated dry cleaning center, you can lengthen their life, for frequent cleaning removes tiny razorlike particles of grit that will cut and weaken fibers.

Some rules to follow if you want the job done well:

1. Take down the draperies and fold them carefully. Remove slip covers and fold. (Never crumple when carrying them or stacking them, for this can add wrinkles.)

2. Remove all drapery hooks and weights; close slipcover zippers.

3. Check seams for any breaks and repair these before you take the items to the cleaning center.

4. Carefully fold draperies and covers as soon as the dry cleaning has been completed and carry home. Hang the draperies immediately. If they have been handled well, they should need no pressing.

5. Slipcovers may need touching up with an iron before being put back on the furniture.

Torn curtain

To darn small holes or tears in lace curtains, place a piece of netting dampened with starch over the holes on the wrong side and then press it down firmly with a hot iron.

Handy marble

Roll a marble through the casing of a freshly ironed curtain, and the rod will slip through easily.

Old keys

If you have a collection of old keys, use them to weight down hems of your drapes.

Tips for caring for down comforters

1. Air a down comforter as often as possible. Apartment dwellers can get the same effect by putting the comforter into a commercial dryer set on "air fluff" or "warm." Put a couple of clean tennis balls inside the dryer to force fresh air through the down.

2. If you wash a down comforter, do so with soap, a free-rinsing product that preserves the life and insulation value while also maintaining fluffiness. Professional dry cleaning by a reliable source is suggested. Washing should be considered as infrequently as once every five or seven years, depending on individual use.

3. For best storage, the comforter should be folded in half and hung in a closet or folded in thirds and placed on a shelf. Never store in an enclosed bag or casing because mildew or mold may grow.

4. Stain-resistant sheets reduce the breathing ability of down, so cotton sheets are suggested.

5. A down comforter (or pillow) should never be "hit" to restore fluffiness. This breaks down the fibers and causes dust to form. Shake instead.

6. Always slip the comforter into a protective cover before use.

Neat trick

To wash white shoelaces, string them through a buttonhole of a white shirt and tie them together before washing both. You won't lose the laces, and they won't become tangled.

Bathroom rugs will last longer

Bathroom rugs with rubber backing last twice as long if they are not put into the dryer after washing. Just hang them over the bathtub and the rubber backing will not chip or flake.

Keep the shape!

To prevent berets from shrinking after washing, slip them over a dinner plate. They will dry beautifully and keep their shape.

Using leftover shampoos

Don't throw away shampoos that aren't right for your hair. Many are excellent for removing oil and grease from clothing. Just pour the shampoo right on the soiled areas and throw the garment in with the rest of the wash.

Give it a "spritz"

Keep a spray bottle filled with vinegar in the laundry room. It saves the trouble of running to the kitchen cupboard every time vinegar is needed for treating perspiration odors or for removing the shine from the seat of a dark skirt or trousers. Also, the spritzer bottle makes it easy to apply the vinegar just where you want it.

Laundry aid

If you have teenagers who help with the laundry, write out simple directions for doing the wash (amount and kind of detergent, bleach, water level, and temperature setting) on a 3″ x 5″ card. Place the card in a plastic recipe-card envelope and tape it to the control panel of your washing machine. You'll prevent a lot of laundry mistakes.

Protect wood buttons

Before laundering a sweater that is trimmed with wood buttons, remove the buttons, for they swell when wet and may crack. Leave the thread clips as a marker for replacing them when dry.

Easy measure

Keep a set of graduated scoops in your laundry. They're handy for measuring powdered detergents, soap flakes, dry bleach, and other washing products.

The scoops included in large-size powdered soft drink cans measure ¼ cup. Use them to portion out detergent and powdered bleach for your laundry.

Washing gloves

Launder your washable leather gloves in cold water, using a cold-water detergent such as those you use for woolens. The gloves will dry soft and will be easier to put on.

Or, wash leather gloves using a hair shampoo with lanolin to help restore the natural oil of the glove skins.

Add a small amount of liquid starch to the rinse water when you wash your white cotton gloves. The starch helps keep them looking new and helps cut down soiling.

Second hamper

Buy an inexpensive hamper to use only for items to be dry-cleaned. This saves time gathering clothes when you go to the cleaner.

Laundry cart

An old bassinet you no longer use makes a neat cart for the laundry room. No more reaching and bending for the clothes—just wheel it right to the washer and dryer.

Washing heavy cottons

When laundering clothes made of a heavy textured cotton—such as a jacquard or tapestry weave—turn the garment wrong side out to prevent snagging the long floating threads that give the fabric its surface interest.

Important instructions

Always write a description of the garment itself on the washing instructions or fabric label that accompanies a new garment. Keep all the instructions and labels in a small file box in the laundry and refer to them when washing.

For just-bought clothing that must be dry-cleaned, mark "DRY-CLEAN" with a laundry pen on an inside seam. If the instruction tag is lost, you will know how to clean the garment.

Check fabric labels before buying. Make sure everything can go from washer to dryer to drawer or hanger with little or no ironing or other special care.

Laundry aid

A bar of commercial laundry soap wrapped in nylon netting provides the cleaning power as well as the abrasion to pretreat most stubborn laundry spots. Using either hot or cold water, depending on the fabric or spot, use this method to remove paint, ink, blood, grass marks, and ground-in dirt. It is especially effective on shirt collars.

The proper load

If it is hard to tell when you have a proper load for your automatic clothes washer, first check the capacity of the machine and then make up your load using the chart below as an approximate weight guide. Remember that you shouldn't put more than two large items such as sheets or tablecloths into one load. Make up the rest of the load with smaller items.

1	set of double sheets	3 lbs.
1	double mattress cover	2 lbs.
1	set of twin sheets	2 lbs.
4	pillowcases	1 lb.
4	bath towels	3 lbs.
6	linen or cotton dish towels	1 lb.
1	dinner tablecloth	2 lbs.
4	dinner napkins	1 lb.
5	men's shirts	3 lbs.
3	women's blouses	1 lb.
4	boy's or girl's shirts	1 lb.
7	pairs of socks	1 lb.
7	pieces cotton underwear	1 lb.
1	pair men's pajamas	1 lb.
2	lightweight nightgowns	1 lb.
4	sets of playclothes	1 lb.
3	wash-and-wear women's dresses	3 lbs.
6	diapers	1 lb.
2	pairs children's blue jeans	1 lbs.
4	hand towels and 4 washcloths	2 lbs.
1	dinner tablecloth	2 lbs.
4	dinner napkins	1 lb.

Time saver

Whenever possible, wash each family member's clothes all at once and separately. This saves time sorting.

Quick spot cleaning

To eliminate the mess of spot cleaning, put some liquid laundry detergent into an empty dishwashing liquid bottle. This way you can apply it directly to dirty collars or spots without the frustration of spills or of pouring too much at one time.

Using extra detergent on those dirty collars and cuffs? Apply it with a sponge, then throw the sponge in the wash.

Water softener

If you run out of your favorite water softener, try adding ¼ cup of vinegar to the final rinse water.

Keeping the fringe straight

To keep long-tasseled fringe from tangling while laundering, tie every six to eight strands together at the tips with string.

Clean sponges

Let your washing machine clean heavily soiled cellulose sponges. They'll come out almost like new.

Slipcover tip

A pleat in a slipcover will hang evenly if you use strips of cellophane tape and apply them vertically to each fold at the back of the pleat. Just remove the tape when you launder or dry-clean the cover.

Taking care of towels

To keep bath towels pretty, fluffy, and bright, give them good care. Before they get overly soiled, wash them in hot, soft water with soap or detergent. Wash dark bath towels separately until the bleeding stops. After the loose surface dye has been flushed away, wash them in the same load with other colored pieces. Fluff-dry in your dryer or shake well and hang on the clothesline. Avoid splintery clothespins that might snag the loops. Never iron bath towels; just fold them carefully and put on a shelf. Try to rotate the towels so that they wear evenly. And mend any rips at once. If a snag does occur, *cut* the thread; don't pull it!

Washing delicate items

Launder lace tablecloths, fine lingerie, and cutwork by placing them in a mesh bag before putting into the washing machine.

Tips on tablecloths

Wash your lace tablecloths in warm water with a light-duty detergent, either in your washing machine or by hand. Don't add bleach. Rinse them well with warm water, then gently squeeze out the excess water without twisting or wringing. Machine drying is not recommended, so hang each tablecloth evenly over a clean, rustproof line. If pressing is needed, use a warm iron while the cloth is still damp.

Tricks with pleats

After you wash a permanently pleated skirt, gather the pleats together tightly and carefully slip a nylon stocking down over the skirt. Hang it up to dry, and your pleats will look freshly pressed.

A Few Helpful Tips...
Your washing machine

1. To clean and unclog soap scum from washing machine hoses, fill the washer with warm water and add 1 cup of distilled vinegar. Run your washer through a complete cycle, then repeat using 1 cup of bleach.

2. If your washer overflows with suds, sprinkle them with salt. They'll disappear like magic.

3. Save energy by using a cold-water rinse and use the recommended water temperature on the garment care label for the most effective cleaning. If you use a powdered detergent in a cold-water wash, dissolve it before you add it to the wash load.

4. Improve the efficiency of your washer and dryer by keeping the lint filters clean. Air flow in the dryer can be increased and drying time reduced if your lint filter is regularly cleaned. After washing heavy, lint-shedding loads, clean the washer filter so that loose lint in the next load will be carried away more easily.

5. To keep lint from clogging your drain, put an old nylon stocking over your washing machine hose. It will collect the extra lint.

Sorting it all out

The simple act of sorting your laundry before you wash can save you many ruined clothes. Failure to sort properly can result in unsightly lint, unclean clothes, and tears or holes in garments. Sorting also gives you an opportunity to look for stains and heavy soils on garments so that you can pretreat before you wash. Be sure to check likely areas for heavy dirt and stains, such as the knees and cuffs on children's jeans; collars, cuffs, and elbows on shirts and dresses; and any other areas of heavy wear on household articles and apparel.

Here are four basic considerations when sorting:

1. Color

Separate whites and pastels from dark-colored fabrics to prevent dye transfer. You can wash colorfast colors together if they have similar surface textures. Always wash noncolorfast fabrics with similar colors only (blues with blue, reds with red).

Don't take chances with your clothes. No matter how often you've washed a "positively colorfast, guaranteed not-to-run" fabric, a number of chemical reactions could cause it to happen. So be sure to sort the colors from the whites and lights.

An added benefit to color sorting is that you can use the most effective and efficient water temperature with each color group. Cotton whites come cleanest in hot water, while synthetic whites and colors fare better in warm water.

2. Fabric type and make

Different fabric types require different laundry procedures. Sheer, knit, and loosely woven fabrics do better with slow, gentle agitation. However, sturdier fabrics can stand more vigorous agitation. If a garment is poorly made or has delicate trim that could catch or tear, wash it separately.

3. Texture

There is nothing so unlovely as lint. And the best way to keep from spending extra time with the lint brush or adhesive tape is to sort fabrics by texture. Some fabrics give off lint, like chenille, terry cloth, and sweater knits. Other fabrics, like corduroy, velour, and knits, attract lint. Don't combine the two types in the same load.

4. Dirt

Dirty laundry is not just dirty laundry. There are degrees of dirtiness: light, normal, and heavy or greasy soil. Keep the worst to themselves to prevent graying or redepositing of soil on the less dirty articles. You can usually wash normal and lightly soiled articles together.

Your laundry

1. Put delicate articles in a pillowcase and fasten with a plastic tie. Wash the case on a gentle cycle.

2. Tie belts and sashes, close zippers, and fasten hooks so they won't catch on other garments.

3. Be sure to test an unexposed part of a garment for colorfastness before washing it for the first time.

4. Check all garments to remove items from the pockets, shake dirt and sand out of the pockets and cuffs, and mend tears and holes.

5. Liquid fabric softeners not only soften fabrics by slightly coating the fibers, they minimize wrinkling and static cling. To prevent a softener build-up, which can eventually reduce absorbency, you may wish to skip the softener every few washings.

6. Stains and soils can be removed more easily when they are fresh, so pretreat before you wash.

7. Be sure to follow all package directions, and never mix stain and spot removal solutions together. If you do use two or more removal products on soils and stains, be sure to thoroughly rinse the first treatment from the fabric before applying any others.

8. Launder all seasonal clothing and tablecloths before storing them. The longer the soils remain, the more difficult they will be to remove.

You wonder where the gray came from

If your white clothes are coming out yellow or gray after washing, and you swear you didn't slip a colorful article in with the load, you have one of those "laundry problems." The following is a brief description of two of the most common laundry problems and how to solve them.

1. Yellowing

Yellowing is caused by a number of things, such as hard water, incorrect bleach type, bleaching when you shouldn't, or dirty wash water. It can also occur when the heat setting on the dryer is too high for the articles being dried. Older synthetic fabrics turn yellow just from age, not from washing.

If your laundry is consistently coming out yellow, check the water hardness or the machine filters for dirt. If it's a once-in-a-while occurrence, you could be misusing bleach or overdrying the articles.

2. Graying

Gray laundry is usually caused by an overloaded machine or too-cool wash temperature. It can also occur when not enough detergent is used, the wash cycle is too short, or the rinse cycle is insufficient. Graying can also be the result of a long wait between the wash and rinse cycle, allowing dirt to settle back on the clothes. Hard water can also cause graying.

Be sure the machine is properly, not overly, loaded. Use sufficient detergent for the load and degree of dirtiness, and make sure the wash and rinse cycles are long enough for the amount and type of load you are washing. Always rinse clothes promptly after the wash cycle.

The Label Says This:	It Means This:
Washable Machine Washable Machine Wash	Item can be home or commercially laundered and dried.
Home Launder Only	Do not commercially launder.
Machine Washable— Cold Water	Wash in cold water only; cold setting on machine.
Machine Washable— Warm Water	Can be washed in warm water up to 110° F.
Machine Washable— Hot Water	Can be washed in water up to 130° F.
No Spin	Remove article from the wash before the final spin cycle.

Machine Washable—Delicate or Gentle	Use gentle wash cycle only or wash by hand.
Machine Washable—Permanent Press	Use permanent press cycle on machine; or else regular wash, cold rinse, and short spin.
Machine Washable—Separately	Wash only with like colors.
Hand Washable	Can be handwashed in cool or warm water; may be dry-cleaned.
Hand Wash Only	Do not machine wash or dry-clean.
Hand Wash Separately	Hand wash alone or with like colors.
No Bleach	The article cannot be bleached.
Tumble or Machine Dry	Follow label directions for dryer temperature setting; item can be tumble dried.
Tumble Dry—Remove Promptly	Remove article as soon as the drying cycle is over.
Drip-Dry	Do not tumble dry; hang the article while still wet and let dry.
Do Not Twist, Wring, or Squeeze	Article must be hung or drip-dried or dried flat.

Dry Flat	Article must be placed on a flat surface to dry.
Block To Dry	Article must be shaped and sized while wet and dried on a flat surface.
No Chlorine Bleach	Do not use chlorine bleach. All-fabric bleach may be used.
Hang Dry or Line Dry	Hang damp and allow to dry.

Time-saving laundry tips

1. Buying new sheets? Pick a different color or pattern for each size bed, and sorting after laundering will be faster.

2. Wash dark things inside out, to keep right side from collecting lint.

3. Prevent tangling in the machine by buttoning shirt and blouse sleeves to front buttons.

4. Close zippers to protect them; fasten hooks to prevent snagging on clothes.

5. Brush lint from pockets and cuffs before laundering to keep it from getting on other wash.

6. Bulky items like blankets and bedspreads should be washed alone for best results.

7. Read labels and instructions to be sure you are using the right amount of detergent; amounts can vary based on strength of formula, size of washer, amount of soil, and hardness of water.

8. Wash bath mats less often by protecting them with a used towel when kids take a bath.

9. Put up kiddie-height towel racks to remind youngsters to hang up and reuse towels.

10. Spray sneakers lightly with starch; it protects them from soil without making them stiff.

11. Dewrinkle corduroy and velvet by tumbling 15 minutes in the dryer with a damp towel.

12. Save a wash by using your dryer to fluff and remove dust from shag rugs, sofa pillows; same for draperies and bedspreads, but hang or spread them right away to avoid wrinkles.

13. Wash knits inside out to protect against snags.

Use fabric softener sheets for the dryer several times; because they're so lightweight they always end up a mess in the lint catcher. Pin each new one to an old washcloth and toss that into the dryer with each load until the softener sheet is used up. The extra weight keeps it out of the lint catcher.

Get the most from your sheet fabric softener by simply tearing it in half. No difference in the results; clothes are just as soft and static-free.

Or, one single strand off a sheet works just as efficiently as an entire one to take the static out of permanent-press items. On one brand, each sheet has seven strands. So, one roll of 40 sheets will take care of 280 loads!

Fasten a small length of chain to one end of your clothesline. Then, if the line sags, place the next link of the chain over the hook. It's easier than trying to pull the line tighter.

If you are only drying a few items by machine, throw a clean bath towel in with the load. The towel absorbs moisture and the clothes will dry faster.

If you must hang out the clothes on a cold day, wear a pair of rubber gloves over cloth gloves. They keep hands dry and warm.

Add a pocket to the clothespin bag to hold a sponge to wipe the clothesline before hanging laundry to dry. It will be handy but not in the way when reaching for the pins.

When hanging wash, hang clothes to be ironed on the first lines and clothes that need only to be folded on the last lines. Cuts down time spent sorting.

Keep a pair of sunglasses pinned to your clothespin bag so that you have them handy when needed while hanging out clothes to dry.

A babystroller makes a convenient carryall for a clothes basket when hanging wash to dry. Just push the stroller as you go, and the height of the stroller keeps you from having to stoop too far.

Pants stretchers are a wonderful invention, but they're hard to secure to a clothesline. To solve this problem, take a shower-curtain clamp, hook it through the cuff end of the stretcher and over the clothesline, then snap the clamp shut.

Carry an old cloth shoulder bag to hold your clothespins. It will keep you from having to run back and forth to get and put away the pins.

Before hanging up wet blankets, string cardboard tubes (from paper towel, waxed paper, and the like) on your clothesline, then hang the blanket over these to prevent a line mark on the dried blanket.

After laundering a pleated skirt, hang it by the waistband to the clothesline. Then clip a spring-type clothespin to the bottom of each pleat. The pleats will dry in place, and the skirt will need little ironing.

Remove the lint from the catcher in your automatic dryer by using the dusting brush of your vacuum cleaner.

Speed the drying of a bulky sweater by inserting a folded bath towel between the front and back. It will absorb moisture and allow air to circulate more freely.

To prevent jean hems from turning up after washing, clip two or three clothespins along the very bottom of the pant-legs and let dry. This gives them the stylish no-ironed look, only a little neater.

Solve the problem of drip-dry laundry by attaching a folding garment hanger above your bathtub. Hang wet clothes to dry. After removing them, fold the hanger to one side.

A place for empty hangers

Empty coat hangers seem to have a life of their own. They either get lost in closets or tangled into a hopeless jumble in the clothes basket. Fasten a towel rack to the wall or a cupboard near the dryer. Family members are glad to hang them there just to get the pesky things out of their closets, and you have an easy-to-reach, orderly supply on laundry days.

IRONING AND REMOVING STAINS

Easier ironing

When ironing, keep an ice cube wrapped in a thin cloth handy for dampening corners and any other small dry areas.

When not spraying houseplants, keep the plant mister on the ironing board. It sprays a fine mist that's perfect for dampening clothes before ironing.

Because organdy curtains dry so quickly while being ironed, fold a large bath towel in half and pinch each end of it to the back of the ironing board. Keep the curtain rolled in the towel and pull it out as you iron.

Quick repairs

Keep sewing needles with basic colors of thread near the dryer and the ironing board for quick repairs when folding or ironing clothes.

Whisk the lint away

Keep a whisk broom hanging on a hook underneath your ironing board. You'll find this handy when pressing clothes that are covered with lint.

Save time and wrinkles

To prevent wrinkling, smooth and fold or hang clothes as soon as they are dry. Keep your ironing board set up near the dryer to do necessary touch-ups immediately.

Give it body

To add body to frequently washed knitted shirts, spray lightly with starch and press with a warm iron. The shirts will keep their shape and stay clean longer.

Give frequently washed corduroy garments more body: Turn them inside out, spray with starch, and then iron.

Cheesecloth makes a good ironing cloth. It leaves no lint and retains little moisture, and clothes don't get too wet.

Handy dispenser

A clean catsup dispenser makes an ideal container for filling steam irons. Keep it near the ironing board to save steps.

Removing starch residue

Remove that "cooked-on" starch residue from your electric iron (after letting the iron cool) with rubbing alcohol. Wipe with a clean damp sponge and let dry thoroughly before reusing the iron.

No waste

Freeze leftover starch in an ice cube tray, clearly label it, and store in your freezer. You'll have cubes of starch handy when a small amount is needed.

Keep them flat

Starch rag or braided rugs heavily and they'll lie flat.

Easy zip

When ironing shorts, jeans, or overalls, check the zippers and, if they stick, lubricate them by rubbing with a wax candle.

Tight fit

Your ironing board cover will fit tightly and smoothly after washing if you fasten it on the board while it is still damp.

Protecting ironed clothes

When ironing, put a discarded (but clean) oilcloth or plastic tablecloth on the floor under the ironing board. This protects any dangling garments while they are being ironed. When not in use, roll the cloth on a broom handle for storage.

Easier ironing

When ironing flat pieces, turn the ironing board around so that the iron rests on the narrow end of the board. This arrangement gives you more ironing surface for large pieces.

Quick mending

Keep small slips of assorted colored paper next to the ironing board. As you iron and discover mending to be done, pin a colored slip to the garment—blue for missing button, green for ripped hem, red for tear, and so on. This saves time and jogs the memory when you get around to mending.

Ironing board protection

The long paper bags that dry cleaners use to cover cleaned clothes make wonderful ironing board protectors. Slip one over the folded board before storing.

Ironing pleats

When ironing pleated cotton skirts or dresses, spray the edges of the pleats lightly with starch. This helps to keep the pleats in longer.

Keep it neat

Keep a pair of scissors near your ironing board and trim off any ravelings or threads as you iron.

Hold that spot

Before laundering stained linens or garments, hold spotted areas firm by placing them in embroidery hoops, then treat the stains.

Help for working mothers

As an instant reminder that an article of clothing needs special treatment for a stain before it is laundered, have your family members tie a knot in the pant leg or sleeve before they toss it into the hamper. If this is not possible, a large safety pin attached in a conspicuous place will do. Most working mothers have to do laundry in a hurry, and this is a time saver!

Quick spot remover

If you spill something on your clothes while eating out, ask the waiter for a glass of club soda; use a clean napkin and try to remove the spot.

Cleaning rain slickers

An easy way to clean those unsightly smudges on rain slickers, especially the light-colored ones, is to sprinkle some baking soda on the soiled areas and gently rub it in with a damp cloth. The slicker will look like new!

Mildew removal

To remove mildew from leather bags or shoes, wipe them with a cloth moistened in a solution of 1 cup denatured alcohol and 1 cup water. Dry carefully in an airy place.

Fruit or berry stains

Stretch material over a large bowl and pour boiling water through the stains. If they remain, bleach with hydrogen peroxide or chlorine bleach.

Removing oil stains

Use white chalk to remove grease or oil stains. It can be rubbed onto a washable fabric before laundering or ground up and worked into a carpet, then vacuumed after it has absorbed the grease.

Coffee stains

Soak overnight in a large pan of strong vinegar water and hang in sun while dripping wet. Then wash as usual or try one of the commercial coffee pot cleaners.

Chewing gum

Put garment in a plastic bag and freeze. Gum should flick off easily.

Brown spots

Leaving wet articles in the laundry basket for long periods can cause browning due to mildew. Brown spots can also be caused by iron particles in the water being "rusted" by bleach.

Wash and dry wet clothes promptly. If you suspect the cause of the spots is iron in the water, you should consider buying a water softener.

Lint

The primary cause of lint is an overloaded washer or dryer, causing the clothes to rub against each other. In some instances, it is the result of clothes being allowed to dry too long in the dryer.

If you have sorted the articles properly and are still having lint problems, check to see if you're using enough detergent and make sure not to overload the washer and dryer. If the problem is not apparent after washing, be careful not to overdry the load.

Pilling

Those balls of fuzz usually found on the collars, cuffs, and elbows of synthetics and permanent press are called pills and are caused by abrasion. Pilling is, unfortunately, permanent. To prevent it, turn the garments inside out before laundering and take care not to overload the machine. A fabric softener in the final rinse will also help reduce pilling.

CLOTHES CARE

Shoe business

To clean white rubber on sneakers, use a moistened soapy scouring pad. For extra soil marks, dip pad in heavy-duty cleanser.

Glue a little name-and-address label on one side of a spring-type clothespin and carry it in your purse. Snap it onto overshoes when they are left together with others. It's a help in identifying them quickly.

Coat the eyelets of white shoes with clear nail polish to prevent discoloration of laces.

Put your girls' newly cleaned and whitened gym shoes into plastic bags. This prevents the cleaner from rubbing off on clothes and keeps the shoes together on the return trip to school.

Keeping shoes dry

Polish and shine your shoes and put a light coat of floor wax on them. This waterproofs them and keeps them clean and shining a long time.

The family's canvas shoes will stay dry on damp days, require fewer washings, and keep their good looks longer if they are treated with waterproofing, available in spray cans.

To dry rubber boots that are damp, use the blower attachment of your vacuum cleaner. Warm air will speed up the drying.

Spray new white tennis shoes with starch. This will keep them white longer and make them easier to clean when soiled.

Shoes that shine

Good care of family shoes will help them wear well. Brush and air them after each wearing. Stuff the toes with tissue paper or shoe trees. Once or twice a week apply a neutral paste polish or one the color of the leather. Let the polish dry thoroughly. Then rub with a soft cloth and buff with a soft brush. When shoes are new, it's wise to treat the leather with paste wax before the first wearing. Then stroke with a soft brush and follow with a regular shoe polish.

Recycle your torn nylons and kneehighs! They are just the ticket to add a final brilliant shine to freshly polished shoes.

To give new life to shoes with wooden heels or wedges, apply a small amount of pure lemon oil to the wooden parts with a soft clean cloth. This will restore the natural oils and will clean and polish the wood.

Shoes with wooden heels and wooden platforms often become marred and scratched and start looking bad before the rest of the shoe wears out. Lightly sand the wood and refinish it with furniture stain to make the shoe look brand-new!

Use the dusting brush on your vacuum cleaner to clean suede shoes. It not only removes embedded dust; it raises the nap.

Ever wish you could get more of those nifty shoeshine mitts that motels and hotels put in the rooms? Well, you can—and it's easy and free. The used fabric softener sheets you put in your dryer do a great job of touching up shoes or putting that shine on after you polish them. Also, when you travel, pack one unused fabric softener sheet in your suitcase. It keeps the clothes smelling good and static free when unpacking.

When cleaning and polishing sandals or open-toed shoes, slip the hand that holds the shoe into a small plastic or paper bag. Your hand won't get stained.

Use paper toweling instead of a cloth to apply paste shoe polish.

Before discarding an old sweater or wool shirt, cut off the sleeves. They make fine buffers for shoes.

When patent leather gets that dull look, work in a small amount of petroleum jelly and buff with a soft rag. This will bring that sparkle back!

Clean your patent leather bags and shoes with a solvent glass cleaner. Just spray it on and polish dry with a soft cloth.

Protect the back of shoe heels from scuffing by coating them occasionally with colorless nail polish.

Protective coat

Use a cleaner-polisher wax on your plastic or vinyl pocketbooks, jackets, and shoes. It not only cleans them but coats them with a protective film that helps delay soiling.

Cleaning hats

Use the suds from an upholstery cleaner to clean a soiled felt hat. Follow the directions carefully and, when dry, brush with a stiff clothesbrush.

Try using the upholstery attachment of the vacuum cleaner to dust your husband's hats and your own. This not only removes the dust and lint, it plumps up the nap.

Storing winter clothes

Store winter clothes clean. Wash or dry-clean all wool knits—socks, sweaters, gloves, and scarves. Store with mothballs, flat, in clean boxes, plastic bags, or wrapping paper. Be certain that all openings are sealed with gummed tape. Store the garments in a cool dark place.

Neat-looking ribbons

Hair ribbons constantly become wrinkled and messy with use. An easy way to make them fresh and neat looking again is to slide them through a heated curling iron.

Hang them up

Hang belts—or your daughter's hair ribbons—on a rotating necktie rack to keep them in order and easily accessible.

A convenient way to store belts is to hang them on cup hooks screwed to the underside of a wooden hanger.

Ways to remove lint

A sponge powder puff is great for removing lint from velvet jackets, skirts, and the like.

To remove lint from clothing, use a damp sponge. It will pick up most of the clinging hairs and the like that collect on suits, coats, and other garments.

Brush woolens with a dry cellulose sponge to remove lint from the fabric. This does a good job!

A slightly dampened clothesbrush will remove lint from clothes quickly.

Repairing an umbrella

Tips often pull off the ribs of an umbrella. When they do, apply a few drops of clear nail polish to each tip, then force ribs into place. When the polish is dry, the tips will stay put.

Easy reach

Slip a safety pin or two on your key ring, so you will always have one in case of an emergency.

A quick wipe

A quick way to clean dirty, smudged eyeglasses is with white vinegar. A small squeeze bottle kept in your purse or desk allows for quick wipes with a tissue.

Preserving your canvas bags

Prevent a canvas bag from soiling too quickly by spraying it with a stain-resistant product. Your bag will keep free of soil for a much longer time.

Keep them from stretching

To keep cuffs of sweaters and mittens from stretching, weave several rounds of elastic cord through the underside of the cuffs. Make sure the elastic is not pulled so tightly it impairs circulation. If desired, white elastic cord can be dyed with commercial dye to match the color of the garment.

Cleaning fleece

Vacuuming fleecy jackets or fleece coat linings with the upholstery brush gets the dust out and smooths the fleece.

Easy identification

Tape an address label to the shaft of your umbrella. It's an easy way to identify it, and, if you lose it, it can be returned by the finder.

Quick wrinkle remover

When the season changes, put stored clothes into the dryer for a few minutes. It takes out wrinkles and fluffs up nap.

For your hatpins

A piece of felt, glued to the inside of your hatbox lid, is a handy place to keep hatpins.

Keeping the moths away

Have you ever wondered what else to do with your family's mateless socks besides giving them to the dog? Stuff a few moth balls in the toes and suspend them from hangers in storage closets or garment bags. Not only are the clothes protected from insect damage, but the mothballs do not directly touch the clothes and there are no camphor remnants in pockets or linings!

Moths bugging your clothes? Make "moth tape" to put them on the run. Just dust moth crystals on the sticky side of plastic tape and hang in the closet. Moths will stay away!

Helpful marker

Keep an indelible marker in your dresser. When you find a pair of ruined pantyhose, mark an "X" on the label. After washing you can easily identify which ones go in the drawer to be worn under slacks.

Keeping wire hangers apart

Empty thread spools placed over the hooks of wire coat hangers will keep the hangers separated and your clothes uncrushed. It surely saves time, tension, and temper.

When you buy clothes

Look for these details, which are the marks of good tailoring:

1. Smooth fabric with no puckering at seams.
2. Buttonholes sewn on both sides of cloth.
3. Firm, closely woven fabric lining and pockets.
4. Pinked or overcast skirt seams.
5. Seams wide enough to permit letting out.
6. Good tape binding in hems.
7. Even close stitches.

8. Collar and lapel which will snap back when rolled up and then released.

9. Pants crotch without small triangles of cloth.

Better care means better wear

Proper care of your clothes is an easy matter; just observing a few simple ground rules does it. It will more than pay off in lengthening the life and trim appearance of your clothes.

Do's

1. Do—thoroughly brush your clothes regularly.

2. Do—thoroughly dry rain-soaked or damp garments in a cool, well ventilated place before hanging in the closet.

3. Do—have garments dry-cleaned regularly; even nominal accumulation of perspiration, grease, grit, and dust particles impairs the attractiveness and longevity of any apparel.

4. Do—save the hang tags that come with garments you buy. Show them to your dry cleaner for his guidance—and take care of instructions that have to do with home care.

5. Do—immediately send stained garments to the dry cleaner. Exposure to air, heat, and light sets stains and can make their removal impossible.

6. Do—tell your dry cleaner when a garment has been stained. It is important for successful stain removal.

Don'ts

1. Don't—press a garment if it is stained. The heat of pressing will set the stain and likely make its removal impossible.

2. Don't—use untested home stain removers. They aggravate the condition or may create permanent damage. Take the garment to your dry cleaner immediately.

3. Don't—use an underarm deodorant without using a shield to protect the garment from the deodorant. Allow deodorant to dry before dressing.

4. Don't—store garments at home without first having them cleaned and mothproofed before storage. Be sure that the storage bags, boxes, or cedar chests used are kept in a dry place.

5. Don't—use nail polish remover to remove nail polish stains from a garment. You may damage the garment's dye or, if the fabric is an acetate type, create a hole.

6. Don't—hang knitted garments. It pulls them out of shape and causes a sagging hemline. Knitted garments fare best stored in a drawer, or, if that's not feasible, fold the garment over a horizontal, padded rod of the hanger.

Facts about accessories

Accessories and trimmings add glamour and sparkle to your clothes. But what a headache if they won't clean. Sometimes they are replaceable, but at the cost of extra time and money. Check when you buy.

Belts

Seek out belts that are clearly marked "dry cleanable." Some uncleanable belts have glued backs—they dissolve in dry cleaning. Some backings become brittle and come apart.

To keep belts, ties, scarves, and any detachable accessories matching a garment perfectly, be sure to include them with every dry cleaning or laundering—even if they have not been worn. Colors and designs change ever so slightly, but progressively, and this assures that there will never be a tell-tale contrast.

Buttons

Buttons may bleed; some metal buttons will rust; some plastic buttons dissolve or soften in dry cleaning. There's no need to settle for problem buttons—serviceable buttons to suit every need and taste are available.

KEEPING NEEDLEWORK ORGANIZED

Bobbin storage

The round plastic cases that pins and sewing accessories come in are fine for storing your sewing machine bobbins. The cases keep the thread clean and prevent it from unrolling.

Organizing leftovers

After finishing cutting out a garment, place all the pieces of leftover material and trimmings used in a clear plastic container. This way you keep all the pieces together for possible later use and they can be seen at a glance.

Button storage

When removing buttons from an old garment, thread them on a fine hairpin, twist the ends together, and store in your button box for future use.

It's easy to keep buttons sorted by colors and sizes if you put them into a compartmented fishing-tackle box.

Keep track of loose snaps in your sewing basket by snapping them through a strip of cheesecloth.

To save buttons from discarded clothing, take a piece of freezer or adhesive tape about 8" to 10" long, depending on how many buttons you have. Press the buttons flat side down along the sticky side of the tape. Fold back ends, sticky side together.

Neat sewing basket

Rubber bands slipped over spools of thread keep the ends of the thread from unwinding and cluttering the sewing basket.

In order to avoid tangles in the sewing box, keep a roll of cellophane tape handy. Loose thread ends can be secured with a bit of tape, leaving the sewing box neater.

Wind remnants of bias binding, seam binding, elastic, or lace around empty thread spools and fasten the ends with cellophane tape.

Useful tape dispenser

An empty adhesive-tape dispenser makes a great holder for a tape measure. It rolls up neatly and is handy for the family seamstress.

Emergency sewing kit

Small plastic medicine vials make excellent holders for emergency sewing kits. Put a bobbin with thread on the bottom of the container, add some needles, buttons, and safety pins. It can be carried in a purse, suitcase, or car.

A storage place

If you do a great deal of knitting and crocheting and often have one or two different projects going at once, purchase two plastic vegetable bins and stack one on top of the other. Not only can you put your crocheting in the bottom and knitting in the top, or vice versa, but the legs are hollow and make a perfect place to store extra knitting needles.

Yarn caddy

Here is an inexpensive and practical use for those soda bottle cartons with either six or eight compartments. Fill paper cups with assorted yarns and place in each compartment. It is a handy carry-all and a convenient method for picking the right colors at a glance.

Protecting patterns

To prevent your sewing patterns from falling apart after repeated markings with the tracing wheel, apply clear adhesive tape over the areas where the wheel will be used (darts, dots, stitching lines, and the like). The tape reinforces the pattern at these points, yet leaves it clearly visible for markings.

A fabric box

If you love to sew and often stock up on fabric you find on sale, then store it in a large box in a closet, do you find much later the you have forgotten about it? Solve the problem by cutting small swatches of the fabric and taping them to the outside of the box. Write the approximate yardage of the fabric on the scrap with a felt-tipped pen. No more digging, no more wasteful spending. When you use a fabric, simply remove the sample from the outside of the box.

Scissor safety

To keep scissors closed while they are being stored, slip the points into a piece of cork.

Good use for a spice rack

Give your unused spice rack a new life. Make it a convenient yet attractive storage rack for your collection of thread spools.

Storing small items

Use the small plastic boxes tiny breath mints come in to store glitter, sequins, pins, and the like for your craft projects.

Neat and clean

Store your stock of sewing fabrics in clear plastic garment bags—keeps them easily viewed.

DARNING AND EMBROIDERING

Easy mend

Mending a knitted garment? Place the raveled or torn part over the bristles of a brush. The bristles will hold the fabric and prevent stretching in the area being mended.

A golf ball, placed inside children's socks that are too small for a darning egg makes mending easy.

A marble makes a perfect darning egg for use in the fingers of gloves that need mending.

To repair a hole in a sweater or any other woolen item, place a patch of mosquito netting on the wrong side of it, then darn through the holes in the net.

Neat way of mending

Whenever possible, extend the life of a dress or a blouse by covering a small hole with a bit of colorful embroidery.

Invisible mending

When darning multicolor material, choose a long-eyed needle, insert strands of various-colored threads (choose the ones in the material). The mend will be almost undetectable.

KNITTING, CROCHETING, AND NEEDLEPOINT

Tangle-free yarn

To keep embroidery yarn untangled, wind each color in a little ball and put it into an empty pill bottle. Pull the end of the thread through a hole punched in the plastic lid.

Wrap embroidery thread around unfolded empty matchbooks. With the flap closed, there will be no loose ends to tangle.

Easy tracing

A ball point pen that has gone dry is ideal for tracing embroidery designs, for it will not tear the paper pattern the way a pencil does.

Keep needlepoint canvas clean

To keep needlepoint canvas clean, save the tubes from paper towels and wrapping paper and roll the canvas inside. It will stay beautifully clean and ready to use.

Blocking needlepoint

Use your plant mister to block finished needlepoint. Tack the canvas to a board, spray with mister, and let dry overnight. Repeat if necessary.

Attractive storage boxes

Fireplace matches come in such beautiful containers. Use the empty ones to store crochet hooks and short knitting needles.

Use an empty food-wrap box in either the 12″ or 15″ size to store regular or long needles. To make them more attractive, decorate the boxes with colorful self-adhesive paper.

A plastic toothbrush holder makes a good crochet hook holder that is safe and unbreakable.

Winding yarn

When you wind yarn into a ball, start by winding it around a mothball. This will keep it free of moths while you store it or while you knit.

Knitting a sweater

Knit with two skeins of yarn instead of one when working on the elbows of a child's sweater. This makes the elbow wear longer.

Thoughtful gift

After completion of a crocheted afghan intended as a gift, clip the washing instructions from the yarn label and pin them to the afghan.

This makes the care of the present easier for the recipient. Include also tiny samples of yarns to use for mending.

First aid for garments

Machine-knitted clothes are great, except when they get snags. A tiny, flat needle-threader works well to mend them. Insert the threader wire from the wrong side exactly at the snag spot, retrieve the pulled thread, and work it back to the wrong side. The inexpensive, lightweight threader can be tucked into a purse for on-the-spot garment first aid.

Neat trick

When using a safety pin to hold knitted stitches, put a small button on the pin before slipping on the stitches. This prevents the yarn from catching in the spring end.

Color embroidery sheet

After transferring an embroidery design onto fabric, color the transfer sheet with crayons to show the various colors the pattern calls for. This saves time because you won't have to refer constantly to the chart.

PATCHING AND SEWING

Ways with the iron-on tape

When applying iron-on tape, put a piece of aluminum foil under the hole in the garment so that the tape will not stick to the ironing board.

Instead of waiting until jeans are torn and need mending, put iron-on patches on the inside of the knees of your children's brand-new jeans.

Having trouble with your denim skirt's hem rolling up, no matter how much you press it? Why not iron some mending tape (in matching color) just inside the hem edge!

Use a small piece of iron-on tape to cover rough zipper ends on pullovers and tops. No more scratchy parts against your skin.

Commercial iron-on patches will adhere longer if you pink them before applying. Similarly, use your pinking shears when cutting patches from iron-on tape.

If the feet of your child's pajamas wear out before the rest of the garment, reinforce them with inexpensive iron-on corduroy patches.

Hide that hole

During a dinner party or cocktails, many fine linen tablecloths have been spoiled by a cigarette burn. To repair them, purchase an unusual assortment of sew-ons: A tiny rose or delicate daisy can transform a plain tablecloth into an attractive conversation piece. At the same time, no one knows about the cigarette burns, and a cloth is saved.

Easy identification

Cut children's initials out of material for blue jean patches and press them on the youngsters' cotton caps and jackets. This makes their clothing easy to identify.

Patch jobs

An easy way to sew patches on jeans, uniforms, and the like is to glue them into place first with commercial household glue. After the patch has been sewn securely, the glue washes right out.

Before patching sheets or pillowcases, dip the area to be mended into a light starch, then dry and press. This makes patching easier.

Patching up jeans

To patch jeans, take the pockets from old ones and sew them right over the holes or worn spots. It looks quite attractive, and children enjoy wearing them with these patches.

Use the children's stencils to cut patches shaped like animals. These make more attractive patches than the squares generally used.

An old purse...

If you have a worn, soft leather purse that is no longer in style, save it to make elbow patches for an old cardigan sweater or to update a favorite tweed jacket. These patches are almost impossible to find in the stores!

Recycling old leather gloves

Use the worn-out parts of your old leather gloves for garment trim or to cover leather buttons.

Save old elastic bands

Save the elastic waistbands from discarded panty hose! Carefully snip the panty portion from the waist and cut through the band at the seam. They are useful for children's playwear, pajamas, or for gathering sleeves or waists on blouses and dresses. A good budget stretcher!

Simple stitching

If you've had problems sewing fabrics with foam backing, try putting a piece of plastic wrap between the sewing machine pressure foot and the material. Use a longer stitch, too.

Accurate stitching

To trace designs or make even rows, pin pattern to the fabric and then stitch along the lines, using the sewing machine and an unthreaded needle. Then remove the pattern and thread the needle. You are assured of an accurate job.

Cutting it out

Lay a discarded plastic tablecloth on the table when cutting out a pattern. The tablecloth protects the surface, and the scissors slide easily over the plastic.

When cutting out a garment, cut the front pieces with pinking shears and the back with plain scissors. Speeds up the job and it's easier to match the pieces.

When cutting a pattern from material that frays easily (like denim or flannel) apply a thin coat of clear nail polish along seam edges to prevent it from fraying when being sewn and laundered.

Sewing doll clothes

Doll clothes can be quite expensive, so when sewing your own, cut out a pattern for doll clothes as well. Sewing the doll's outfit when the machine is properly adjusted and threaded for the fabric takes little extra time. Little girls always love new clothes for their dolls—and they are ideal budget-saving gifts.

Patchwork tablecloth

Rather than using old linen calendars as dish towels, save them and sew them together for an unusual patchwork tablecloth. Then, each year, add to the calendar tablecloth. A novel idea!

Care for various fabrics

When sewing curtains or clothing, sew in a label with the care instructions and fiber content so you don't have to worry when it comes to dry-cleaning or washing them. Merely check the label and follow instructions!

Sewing buttons

Before sewing a row of buttons, tape each one exactly where it belongs with strips of adhesive transparent tape. After the first stitches through buttons are made, remove the tape.

Hang them up!

Before you discard pants or slacks, check to see whether they have belt loops. If so, cut them off and sew on the inside of children's coats and jackets for a coat loop. You have just eliminated the "lost coat at the bottom of the school closet" problem.

Bias tape

Simplify cutting bias strips by pressing masking tape on the bias of the fabric and cutting along the edges of the tape. When you gently pull off the tape your strips will be straight.

Rickrack trick

When sewing on tiny rickrack, lay a narrow strip of waxed paper over it. Sew and then tear the paper away. It keeps the braid from catching on the machine pressure foot.

Avoiding pinholes

To avoid pinholes when hemming delicate garments, mark the hemline with tailor's chalk and use hair clips to hold the fold in place. No need for pinning or basting!

Mending lace trim

Lace trims, especially at hemline and top edges, are often the first places to wear out or tear on a slip. Try replacing the torn parts with flexible nylon lace hem facing, available in at least two widths and many colors. The hem facing is pretty but more durable and stretchable than ordinary lace trim.

Handy notes

You can prevent future errors in sewing by slipping a memo into individual patterns explaining any size alterations or changes that had to be made for that particular item.

Planning ahead!

When preshrinking fabric in preparation for a sewing project, toss the zipper, seam tape, and any other washable notion in the washer as well. You will not be disappointed with a puckered seam, and the finished product will look more professional!

Old towels

Save money by trimming old frayed towels with cotton bias tape in matching or contrasting colors. They look pretty and perk up the appearance of the bathroom.

Terry towels and washcloths resist fraying and wear longer if hems are reinforced with a row of zigzag stitching in a matching or contrasting color.

Colorful bedspread

Sew your children's souvenir pennants onto blankets. They make colorful throw covers for their beds.

Secure that drawstring

Sew a large button on each end of the drawstring on your husband's pajamas. This will keep the string from mysteriously disappearing.

No slip-up

Wearing an apron made of terry cloth when you're sewing a slippery fabric will prevent its sliding off your lap as you work.

Pretty pillow cases

When cotton curtains or floral cotton bed sheets become a little faded from washing, try to salvage the best parts, and sew pillowcases from them.

Clear match

For hard-to-match threads in mending, keep a spool of clear nylon thread on hand. It is transparent and will pick up the color of the fabric. This also works well when a bobbin runs out and the spool is almost empty; just put the clear thread on your bobbin.

To help you with appliqué work

Here's a tip for appliqué work: Dip the pieces into a weak solution of cold laundry starch, then iron them in place before stitching with a zigzag sewing machine. This prevents wrinkling and slipping.

Quick transfer

Use your steam iron to stamp transfer patterns on fabric. You'll get a much clearer print.

Ironing table

Adjust your ironing board to a sitting height and place it at a right angle to your machine when sewing. It's easy to iron as you sew and saves energy and time.

No more confusion

If you and your teenage girls all wear panty hose and you can never tell which pair belongs to whom, try sewing a thread of an assigned color to the top of each pair. It takes little time to do and solves the identification problem. This device can also be used for socks and other clothing.

Some neat dyeing tricks

A practical dyeing idea is to run a few strands of white thread through garments to be dyed. When finished, remove the threads and wrap around a spool; they can be used for future mending or hemming.

When you dye or batik fabric, always do an extra piece and save it for patching. Otherwise it's nearly impossible to duplicate the designs and colors.

Kitchen tongs come in handy to lift and turn articles during dyeing. The tongs prevent scalded fingers and make it easy to move fabric through the dye, resulting in more even absorption.

In and around the sewing machine

After oiling your sewing machine, run the needle through a blotter. It will remove any excess oil and keep materials from getting stained.

Mascara brushes, washed clean, are very handy for cleaning the crevices of the sewing machine and other tiny places.

Put a thin sheet of foam rubber under the foot control of your sewing machine to prevent the control from sliding around when you use it on an uncarpeted floor.

Attach a magnet to your sewing machine to hold an extra supply of needles, and keep one in the sewing basket to attract loose pins. Glue a small magnet to the end of a wooden yardstick, for easy pickup of pins.

To speed up oiling your sewing machine, mark all the places to be oiled with a dab of red nail polish.

Erase tell-tale creases

When lengthening a garment, there is always that inevitable shine and crease from the previous hem. To prevent this tell-tale giveaway, apply white vinegar to the wrong side of the fabric and steam press. Both shine and crease will disappear.

Repairing braided rugs

When the braids in your braided rugs rip apart, instead of resewing them, use clear fabric glue to repair them. It's much faster and easier to do, and the braids will not tear again so quickly.

Sew your own table pads

Custom-cut tablepads are quite expensive. A much more economical substitute which serves the purpose just as well is to make your own from a new or used quilted mattress cover. Place the cover on your table top and trim with scissors for a custom fit. Bind the raw edges with bias tape, and you'll have a sturdy, heat-absorbent table pad to protect the finish of your table at a great saving.

Quick cleanup

After a busy day of sewing, wring out a sponge mop in clear water and brush it lightly over the rug. It will remove all the threads and lint.

Restoring old buttons

Apply a coating of clear nail polish to old pearl buttons to give them a new gloss.

Aid for accessories

After buying or sewing clothing, staple a small fabric sample to a 3″ x 5″ index card and carry it in your purse. It will make the selection of accessories much simpler.

Easy threading

Having difficulty threading a needle? Push it through a sheet of white paper and the eye will be easier to see.

Quick repairs

Carry a twist tie (the kind used to tie bread packages) in your purse for those emergencies when a button falls off. After repositioning the button, push the wire through the buttonholes and material, and twist to a close on the other side.

Easy throw pillows

Washcloths can make colorful and economical throw pillows. Stitch three sides of two washcloths together and stuff with cut-up nylons. Stitch up fourth side. They're the perfect size for using with sleeping bags or on trips to the beach.

Six

370 WAYS TO KEEP
THE REST OF THE HOUSE

GENERAL CLEANUP

Getting organized

Here are some tips to help you organize and speed up your cleaning chores:

1. Concentrate on doing one job at a time. Set aside one day for doing the laundry, another for vacuuming and floor washing, a third for dusting and "smudge" work.

2. Certain cleaning chores that require little or no moving of objects can be done all at once with a glass spray cleaner. It takes care of cleaning windows and windowsills, light switches and fixtures, door knobs, mirrors, kitchen and bathroom sinks and spigots, cabinets, shelves, and countertops. You can move from room to room, spray cleaner and clean cloth in hand.

3. Organize your cleaning aids—store floor cleaners with mops, furniture dust and polish aids with feather dusters and polishing cloth, and so on. Keep duplicate sets on each floor of your home, or carry them conveniently in a caddy.

4. Large jobs, like major room overhauls, should be done individually. Plan to do just one or two rooms a day, so you can give them a careful, thorough cleaning.

5. Practice the reward system. When the job's done, enjoy yourself... lunch with friends, spend the afternoon reading a good book, or just put your feet up and relax.

Alternating chores

If you are holding a job you will probably need help with housework from your family. Make a list of daily chores for the children. To keep it from becoming a tedious routine, they can trade lists at the end of each week. This also helps to eliminate such misconceptions as "that's man's work" and "that's woman's work." It all comes under the heading of housework. One child is just as good at cleaning the bathroom and setting a dinner table as the other is at mowing the lawn and cleaning the garage.

Breaking a habit

If you are a working wife and your family has the habit of leaving their clothes scattered all through the house after returning home from work, try this: Set a kitchen timer for 10 minutes, and ask everyone to get busy putting things back where they belong. The house looks tidy quickly, and the whole family realizes just how much of a mess they left each night for Mother to take care of.

The big cleanup

Before giving your home a major (spring, preholiday) cleaning, tidy up your equipment as well. Soak smelly sponge and string mops, brooms, sponges, and mesh pads in baking soda solution. It will remove dirt, grime, and odor, leaving them fresh and clean.

Clean sponges

Keep cellulose sponges bright and clean just by tossing them into your washer with a load of clothes. (Don't add bleach, though.) Sponges that you use in the kitchen can be washed in the dishwasher along with a batch of dishes. Either way the sponges will come out fresh and soft.

Easy measuring

Mark your cleaning bucket as a measuring cup is marked—with lines (use paint or red nail polish) to indicate quarts. This makes it easy to mix cleaning solutions to the proper strength.

Hang it up

Run a shower-curtain hook through a hole in your broom handle. Makes it easy to hang up.

Save your walls!

Cut the finger from worn rubber gloves and slip onto the handle of your vacuum cleaner, electric sweeper, or broom. When the handle falls against the wall, it will not leave a scuff mark.

Your cleaning closet

Tools:

1. A vacuum cleaner with a set of attachments for carpet and rug cleaning and dusting.

2. Floor polisher/scrubber, dust mop, and steel wool for wood floor maintenance.

3. Brushes, sponges, mop with detachable head, and bucket. Get one that's divided for washing and rinsing, so you don't have to run back to the sink for a refill.

4. Clean rags for dusting and polishing.

Cleansers:

5. Baking soda to clean glass, wall tile, and porcelain enamel.

6. Ammonia to wash windows and mirrors, loosen wax, and clean ovens.

7. Bleach to remove stains and whiten laundry. It's an inexpensive toilet bowl cleaner, too.

8. Liquid and powder detergents for dishes, clothes, and household cleaning; all-purpose cleaners to remove grease and grimy dirt; cleansers and scouring powders to remove tarnish and stains.

9. Polishes, waxes, and oils for wood, leather, and metal surface cleaning and polishing.

10. Spot removal products for carpets and upholstery.

Storage:

11. Peg board for hanging tools.

12. Shelves for storing supplies.

13. Stepladder or stool for cleaning hard-to-reach places.

14. Basket for carrying supplies from one room to another.

For a quick wipe

Carry a damp cloth or sponge in a small plastic bag in your apron pocket. It's handy to wipe up the spots and fingerprints you find while dusting or straightening up.

Double-duty brushes

A wire brush cleans a carpet sweeper brush nicely.

A sturdy vegetable brush is a dandy cleaning tool. Keep a fresh one with your vacuum cleaner to get into corners and next to baseboards. You will find it easier to use than a whisk broom or a straight scrub brush.

Keep a 4″ nylon paint brush with cleaning supplies. It is great for dusting piano keys, the tops of books, corners of windowsills, window screens, lampshades, and any other hard-to-get-at places.

Disposable dustpan

To make a quick throw-away dustpan for messy cleanups, cut a disposable foil pie pan in half. These come in handy in a workshop or garage, too.

Handy apron

Wear a cobbler's or any other large-pocketed apron when cleaning the house. That way you can pick up the mislaid button or the small lost toy as you go along. Also carry a small pair of scissors to clip a rug thread or a drooping leaf and a small note pad and pencil to jot down reminders like "Toy box hinge needs repairing."

Useful eraser

Keep a large pencil eraser with your cleaning supplies and use it on painted walls and woodwork to remove those marks that won't come off with ordinary cleaning.

Caring for the mop

To keep cleaning mops from becoming stiff after use: Add a capful of fabric softener to a pail of water and rinse thoroughly. They come out soft and fresh smelling.

Clean your dust mop between washings by vacuuming it. Place it on a newspaper on the floor and run the upholstery attachment of your cleaner over it until the dust has been removed.

When storing the dust mop, pull a plastic bag over the head. If you use oil on the mop, the bag will prevent its evaporation and protect the other tools in your cleaning closet.

To keep a new string mop or mophead replacement from tangling and fraying, tie a knot on the end of each strand. For best results and longer life, do this before its initial use.

Books and shelves

Unstick the pages of a book on which water was accidentally spilled by putting it into a frost-free freezer compartment. The freezer operates by continuously drawing out moisture and eventually will unstick the pages of your book.

Clean the leather bindings of your books with a lather made from saddle soap. Wipe dry with a clean soft cloth.

Clean your bookshelves and books regularly with the dusting tool of your vacuum cleaner to guard against dust damage.

Bookends

Fix a piece of double-faced tape underneath bookends to keep them from sliding out of place.

Caring for rugs

Hang a small whisk broom on a hook attached to an upright vacuum to brush out corners you can't get into with the machine.

After spot-cleaning spills on your carpet, rug, or upholstery, use your hair dryer to direct warm air over the damp area. This not only speeds the drying; it helps to lift the nap.

When vacuuming scatter rugs, lay them on top of large carpets. The small rugs will stay in place while you run the vacuum over them.

To remove crayon marks from vinyl-tile or wood floors, wipe with a cloth dipped in paste or cleaner-polisher wax.

To vacuum fine dog hairs from your carpet, spray it first lightly with water from a plant mister.

Rather than shuffling furniture from one room to another in order to shampoo the carpet, you can save a lot of time and back-breaking effort by securing a small plastic bag over each furniture leg with a rubber band. Then simply move the furniture aside to shampoo the area and return it to its original spot immediately; the bags can be removed after the rug has dried.

Buy a 30' heavy-duty extension cord for your vacuum cleaner. This enables you to clean the entire hallway and staircase without un-plugging the cord. Then vacuum your way downstairs and wait till you have to go up for another reason to disconnect the cord.

A small plant sprayer kept filled with liquid rug shampoo and stored in a closet close to your carpeted rooms makes it easy to spray and wipe up spills and soiled areas immediately.

If you lose a contact lens on a high-pile carpet, place a nylon stocking over the mouth of your vacuum cleaner attachment. The suction will scoop up the lens onto the nylon.

Save your floors

Unsightly black heel marks on your light linoleum floors can be rubbed out with a pencil eraser. Works great!

When waxing a linoleum floor, wax the bottoms of chair legs as well. It will prevent unsightly scratch marks.

Most stains can be prevented or minimized by keeping floors well waxed and by wiping up any spills immediately. Begin at the outer edge, and work toward the middle to prevent the stain from spreading. To remove stains caused by standing water, heel marks, or cigarette burns, rub steel wool over the area and re-wax.

If your rocking chair marks up your bare wooden floor, affix strips of inexpensive self-stick indoor-outdoor carpeting underneath the rockers.

Caring for furniture

When cleaning Lucite or Plexiglas furniture, dust first, then wash with warm, sudsy water. Scratches will be less noticeable if you apply a light coat of paste wax.

Clean the casters on your furniture and spray or paint them with shellac to prevent staining carpets or wood floors in humid weather.

Try saddle soap to clean leather and vinyl upholstery. Just follow the manufacturer's directions for good results.

To keep tubular aluminum outdoor furniture from becoming pitted, apply paste wax and repeat as needed.

Clean the textured-plastic coverings of kitchen chairs, baby strollers, outdoor furniture, and the like with upholstery shampoo. Rinse and dry with a soft cloth.

Clean piano and organ keys with a soft sponge wrung out of lukewarm suds. Dry with a soft clean cloth. Modern keys are made of a plastic that will crack or craze if cleaned with the denatured alcohol recommended for ivory keys.

Big powder puffs are great for dusting and polishing furniture. And, if fastened one around each knee, they provide ideal protection for times when you're kneeling to pull weeds.

Cleaning walls and woodwork

Walls and woodwork should be washed from the bottom up. When water runs down a soiled surface, it leaves streaks.

Put an end to daily washing of a stairwell wall after it's redecorated by choosing a sand-textured paint. The roughness discourages youngsters from sliding their hands along the wall as they go up and down the stairs.

To clean walls covered with a washable wallpaper, attach a clean sponge refill to your floor mop, dip in warm detergent suds, and wash the walls as you would a floor.

Or, wash your painted walls and ceilings with a paint roller dipped in warm water and a general-duty liquid detergent. The roller covers a large area quickly and easily. Rinse with clear water, using a sponge.

Wash walls to avoid the expense of a new paint job. Dust first (from bottom to top) with a dry mop. Wash with a mild detergent, rubbing gently (2 tablespoons ammonia, 2 tablespoons liquid detergent, 1 quart warm water). Sponge off with 1 tablespoon borax to 1 quart rinse water. Wipe dry.

Your wallpaper

Whether it is water sensitive, water resistant, or plastic-coated, wallpaper can be kept clean and will last for years if you give it good care.

Before you clean any paper, be certain which type it is. If in doubt, test a remnant or an inconspicuous spot with a damp cloth. If the paper is water sensitive, it will absorb water, and a water ring may form around the dampened area. Other types of paper will repel rather than absorb the water.

If water-sensitive paper is slightly soiled, rub the area with large pieces of semi-stale bread from which the crusts have been trimmed. Work from ceiling to baseboard in sweeping strokes. Be sure to overlap cleaned areas and, as bread becomes soiled, use a new slice.

If your paper is heavily soiled, use regular wallpaper cleaner.

Wallcoverings

Some vinyl and fabric coverings can be washed with detergent and water. On paper wallcoverings, use a commercial dough cleaner, or, make your own: Mix 2 cups flour, 4 teaspoons baking soda, 1¼ cups water, 2½ tablespoons ammonia, in the top of a double boiler over 2 cups of boiling water. Cook, covered, on low heat for 90 minutes; cool. Rub onto soiled surface; brush off.

Cleaning windows

Dry the inside of each window with an up-and-down stroke; the outside, with a crosswise motion. If any streaks show, you will know which side needs the extra cleaning.

Out of window spray? Refill an empty dispenser with water and vinegar or rubbing alcohol and water. Either mixture will clean your windows very well.

Windowsills can be cleaned with almost no effort if you have given them a coating of wax. It protects the paint, and rain and dirt will wipe off quickly.

When tape, stickers, and holiday decorations leave a gummy residue on windows, saturate a cotton ball with nail polish remover, and the sticky adhesive will come off like magic.

Before putting up your window screens for the summer, wash them with warm detergent suds. After they dry, coat with self-polishing wax. They'll be easy to keep clean—just dust them off occasionally, with the dusting tool on your vacuum cleaner.

Washing Venetian blinds

To prevent a Venetian blind from banging against the window as you dust it, work from the bottom up, holding on to the bottom of the blind. After dusting a few slats, raise the blind and dust the next slats, still holding the bottom firmly.

Wash Venetian blinds in your children's plastic wading pool, hang them on the nearby clothesline, and rinse with a hose.

Clean Venetian blinds with rubbing alcohol. They will shine, and no drying is necessary.

Cleaning Venetian blinds that can't be removed is a problem—cut fingers, poor cleaning, and the like. Use an oven mitt soaked in cleaning solution and run it across the slats. No more cut fingers, and you can clean both sides of the slats simultaneously. The mitt can be machine washed and reused.

Caring for screens and storms

Before you store away your storm windows at winter's end, coat both sides with a glass cleaner. In the autumn just polish the glass and install. They'll be clean and clear.

Make copper window screens look like new. Scrub them using a stiff brush and one of the copper cleaners available in your housewares store. Rinse the screens with a hose and wipe dry.

Cleaning wicker

A small, soft brush moistened with a few drops of furniture polish is great for dusting wicker furniture. The brush reaches into crevices, while the polish absorbs and removes the dust.

An effective way to clean a wicker basket is to swish it through rich warm suds several times. Use a brush to loosen any caked-on dirt. Rinse, then dry away from heat. The wetting-down also prevents the wicker from becoming brittle.

Lamps and shades

The easiest way to quickly dust a pleated lampshade is to use a portable blow-dryer. Plug it into an outdoor electrical outlet and blow off the dust and dirt in the privacy of your yard. It also keeps the dust from resettling in the house.

If the vinyl cord of a hanging lamp looks gray and dingy, coat it with white shoe polish—it will look like new again. Use a "kid's scuff-coat" polish in a bottle with a sponge-tip applicator.

Shampooing your upholstered furniture or rugs? Do your fabric lamp-shades, as well. First be sure, however, that they are stitched, *not glued*. Put a small amount of shampoo in a pan and use only the suds and a soft sponge.

Glass or ceramic lamp bases clean easily when sprayed with one of the spray-on liquid glass cleaners. Polish the bases dry.

Cleaning vases

To clean small-neck glass vases and decanters, drop a spoonful of raw rice into the bottle, add warm detergent suds, and shake well. The friction will dislodge clinging particles. Empty and fill again with suds. Rinse with hot water. Air-dry inside, but polish the outside with a soft towel.

To take off stubborn stains from the inside of glass vases, dampen the interior and sprinkle with any toilet-bowl cleaner. Let stand for 5 to 10 minutes, and stains or film will disappear.

Sometimes it is difficult to get to the bottom of those slender vases and bottles. Fill them with water and dissolve a denture cleaning tablet in it. The result will be sparkling.

Pictures and frames

Clean wooden picture frames with a cream wax and you'll improve their appearance.

If the picture has glass, clean the glass with a damp cloth wrung out as dry as possible. Even a small amount of moisture on the glass may seep under and ruin the mat or picture. If you use a commercial glass cleaner, be sure to polish the glass until no film remains. If the picture is framed without glass and has been given a coating of clear plastic or varnish, clean it with a damp sponge or cloth wrung out as dry as possible. If the picture has acquired a film of grease or is spotted, add a small amount of detergent to the water. Work quickly and dry the picture as you go along. Dust your pictures once a week with a soft cloth. Clean an ornate frame with a soft paintbrush, then polish the frame with a clean cloth. Don't forget to dust the back of a picture and mend any tears in the paper. Replace an old paper back when it is badly torn.

Hints for the fireplace

Waxing a natural brick fireplace makes it easier to keep clean.

Clean glass fireplace doors with a scrub pad that is designed for nonstick cookware. It will not scratch the glass.

Do you enjoy a fire in the fireplace but hate to clean up the ashes? Spread a wide sheet of aluminum foil underneath the grate. Then, when the ashes are cold, simply gather up the foil with the ashes and discard.

An empty milk carton stuffed with newspaper makes an excellent starter for fires in fireplaces. Poke holes into all sides and light.

Need kindling for the fireplace? Save all paper bags and fill them with the twigs and branches that accumulate in the yard. In each bag, place just enough to start one fire. Store them in the basement or garage until time to use. Besides a handy kindling supply, you get a clean yard as a bonus!

To hold firewood

Old crocks can be put to good use as attractive containers for kindling and wood near the fireplace.

Candles

To easily remove candle stubs from long-stemmed glass candle holders without risking breakage, fill the stems with hot soapy water and let stand for about 30 minutes. Then insert a nut pick into the stub, and the candle will lift right out.

Candles sometimes become dull and lose their gloss after being used for decorative purposes. To renew their shine, spray liquid wax on a cloth and wipe the candles; they'll look like new again.

Also: A cloth dampened with denatured alcohol will do a good job of cleaning dusty candles without removing their luster.

Wastebaskets

Wax and polish the inside of metal and wooden wastebaskets. Dust, pencil shavings, and loose dirt will not stick to the basket.

Cleaning playing cards

Clean your much-used playing cards by wiping them with a cotton swab soaked in alcohol. Then sprinkle on some talcum powder. When dry, rub the cards with a woolen cloth.

Summer clean ups

Use a solution of automatic dishwasher detergent to soak outdoor grill grates, then scour them with a wire brush. They are clean in a matter of minutes!

Your telephone

Clean your telephone with a cleaner-polisher wax. It leaves a protective coat that prevents soiling and keeps the phone looking like new.

Easy number reading

Keep a magnifying glass near the telephone as a handy aid when dialing a number from the phone directory. It will eliminate mistakes in reading the small print.

Useful pipe cleaners

Use pipe cleaners for any hard-to-reach area of your typewriter or sewing machine.

Easy removal

To remove cellophane tape from paper or cardboard without marring the surface, run a warm iron over the tape to soften the adhesive. Then gently pull off the tape.

If paper is stuck to a polished surface, soak it with olive oil: removal then doesn't damage the surface.

Clip it back

Use pin-curl clips to hold back sheer curtains when airing bedrooms. The clips won't damage or mark the curtains.

Catch those drips

Cut a piece of foam rubber to fit the inside base of an umbrella stand to soak up the drips.

For latecomers

It's easy to locate keyholes at night if you place a strip of reflector tape over each lock and cut out the keyhole.

Put a patch of masking tape on the house or apartment key. The rough texture of the tape makes it easy to single out the key on a chain in the dark.

Key identification

If finding the right key to your apartment, house, or other area is a problem, simply tape a large identifying initial to the key. A big "O" for office, "A" for apartment, "FD" for front door, and so on.

Cleaning fish tanks

Algae that accumulates on the sides of fish tanks can be easily removed with a plastic scouring pad sold in grocery stores. Be sure to use the kind without soap. These are cheaper and much easier to use than algae scrapers sold in aquarium-supply stores.

Snow shoveling made easier

Before shoveling snow, coat your snow shovel with any kind of household liquid wax and even the wettest snow won't stick to your shovel.

Easier bed making

Speed bed making by using a pen or marker to make an inconspicuous dot at the middle of the hem lines on each sheet. You'll eliminate the need for adjusting side overhang.

THE BATHROOM

Mats and rugs

Prevent a rubber bath mat from mildewing or becoming slimy by drying it after each use. Hang it on a towel rack or roll it loosely and stand it in the tub or shower.

If the nap of your nylon bathroom rug is flattened by laundering, use a pet's brush to fluff it up.

Cleaning aids for tiles and tubs

Weary of scouring the grout between tiles in the shower? Try one part chlorine bleach to nine parts water in a spray-pump bottle. In a short time mold is dead and grout turns white.

If a bath mat has stained the side or bottom of the tub, remove the stain by applying a chlorine bleach solution (following manufacturer's directions). Allow it to stand 20 minutes, then wash with suds and rinse. To keep the bath mat clean, soak it in a similar solution for 20—30 minutes, then scrub with a sudsy brush, rinse, and dry.

Keep an inexpensive squeegee in the shower to wipe clean the walls and glass doors. Children find it fun to use, and it keeps the ceramic tiles shining.

After cleaning ceramic tile and grout, apply a thin film of ordinary furniture polish to prevent mildew and to discourage soap film from building up.

For cleaning tile joints, mix enough dry detergent and vinegar to make a paste and apply to tiles. Rinse off and tiles are clean.

After cleaning the shower, dry the wall tiles, glass doors, and fixtures and coat them with liquid car wax. When the wax dries to a white film, polish the surfaces with a soft cloth. The whole shower sparkles and stays shiny much longer. Car wax also works well on counter tops and appliances.

Shower curtains and mildew

When your plastic shower curtain starts to accumulate scum and mildew at the bottom edge, simply trim off the hem with pinking shears.

Sparkling fixtures

A quick way to clean and shine chrome fixtures in the kitchen and bathroom is with a spray bottle filled with vinegar. Spray a little on the fixtures and simply wipe away water spots and residues.

To remove the mineral deposit that so often clogs a shower head in hard-water areas, unscrew the head, place in a pan, and cover with vinegar. Bring to a boil and simmer 15—20 minutes. Cool and rinse in cold water.

Keep pieces of nylon mesh near your bathroom and kitchen sinks. They come in many pretty colors to match your color scheme and are great for cleaning chrome faucets and the greenish stains in basins, and for general wipe-ups. They don't scratch and can be thrown into the washing machine when dirty.

Water that comes out in a stream instead of a spray can be annoying. The shower head may be clogged with mineral deposits. To clean it, remove the face and free the holes with a thick sewing needle. Then clean the back surface and replace the parts.

Simple clean-up

Ever been annoyed by the soap film and crust that builds up all over the bathroom soap dish and makes the bathroom look messy? Solve this problem very simply with a sponge. Cut it to fit the size of the soap dish and place the soap on top. Now all the film runs into the sponge and makes cleaning up a simple matter of rinsing the sponge.

Keeping it neat and tidy

It's hard for kids to fold towels neatly on a rod, but they can easily pull towels through a ring. When you buy towel rings, get the stick-on kind and affix them at child level.

Hang a small towel bar at preschooler eye level in the bathroom. This encourages them to hang up their own towels after bathing rather than leaving them on the edge of the tub or on the floor. An expandable rack with hooks used in the same manner in the bedrooms encourages them to hang up their clothes.

Handy wastebasket

Have a wastebasket in each bathroom for crumpled tissues, used cotton balls, cotton swabs, and other things that should not be flushed in the toilet.

Easy cleaning

Save time cleaning the toilet by pouring in ½ cup of bleach. After it sits for a while, scrub the bowl with a toilet brush and then flush.

Sparkling mirrors

When you accidentally spray hair lacquer on a mirror, make the glass spotless again simply by wiping it off with a sponge or cloth that has been dampened in rubbing alcohol.

Keep a roll of paper towels in the bathroom and use them to wipe up spills or to clean a splashed mirror. Paper towels are available in colors to match or complement your bathroom decor.

Easy glide

Wax the shower curtain rod with paste wax, and curtain hooks will move smoothly across the rod without sticking.

Rust prevention

Coat the metal bathroom scale with paste wax. This prevents the rusting that often occurs when the scale is splashed with water from the humidity build-up.

Handy table

Put your pastry board across the washbowl before cleaning out your medicine cabinet. This makes a handy table to hold the bottles and jars while working.

Shower curtain care

After washing and drying plastic shower curtains, coat them with cream wax. This coating will prevent soiling, and the folds will not stick together.

Bathroom beauty

Want to give the bathroom a new and different look? There are lots of ways to do it. Some of these decorating ideas may be right for yours:

1. Cover walls with a bright, colorful wallpaper. If your bathroom has a window, have the shade made from extra wallpaper to match the walls.

2. Hang a fancy shower curtain. Almost any washable material can be used, as long as you protect the wet side with a waterproof shower sheet.

3. Keep it shining. A clean bathroom is always a pleasure. Protect your family from illness—disinfect and deodorize the bathroom while you clean it with a commercial bathroom cleaner. Spray tub and basin, floors, tiles, counter tops, and other washable surfaces with the cleaner and wipe off with a damp sponge. In addition to killing staph, strep, and other household germs, you'll also help prevent mold and mildew growth for up to two weeks.

4. Add some decorative shelves. A few gold- or silver-trimmed shelves will provide extra storage space and lend an elegant look to the room—use them to show off pretty bubble bath, bath oil, perfume, and cologne bottles.

5. Cultivate a green thumb...plants look great in any room, including the bathroom. Choose plants which adjust well to moisture and don't need a lot of direct light.

6. Select the largest and prettiest seashell from this summer's collection. It will make a great soap dish and bring back memories of warm and sunny days spent at the beach.

Every little bit helps

Solve the lack of counter space in small bathrooms and be decorative at the same time. Suspend a rope plant hanger from the ceiling near the sink. Instead of a plant, use the basket or flowerpot to hold brushes, combs, lotions, and the like.

Pretty bathroom curtains

If you need curtains for a new bathroom or are simply tired of the old ones, try using two bath towels that match the decor. Turn down the top border of the towels to the inside 1 or 1½ inches, depending on the style of the rod you use. Slip the rod through the hem and hang.

Attractive bathroom box

Decorate a large oatmeal box and use it as a storage container for extra toilet paper. It holds two rolls and can be conveniently—and decoratively—displayed anywhere in the bathroom.

Equal time

Children need equal time at the bathroom mirror but often have trouble getting high enough to see. To simply and inexpensively solve the problem, affix mirror tiles in an attractive design at varying heights on the opposite wall. Each child will have his or her own mirror.

Handy wicker plates

Wicker paper plate holders spray-painted to match the room decor make excellent cosmetics holders for the bathroom and a good place for men to empty their pockets at night.

Inexpensive towel rods

Decorator towel rods can be very expensive. Take a look through the drapery department and you may find cafe rods suitable for towel bars. They come with their own brackets and are much less expensive than actual towel rods.

Decorative repair

Bind frayed edges of bath and hand towels with bias strips cut from the leftover pieces of fabric after sewing bathroom curtains.

Shelf safety

Line shelves of a medicine chest with strips from a desk blotter. This absorbs spills and prevents bottles from slipping off the shelf.

Broken glass

If you've broken a glass or bottle in the bathroom and think that there may still be some minute particles of glass on the floor, darken the room and examine the floor by passing the beam of a flashlight across it. The smallest particle will gleam in the light.

Instant ice pack

Make your own ice pack by dipping a sponge into water and placing it in the freezer. Wrap it in a small terry towel and it's ready for use.

Medicine for children

Most children's medicines come in liquid form that requires exact dosage. Save time by hanging a set of measuring spoons on a self-adhesive hook inside the medicine cabinet door (but be sure to keep medicines where the children can't reach them). No more worries about the right amount of medication or where to find the right-size spoon in the middle of the night.

235

Safety precaution

A thin layer of clear nail polish spread over the label of a medicine bottle provides a protective coat. Dirt and spillage are easily wiped off while the directions and file number remain legible.

Used blade container

If the problem of what to do with used razor blades is plaguing you, cut a narrow slit in the top of an evaporated-milk can. After pouring out the contents, rinse and give it a coat of paint to match your bathroom decor. Makes an attractive receptacle for used blades.

Doorway to safety

Two pieces of adhesive tape cross-slashed over the bolt of the bathroom door, will prevent that try-anything toddler from locking himself in.

Quick first aid

Give each family member two lip balm sticks, one for year-round lip protection and one to help soothe irritation from minor nicks, scratches, scrapes, and hangnails. Also rub nails and surrounding skin with it when manicuring.

First-aid supply checklist

In every home should be first-aid materials—carefully chosen, labeled, and stored in a special box or cabinet.

Following is a list of the most often needed supplies, which should be checked periodically to restock used items:

1. Individually wrapped sterile dressings (select various sizes) for cleaning and covering wounds

2. Assorted gauze bandages of various widths

3. A roll of adhesive tape (1-inch wide)

4. Some absorbent cotton

5. Tourniquet

6. Scissors

7. Mild antiseptic for minor wounds

8. Calamine lotion for insect bites, rashes, sunburn, etc.

9. Box of baking soda (bicarbonate of soda)

10. Aromatic spirits of ammonia

11. Medicine (eye) dropper

12. Both oral and rectal thermometers

13. Hot water bottle or heating pad

14. Ice bag

Bathtub safety

Stop worrying about small children taking a bath and injuring their heads on the faucet pipe (they can be quite sharp). A solution is to purchase a rubber protector (the type used on furniture legs). These can be found in the hardware section of most department stores. Simply cut a large enough hole in the bottom to let the water flow through and push it over the end of the faucet. No more worry at bath time!

Additional storage space

Short of storage space in your bathroom for shaving cream, toothpaste, and the like? A perfect solution that's attractive and inexpensive is a spice rack—the kind with lattice-work doors. It provides enough additional space for all those bottles and containers that clutter up the sink top.

Are small cosmetics, bobby pins, hairnets, and the like cluttering up your medicine cabinet or counter in the bathroom? An old-fashioned spice cabinet with its many small drawers offers handy and attractive storage.

Handy squeeze bottle

Keep a plastic squeeze bottle—such as the ones made for catsup and mustard—in the shower, filled with shampoo. You will find this is much easier for children to use. There is no top to remove and, therefore, no waste due to spills.

Cotton holder

Stuff cotton from medicine bottles and the like into empty bathroom tissue rolls to use for removing nail polish or any task that does not require sterile cotton.

Use empty boutique-size tissue boxes to hold cotton balls. The decorative box looks nice in either the bathroom or the bedroom and is very convenient as well.

Easy reach

A small magnetic knife holder hung in the bathroom will keep nail clippers, small scissors, nail file, safety pins, and needles within easy reach.

Extra towel racks

When you're expecting company and there aren't enough racks for guest towels, set up a folding wood clothes dryer in the bathroom. If you entertain often, you might paint one of these a color that harmonizes with your decor, keeping the dryer in the linen closet when not in use.

PERSONAL NOTES

Taking care of jewelry

A suitable place to store earrings is a small, inexpensive carpenter's cabinet of see-through plastic—usually used for nuts and bolts—with five small drawers. In each, place earrings of the same color—gold, silver, red, and so on. Just pull out the appropriate drawer to make a selection. Sure saves time and frustration!

Keep costume jewelry pins on a large pincushion—and see at a glance which one you want to wear.

A great way to avoid tangles in your costume jewelry, especially chain necklaces and beads, is to hang them on a curtain rod attached to the wall behind your closet or bedroom door. You can stretch the rod to length needed and see at a glance what you want to wear. It saves time and nerves.

Keep fine chains from tangling in your jewelry box by cutting a drinking straw to half the length of the chain, slipping the chain through, fastening the catch.

Coating costume jewelry with clear nail polish keeps it from peeling and preserves the shine.

Stringing beads

Here is an easy way to string beads: Just dip the end of the string into clear nail polish and let dry. The stiffened part becomes the needle.

Restring broken necklaces with fishing line. It's easy to use, requires no needle, and is strong enough to hold heavy beads.

The "no-no" jar

Everytime you consciously say "no" to that extra piece of candy or between-meal snack, reward yourself by dropping a nickel or dime into a small jar. Use this sacrifice money to splurge on something nonedible that you've been wanting. Then begin the save-spend cycle again. You will gain in the right way!

Prettier feet

Use a pumice stone (from a variety or drug store) on your heels, the back of your ankles, and any other rough spots; then apply some cuticle remover on the areas, wait a few minutes, and rinse. If feet are still not soft enough, spread some petroleum jelly all over them and slip on a pair of socks. After several hours your feet should be silky soft.

Your legs

To prevent friction burns when shaving legs with an electric razor on humid days, dust them with baby powder first.

Taking care of your hands

To avoid nicks in your nails, wear a pair of thin rubber gloves while shampooing—hair strands can damage water-softened nails. Gloves also protect against scalp scratches if you like a firm shampoo.

Clean hair with old nylons

Ever hear of brushing your hair clean with old panty hose? When your next pair runs, don't throw them out. After washing and drying them, cut out a large piece to cover the bristles of a hairbrush. With the material pulled taut, surface dirt and oils will be removed from hair when lightly brushed. Material may be washed and used again—or cut another piece.

Help with diet and exercise

Most women are diet and figure conscious. To help with this on a daily basis, start to keep a "bodybook." It is a simple notebook of diet hints and exercises clipped from various magazines. It certainly helps make dieting and exercising much more fun.

Worn-out emery boards

Get more use from a worn-out emery board by either trimming both outside edges with scissors or cutting it down the center, thus exposing new filing edges.

Pamper yourself

While running your bath water, drop in your favorite skin lotion container, tightly covered. By the time you've finished your bath, the lotion will be warm and creamy. No more after-bath chills.

More mileage from lipstick

If you hate to throw away a used-up lipstick, knowing there's about ¼″ inside the case being wasted, use a lipstick brush not just to outline your lips but to put on color. This way you use every bit.

DECORATING IDEAS

Picture perfect

Wind a little adhesive tape around the center of the picture wire, where it rests on the hanger. The wire will be less likely to slip, so your pictures will stay straight.

If in doubt about where and at what height to hang a picture, cut a pattern exactly the same size out of brown paper or newspaper and, with a bit of masking tape, fasten the pattern to the wall where you think the picture should be. Change the pattern's position until you are happy with the arrangement, then hang the picture at that spot.

Try nylon fishing line to hang pictures and mirrors. It is strong and, because it's almost invisible, can be suspended from molding without looking unsightly.

You can prevent ugly picture marks on your walls by sticking a thumb-tack on each corner of the back of the frame. Allow the tack to extend about ⅛″.

Protect watercolors (and even oil paintings) from dust: Frame them using nonreflecting glass. Unlike ordinary glass, this is virtually invisible and does not affect the appearance of the art.

Tips for rugs

If your throw rugs are constantly moving out of place, sew or glue a used canning-jar rubber to the underside of each corner or put a strip of double-faced masking tape across the short sides.

Train unruly rug fringe by using a damp cake of white soap to rub the strands that tend to curl. Another method of removing the curl is to lay a piece of wrapping paper under the end of the rug, straighten the strands, and tape the very tip of each to the paper; then spray with spray starch and let the fringe dry before removing tape and paper.

Foam sponge towels, which you can buy by the roll like paper towels, work very well to anchor small throw rugs. Besides being cheaper, they are not as thick as some rug anchors are and can be cut to any size to fit under the entire rug.

Small area rugs on top of wall-to-wall carpeting can be kept from "walking" with an old wool blanket or a muslin sheet, cut to size, placed underneath them.

Ways with windows, curtains, and shades

Need tiebacks for drapes? Some room decors are not suited to the heavy cord and tassel kind. Purchase a length of medium-sized gold-tone chain and adjust to the desired length and you'll have an attractive, durable tieback that works well in nearly every room. Purchase inexpensive chain belts from the dime store and spray-paint them to match your decor.

Ball fringe tape makes very attractive tiebacks. It comes in many colors to match your decor, and can be purchased at most fabric and notion stores.

If you have a problem with café curtains sliding back in place after you have pushed them aside, try this: Use two elastic ponytail holders—the kind with marble-sized plastic balls—push the curtains as far back as you want, then wrap the holders around the rod. Colored plastic-coated clips work just as well.

When hanging curtains or draperies, it's easy to handle them if you make three or four loose folds upward to within a foot from the top of each curtain. Then, using spring-type clothespins, gather the folds at each side. Put the curtains on the rod (either at the window or away from it), then remove clothespins.

When putting up curtains on small curtain rods, slip a thimble over the end of the rod. The curtains will glide on easily and no threads will be pulled. Or, prevent snags by covering the end of the rod with cellophane or masking tape.

For a refreshing change in decor, cut oilcloth or similar material to size and affix to an old, worn window shade. Hem the bottom and slip the old stick through it. Presto—a new shade!

A fine-mist plant sprayer is useful for removing wrinkles from already hung draperies or curtains.

Whenever you install or remove storm windows or screens, protect your draperies. Run them through the horizontal bar of a coat hanger and hook the hanger over the curtain rod.

Decorative flowerpots

Paint flowerpots to match the color scheme of the room in which they are used. An easy way to paint the pots is to invert them on a milk bottle and turn the bottle as you paint.

Pretty pulls

Decorate empty thread spools with felt, fabric, yarn, or paint and use them as light or window shade pulls.

Preserving dried flowers

Spray your dried-flower arrangements with hair spray to prevent the fluff from such plants as milkweed from falling out.

Dressing up a vanity table

A great way to attach a skirt to a vanity table: Instead of using unsightly thumb tacks, which tend to come loose, purchase two yards of Velcro™ fastener (popular for use on toddlers' coveralls). Nail the bottom piece of the tape to the vanity rim and sew the top piece permanently to the inside of the skirt. It has a neat appearance and comes off easily for washing.

243

Interesting bedroom walls

Here is a budget-minded way to add interest to bedroom walls, but the idea could be adapted for almost any room. Take an ordinary trellis, spray-paint it a bright color, and use it to support a climbing plant indoors. You can also use one against a wall to hang an arrangement of small pictures. Or, use one as a "hang-all" for jewelry, belts, and scarves around your dressing table. One real advantage of using a trellis for any of these ideas is that you can avoid putting lots of nail holes in the wall, and it can be easily moved as it doesn't have to be a permanent installation.

Useful carpet samples

To liven up a not-so-important stairway leading to basement or attic, carpet the steps and risers with carpet samples. Use double-stick carpet tape, and the entire cost is minimal. Not only will you have a lot of fun coordinating your color scheme, but you'll also add a safety feature, as each step will be easily distinguished from the next.

Handy shopping guide

Make a notebook of rug, wallpaper, and upholstery swatches along with room dimensions and photographs of each room in the house. Take it along when shopping for home furnishings.

Displaying a handcrafted rug

A handcrafted rug is shown off at great advantage when wall-hung on a brass café rod using clip-on rings. Another rod on the bottom keeps it hanging straight!

Decorating with puzzles

If you love to do jigsaw puzzles, it seems only natural to decorate one wall of the baby's room with them. Select favorite characters and, as each puzzle is finished, mount it on cardboard and tack it to the wall.

Table linens

If you enjoy using lovely table linens yet with small children find it impractical, purchase clear plastic by the yard and put it over the tablecloth. The heavier plastic seems to work best; it wipes clean easily and won't slip. Now you can enjoy good linen tablecloths without fear of spotting or staining.

KEEPING IT IN PLACE

Organized closets

Crowded closets are a common problem. Stretching the walls isn't a practical solution; a routine cleaning and reorganization of the closet is. Here's how to go about it:

1. Remove *everything* from the closet and take an inventory. Get rid of items you no longer need.

2. While the closet is empty, clean it—from the top shelves down. Use one of the commercial spray cleaners on walls and shelves and wipe with a clean cloth. Also, remember to clean the rod and lighting fixture.

3. Take advantage of space-saving closet accessories. Specially designed hangers which hold multiple items can help you make the most of available space.

4. When rehanging clothes, group them according to length. This will leave floor space beneath shorter items that can be used for a shoe rack or for extra shelves.

5. Closets will stay neater longer if you place most-used items in easily accessible spots. Off-season items can be stored in basement or attic closets; reserve lower shelves for things used often.

Closet rods

Slip several shower-curtain hangers over one end on your clothes closet rod. Use them to hang umbrellas, belts, or pocketbooks.

If the clothes rods in your closets are metal, try covering them with self-adhesive paper (a wood-grain pattern looks nice) this will eliminate little specks on your clothing and black on your hands that results from metal hangers rubbing against the metal rod.

Wax applied to the rods in your clothes closets will permit hangers to slide back and forth readily. And they stay clean with an occasional dusting.

Closets: clothes and accessories

To store large-brimmed hats without crushing them, use a small lamp shade as a hat stand. It is stable and keeps brims up off the closet shelf.

If you must hang pants on a metal hanger, place a flattened grocery bag folded in half over it. This helps to eliminate creases and wrinkles.

Folding and storing

Fold a tablecloth that is not used very often wrong side out after it is washed and ironed. Then if the crease lines should become discolored it won't show when the cloth is put on the table.

Fold and roll dish towels before you put them away in a drawer. Not only does this save space but you can tell at a glance which towel you want without disturbing the rest.

When putting away knitted, slippery tricot items in a drawer, roll them instead of folding them. They will stay neater and have fewer wrinkles.

You can increase the wearing qualities of your linens if you alternate the way you fold them from week to week. Fold them in thirds one week, in fourths the next.

A towel bar fastened to the inside of a closet door or on the back of the bedroom door is an ideal place to keep your folded bedspread when not in use.

Store slippery quilts or bedspreads in pillowcases. They will be easier to stack, and they stay in place.

The perfect place to store extra blankets is simply folded into your luggage. This saves space and at the same time keeps them neat and dust free.

Organizing your garage

An inexpensive shoe bag hung on the garage wall in the gardening area can serve as an excellent organizer. Pockets hold handtools, nozzles, gloves, and other small items.

Coil your garden hose in a bushel basket. It's easy to carry, and the basket makes a good storage place in winter.

Solve the continual jumble of bicycles, tricycles, and wagons in your garage by marking off parking sections with bold red lines on the cement floor. Also print the name of the vehicle to be parked in each area. It's fun for youngsters to "park" their toys in proper places.

Save the empty spools from your sewing threads and nail them up in the workshop or garage to hang work clothes on. There will be no rust marks when clothes are hung up damp or wet.

A clean driveway

To remove motor oil or grease from your driveway, sprinkle it liberally with kitty litter. Allow to absorb as much as possible, then remove with small shovel. Next, sprinkle again and scrub litter sand into the driveway with a brick, thoroughly going over the entire stained area. Sweep away. If spot remains, repeat second step.

Steady garbage cans

Prevent garbage cans from being tipped over by anchoring them firmly inside an old tire.

Extra bulletin board

An extra bulletin board can be made from a side of a large furniture or appliance carton. Trim neatly and add colorful masking tape or thin molding for a border.

Useful cardboard tubes

Cardboard tubes are excellent for storing candles and unframed pictures and for mailing small plants.

Keep them straight

To keep art brushes neat, clean, and in perfect shape or knitting needles safe and shiny, try putting them in a loosely woven placemat. Roll it up and tie with a ribbon.

Creating space

To provide extra storage and seating space, use old decorated army foot lockers or trunks. Install four wheels on the bottom and paint or cover them with self-adhesive decorative paper. Inexpensive cushions can be made from foam rubber cut to fit and then covered.

Handy egg cartons

An empty egg carton stores golf balls easily and neatly.

Additional storage space

Save cardboard boxes of all sizes. Glue them together at the sides and cover with pretty self-adhesive paper to make storage cubes for a closet or playroom.

Neat dressing table

If your dressing table seems cluttered with cosmetics, try putting them on an inexpensive turntable. It can be either painted or covered with adhesive paper to match your decor.

Useful stepladder

Want to store a short stepladder in your house or apartment? Paint it to match your kitchen decor, set in a corner, and place potted plants on each step.

Paper storage

When you have a roll of wrapping paper on a cardboard tube, unroll it and, after using what you need, reroll the paper and slip it *inside* the tube. Paste a small piece of the paper on the outside for easy identification.

Storage tip

Before storing suitcases, place a bar of scented soap inside. The luggage will have a nice fragrance next time it's needed.

Many uses for wine racks

Inexpensive collapsible wine racks can serve many functions. They provide a convenient holder for guest towels at parties. They make a great place to keep unopened soda bottles when placed on the floor of a pantry closet. And in children's rooms they offer tidy storage for your child's artwork "scrolls."

Old into new

An old 2- or 3-tiered spice rack can be spray-painted and hung over a desk or typing table. It is handy for storing envelopes, note paper, correcting tape, and other desk supplies. Looks neat and attractive, too.

Storing seasonal ornaments

Liquor cartons are perfect for storing Christmas ornaments. The cardboard dividers separate and protect the ornaments and are especially good for the homemade ones.

For storing seasonal decorations such as Easter baskets and artificial Christmas wreaths or trees, use clear plastic bags. They keep the decorations free of dust but easily identifiable.

Desk organizer

For keeping desk drawers organized, cutlery trays are useful and inexpensive. The spaces in the tray can be used to hold pens, pencils, stamps, tape, scissors, paper clips, and the like. It makes for a neater, less cluttered desk.

Telephone cube

In a busy household the personal phone book can easily be lost. To keep the most used phone numbers handy, try using a photocube. Jot down the most frequently called numbers and slide them into the cube. If you feel really organized, type all the numbers on slips of paper, glue them onto heavier sheets, and fill the cube. A phone cube is easy to locate, and the plastic case keeps the numbers clean.

Muffle that sound

If the ticking of your clock on the night table disturbs your sleep, cover it with a large glass tumbler. The sound will be muffled, but you will still be able to see the time.

Staying in place

Slipcovers stay in place if, after they've been tucked taut, you wedge rubber or cellulose sponges between the arms or back and cushions of chair or sofa.

SAFETY AROUND THE HOUSE

Safety tips

When washing outside windows or painting, often the legs of the ladder sink into the soft dirt around the house, causing the ladder to tip or leave big holes in the ground. To solve this problem, place a floor mat under the ladder.

Tape a spare fuse inside the door of the fuse panel so you won't have to search in the dark in an emergency.

Have you ever spent time groping in a dark closet for the string to turn on the light? Paint empty spools from your sewing basket in bright colors and use as easy-to-find light pulls. To help family members with poor eyesight, apply some fluorescent tape around the spool, or fasten two small bells at either end.

A strip of carpet tacked to the last step of a dark staircase will let you know by the feel that you have reached the bottom.

Paint top and bottom cellar steps a bright color. This helps prevent many accidents. As an added safety measure, use fluorescent paint.

Cut pieces of rubber stair pads to fit your wooden stepladder and tack them on the steps to prevent slips.

To avoid dangerous falls from slipping on the ladder of your swimming pool, apply adhesive-backed rubber flowers made for bathtubs. Also place some on the area around the pool for extra safety.

To offer a reachable helping hand to small stair-climbers, run a stout rope parallel to but somewhat lower than the existing stair rail.

Rather than risk small children's probing fingers, affix a double layer of nylon net around the electric fan and air conditioner. The net allows free circulation of air, but the mesh is too fine for their fingers to penetrate.

Put a strip of luminous paint around the handle of your flashlight so you will be able to find it easily in the dark.

Glue a strip of luminous tape to the switch of your bedside lamp to easily locate it in the dark.

HOUSEPLANTS, CUT FLOWERS, AND GARDENING

Plant sitting

We hear of baby sitters, house sitters, and pet sitters. Why not turn that green thumb of yours toward a new service for your friends and neighbors—plant sitter? We all know how dispiriting it is to return from a vacation to a houseful of half-dead or dead plants. While your friends and neighbors are on vacation, take care of their plants and perhaps even their lawns. It will be very much appreciated—and you can ask them to do the same for you when you're away.

Plant care

When you go away for a few days and have no one to look after your plants, cover them with lightweight plastic bags to retain the moisture.

Attach a label to each houseplant with all the information about the plant's needs—how much light, water, and fertilizer, type of soil, and so forth. This helps remind the owner, and a "plant sitter" will have no problem taking care of them.

Windowsill gardening

When fresh onions get too old and begin to sprout, plant them in a small flowerpot, put them on the windowsill, and water daily. Soon sprouts appear and grow into long green stems. Snip off a couple of inches to use in salads, omelets, soups, and so on. The delicate taste is always fresh—and plentiful! The same procedure can be followed with garlic buds.

Protect your houseplants from dust when you're cleaning. Cover them with pieces of dampened cheesecloth until you've finished the job.

Caring for hanging plants

It's a good idea to periodically give houseplants a good soak and a pruning in the kitchen sink. But larger hanging plants always seem to be a problem. To solve this difficulty, attach a decorative hook from the side of a kitchen cabinet next to the sink and simply hang the pot from the hook. This leaves both hands free to work with the plant.

Slip an elastic-rim plastic bowl cover over the bottom of the flowerpot before watering a hanging plant. The cover will catch any drips from the hole in the base.

It's simple to keep your patio floor dry when watering numerous potted plants. Save the wax-coated meat trays from the supermarket and place them under your plants to catch drips. For a decorative effect, paint them with instant-drying acrylic paint. These plates will wash clean, are durable, cost nothing, and will save a cleanup job.

Use a wet sponge to water seedlings in a window box. Just squeeze the water on the plants so that it falls in droplets too small to damage the fragile plants.

Use a baster to add water to small bottles that vines are grown in.

Easy plant-feeding guide

As a reminder to fertilize houseplants, make out a schedule. Put colored golf tees in the pots to match the schedule—red for weekly feedings and yellow for monthly. You can see at a glance which ones to fertilize.

Misting plants

When you spray houseplants, hold an opened umbrella behind the plant to keep the fine mist from settling on walls and furniture.

Pruning plants

Use pinking shears to prune the yellowed tips of leaves like coleus, begonias, and piggyback. This makes the clipped leaves look more natural.

Easy move

Putting heavy potted plants on a lazy Susan makes the job of turning them away from the sun a simple one. Just a touch of the finger and they revolve easily without danger of marring furniture. It also prevents moisture from damaging furniture.

Drainage for flowerpots

Don't throw away nut shells—they provide ideal drainage in the bottoms of flowerpots.

After cleaning the aquarium filters, save the charcoal for use in flowerpots for drainage. You can also put the used charcoal in water where you root plant cuttings.

Doll dishes that are no longer used by children make convenient and decorative drainage saucers for small plant pots.

Plant trays

Save the plastic liners from ready-made piecrusts. They make excellent trays for potted plants, and since they're transparent, they do not interfere with the decor of a room.

Repotting plants

Place a square of cotton fabric cheesecloth or nylon stocking over the hole in the bottom of each flowerpot before adding soil. This holds the dirt in and helps to keep saucers and jardinieres clean.

Easy transplanting

A shoehorn makes a good trowel for transplanting small houseplants.

Plant aid

Save the stirrers from cocktails and the chopsticks from Chinese restaurants and use them to help prop up limp stems of small plants.

Pretty pebbles

Brush clear nail polish on clean, small pebbles you have collected at the beach. The polished stones make pretty additions around potted plants.

Plant holders

A wire rack for glassware—the kind used for holding and serving drinks—makes a good container for small potted plants. They can't be knocked over easily, and the entire receptacle can be taken to the sink when the plants need watering.

Attractive and different planters

A little creativity can turn an old set of canisters into an eye-catching display of planters. Drill small drainage holes in the bottom of each canister and use the lids as water trays. Decorate with self-adhesive paper or spray-paint them.

Before throwing away any "useless" kitchen item such as a discolored cup or an old saucepan, consider its possibilities as a planter. Ferns look lovely in percolators, and small hibachis are perfect for baby's tears. These novelty planters also make delightful gifts.

If you want new and different-looking hanging planters, try sawing coconuts in half and cleaning them thoroughly inside. They look even prettier with brightly colored yarn holders made from scraps.

Hanging planters can be quite expensive; try to use empty butter or margarine tubs. Poke three holes into the rim with an ice pick and use a decorator chain to hang. Spray the tubs with paint and you have inexpensive and pretty little hanging planters.

If you have been looking for a large pot for an indoor plant, why not use a colorful plastic wastebasket? They come in many sizes and colors at very low prices. Simply cut a drainage hole in the bottom. A large "saucer" can be made by cutting the bottom off a plastic laundry basket.

Wall of privacy

Create a wall of privacy on your porch by hanging both long and short rope plant hangers alternately side by side. The pots, vining foliage, ropes, and hanger tassles make a screen that is not easily seen through.

Extra shelves for plants

Need additional space for your houseplants? Consider purchasing a plastic bookcase. The shelves won't rust if water should leak from one of the containers, and clay pots won't stain its surface.

Window garden

Do you have a window with an unsightly view and little light? Install colorful plastic shelving directly in front of it and place your plants on the shelves. Many plants need surprisingly little light and provide an abundance of foliage. Instead of an eyesore you will have a showpiece.

Fastening window boxes

Use door hinges to fasten outside window boxes, attaching a hinge to the upper back corners of each box. To take a box down for planting or painting, simply remove the pins from the hinges, freeing the box.

Keeping that soil

Put a layer of gravel on top of the soil in a window box to keep the rain from spattering dirt on your windows.

Ideal Christmas tree for a small apartment

Apartment dwellers with limited space will love the Norfolk Island pine. It's a natural mini-Christmas tree that is a charming houseplant throughout the rest of the year. It requires little water and flourishes during the winter when placed in indirect sunlight. To keep the branches from sagging, hang the Christmas trimmings back a bit from the branch ends.

Pretty centerpiece

Keep a copper or another attractive bowl of houseplant cuttings in water on a table in the living or dining room. While waiting for roots to sprout, you have a pretty living centerpiece.

Display plant cuttings

You can recycle your chipped stemmed glasses by using them to display plant cuttings that are rooting. Fill the glass with colored aquarium gravel and a few bits of charcoal, add water, and insert the plant cuttings. The charcoal will keep the water fresh, and the gravel will hold the stems securely.

Recycling an old barbecue grill

Don't discard that old outdoor barbecue grill. Paint it, line the bottom with gravel for drainage, and use it on the patio for potted plants.

Use your portable barbecue grill as a plant stand indoors during the winter. The grill is easy to move when house cleaning, and the charcoal pan will catch dead plant leaves and any dripping water. If the grill screen rotates, a quarter-turn a day will keep plants from growing lopsided.

Hanging baskets

Use assorted flower seeds to plant your own outdoor hanging baskets. The savings will enable you to change them with the seasons.

Flowerpots on the porch

Flowerpots placed decoratively on a porch railing often get blown off or knocked off. To prevent this, drive a 3″-long, large-head nail into the railing at the spot where you want to locate a plant. Then push the pot down over the nail, forcing it into the hole at the bottom of the container.

Bringing flowers home

If you plan to carry flowers home from the country, cut them several hours ahead of time. Immerse them in cold water almost up to the blooms. Drain and dry them just before leaving and dip the ends in melted paraffin. When you arrive home, trim off the ends and arrange the flowers in cold water. They'll be as fresh as they were when you cut them.

Arranging flowers

If you find that the stems of the flowers you are arranging are too short, stick them in clear drinking straws and trim the straws to the desired length. The clear straws are not noticeable even in glass vases.

Short-stem flowers take special arranging. One method is to fill a bowl three-quarters full of water, put a cut-out plastic doily over the bowl, and thread the flower stems through holes you have made in the plastic.

The plastic baskets that berries are sold in can make good holders for short-stemmed flowers such as pansies, sweet peas, and daisies. Invert the plastic basket in your flower bowl (you can trim the basket down if it is too high) and arrange the flowers as you would in the more conventional frog.

With a small amount of slightly cooled melted paraffin, anchor your flower frogs to the bottom of flower bowls and let the paraffin harden. Bouquets will not topple over.

If you haven't a flower frog, place a plastic or metallic mesh scrubber in a vase and push stems through the scrubber.

Double the life of cut flowers

To extend the life of flowers, cut the stems on the diagonal and place in a solution of distilled water and floral preservative. You can use distilled water on your houseplants as well, and the benefits gained by spraying and watering with it will contribute to the lushness and longevity of your indoor garden.

Everlasting bouquets

Save baby's breath, statice, and strawflowers you receive in a florist's flower arrangement. After all the other blooms have faded, these three commonly used "filler flowers" are lovely in dried arrangements.

Flowers for a friend

Make attractive flower holders by cutting off the tops of plastic liquid-detergent containers. Decorate them with decals, colored tape, or ribbon and use them to take flowers to sick friends.

Spruce up artificial flowers

Perk up organza or other fabric flowers by holding them over steam for a few seconds; then shake gently. They will look fresh and new.

Support for plants

A useful hint to tie climbing plants on stakes or trellises: Use leftover ties from disposable plastic lawn bags. The ties, which are frequently green, are almost invisible.

A small sash rod can be put into soil to support a sagging plant. As the plant grows, the rod can be extended accordingly.

Easy mark

Save ice cream and popsicle sticks for garden markers. With a felt-tipped pen write on them names of seeds and dates planted. Cover with clear nail polish for protection.

Many people like to label the seeds sown in each row of a garden with the seed packet. But some seeds germinate slowly, and the seed packets rot after a while when they get wet. Save small medicine containers or spice jars, put the empty seed packet into one, and place it at the end of each row. No more need to guess what has been sown!

Storing seeds

Use plastic pill bottles to hold flower seeds from the garden—one species to a bottle.

Easy seeding!

Don't throw away mismatched salt and pepper shakers. Save them to use as seed shakers when planting tiny, hard-to-handle seeds. It will make it easy to space them thinly, and there is no waste.

A miniature greenhouse

Don't throw away old plastic "bubble" umbrellas—they make great miniature greenhouses for starting seedlings and cuttings. Just remove the handle and push the center pole into the ground; you have an instant small greenhouse!

Instant scarecrow

Suspend aluminum foil pie pans in your vegetable garden so they will hit together in the breeze. They are the perfect weapon against birds, rabbits, squirrels, and other uninvited nibblers. The pans can be hung by string from tree branches or stakes supporting running plants in the garden.

Utilize old Halloween masks for making unique scarecrows for your next planting season. Prop the mask on a long stick, or hang it from a branch. Drape an old shirt over a clothes hanger, attach to a colorful mask, and place near your newly seeded area. Birds won't go near the scary sentry.

To keep birds from eating growing lettuce, place toy "windmills" in the garden at strategic points. The breeze turns the windmills, keeping away the birds.

Measuring hoe

Use your hoe as a measuring stick in the garden. Paint stripes on the handle indicating 6″, 1′, 2′, and 3′ lengths.

Watering your lawn

In order to maintain a reasonably attractive lawn without using too much water, raise the mower to its highest setting. This way the lawn doesn't dry out as quickly and doesn't need to be watered as often. Thus you can keep a fairly nice-looking lawn and conserve water as well.

Water an entire lawn with an old hose which has been punched with holes. Stretch it out the length of the yard and move it now and again.

Make sure to plug up the end of the hose to make the water squirt out of the holes.

Use a kitchen timer to remind yourself when to move the sprinkler while watering the lawn. This assures even watering and helps cut down the water bill.

Make your garden grow

To water a newly planted tree or shrub, take an old bucket or metal can and put a hole in the bottom of it. (You can do that easily with a nail.) Then place it beside the tree or shrub and fill with water. The water will seep out slowly and soak into the earth—rather than running off.

Picking up leaves

In the fall, when it's time to rake up leaves and twigs, take a large cardboard carton, run a cord or rope through two opposite sides near the corners and about halfway down, and tie the cord on the outside to form a handle. As you rake, fill the box with the leaves. The carton slides over the lawn easily and holds much more than a basket.

Getting rid of leaves is easy if you collect them into piles, then rake the piles onto an old tarpaulin, and drag it to the compost heap. Empty and return for another load. If you alternate a layer of leaves with a layer of garden dirt, you'll quickly have a good supply of rich soil.

Starting your own compost

Since burning leaves is forbidden in most communities, put them to good use in compost. Start with a metal bin and autumn leaves and add weeds, coffee grounds, and vegetable parings, with a layer of dirt added occasionally to prevent flies. Next fall, fork out sweet-smelling, partially composted material for top-dressing your garden. Nature will take it from there while you start a new batch.

Gardening tools

Wrapping the rough handles of gardening tools in colorful plastic tape serves a double purpose. Not only does it protect you from bothersome splinters, but it also helps in the identification of your hoes, rakes, and trowels when tools are borrowed by neighbors.

Here is a foolproof way to identify your gardening equipment. Fashion a tiny branding iron out of a wire coat hanger and scorch your initials onto the wooden handles of each tool.

Paint the cord of your electric hedge clipper bright red or yellow so you'll see it clearly and won't clip it accidentally while hedge-trimming.

When storing garden tools for the winter, clean them thoroughly, coat with oil, cover the head of each with a plastic bag, and fasten with rubber bands or cellophane tape.

Outdoor equipment care

Many families are probably guilty of neglecting outdoor tools and equipment. We expect them to last forever. For them to do the job they are intended to do, cleaning them at the end of each season should become a matter of course. Rust and corrosion are common enemies of outdoor equipment. Here are a few hints to follow for easy care:

1. Scrape the mud from hand tools. Fertilizers attract moisture and invite rust, so remove all traces of fertilizer from your spreader and wash with detergent. Rinse and let dry. Remove any rusty spots with steel wool and coat the metal with lubricating oil. Store the tools in a dry place.

2. Insecticides left in a sprayer can ruin it in one season. Wash thoroughly, rinse, and dry.

3. A garden hose containing water can spring a leak in cold weather. Empty the hose of water and store on a reel or coiled on a flat surface.

YOUR PET

Keep it in place!

If Fido can't keep his dish in one spot, try gluing a rubber jar ring to the bottom of his dish. This will help keep it in one place while he's eating.

When a baby outgrows his suction-cup cereal bowl, use it for the dog. The bowl will stay in one spot.

Use a tubular cake pan as a backyard water dish for your dog. A stake driven into the ground through the hole in the pan's center will prevent it from tipping over or moving about.

Dishes for pets

Save the foam boxes in which you purchase fast-food. Next time you have a picnic, take the boxes along to use as food and water dishes for pets. Handy, disposable, and, best of all, free!

Grooming mat for your pet

Don't throw out that worn bathroom rug. It makes a great sleeping or grooming mat.

Your dog's coat

Keep your dog's coat looking healthy by adding a drop of vegetable oil in his food every day. This is especially important in the winter when the air in homes can be quite dry.

Protective measure

To protect the kitchen door from a dog's nails, put an 8″ x 10″ piece of fine sandpaper (anchored with thumb tacks) at the bottom of the door. When he scratches to go outside, the door is protected, and he files his nails, too!

Bright idea

Put reflector tape on your dog's collar to cut down the danger of his being struck by a car at night.

For animal lovers

Donate extra coupons for dog and cat foods to the local animal shelter where those adopting a pet can start out with savings in caring for their dog or cat.

Pet food storage

Use a small funnel to fill an empty salt box with seed for your canary, parakeet, or hamster. The pouring spout makes it easy to fill small cups without spilling.

Recycling old newspapers

Don't know what to do with old newspapers? Check with your local animal shelter to see if they can use the papers to line the kennels for *their* pups and kittens. Anyone who has ever raised a puppy knows how much paper you can use up in a hurry!

Contributors

A

L. M. Adams
Mrs. Robert Adams
Margaret Adkins
Mary Catherine Ahearn
Detta R. Ahlgren
S. M. Aiken
Jacquelyn Alberstadt
R. Albrecht
Amy Alcott
Mary Ellen Alexander
Sonja E. Alexander
Mrs. W. G. Allen
Maxine Allman
Carol Amen
Mrs. G. L. Ammerman
Mrs. E.W. Ammon
Mrs. Fredrick C. Amos
Marge Anderson
Mrs. O. Anderson
Mrs. J. Andrews
A. Andrewsikas
Mrs. J. T. Anesi
A. E. Anglin
Valerie Anselone
Mrs. M. Apsolon
Cecile R. Archibald
Elizabeth J. Arencon
Mrs. Garnet Armani
Barbara Armentrout
Karen L. Armstrong
Virginia Arral
Mrs. Fred Arthur
K. R. Asbert
Lee Atkinson
J. Atlard
Kathryn E. Avery

B

Lori Babich
T. Bachmann
Mrs. D. Bacykowski
T. Bahill
Jean K. Baiardi
Mary D. Bailey
Peggy Louise Baily
R. K. Baird

Mrs. J. D. Baker
Mrs. James L. Balch
Bonnie Balderson
Joyce Ballard
Susan Bangasser
V. Banks
L. Baranawski
Mrs. J. Barbel
Margaret K. Barber
Evelyn J. Barchard
Mrs. R. W. Bard
Connie Bariteau
Mrs. R. Barkann
Mrs. Ollie O. Barnett
Roberta Baron
A. Barredo
Anna Barron
Paige V. Barrow
Madeline Barry
D. L. Barstow
N. E. Bartlett
Mrs. S. Bass
G. Bassett
Patricia Bates
Kathy Bauch
Barbrasue Beattie
Mrs. J. Beatty
Jane Beauchamp
Robbi L. Beaumont
Pat Becker
Martha J. Beckman
Patricia Bedrosian
F. S. Belote
Colleen M. Benedict
Diane Benjamin
Donna W. Bennett
D. Bennett
Mrs. H. M. Bennett
E. G. Benton
M. G. Benton
Lou Ann Berardi
Robert J. Beran
Mrs. Lisa Berizzi
Shirley F. Berlin
Mrs. R. Berman
Carol Berning
Carole J. Biccum

Linda S. Billock
Doris Bird
Natalie A. Bittner
Madelyn Blade
Dorothy Blake-Kloves
Dolly Bliss
Patricia A. Blundell
E. Bodenstein
Mrs. F. Boggs
Michael Bohaychyk
Jo Anna Bolden
Mrs. Edgar L. Bolejack
V. Bolin
Barbara Boness
Margaret E. H. Bollari
Mrs. Gary Bonitz
Shirley Bosin
W. Bourgoin
Valerie Ann Boutelle
Mrs. E. Bowers
Mrs. W. Bowling
Mrs. R. J. Boyce
S. Boyer
Betsy Boyle
C. Brandt
Nancy M. Brantley
Mrs. R. Brayton
Mrs. J. D. Brazzell
Catricia Breele
Doris D. Breiholz
Bonnie Breitzman
Janet E. Brejla
Vera Brice
J. Bricker
Frances J. Brill
Sallie Bristow
N. Brittner
Elaine Brock
M. Broderson
Pat Brodnicki
D. Brown
Diana Brown
Nancy Brown
Rosemary Brown
Lois Brownlee
A. S. Brownold
Rosemary J. Brozena

Patricia Brule
Marguerite Bruno
Sue A. Buccolo
Mrs. H. Buckley
Joan Budd
Mrs. C. B. Budge
Sara Ellen Bullock
Betty Jane Burdan
Coleen Bundy
Marcia Bures
Florence E. Burgess
Marie Burgess
Marcia Burgoon
K. Burke
Mrs. W. F. Burnett
M. Burosh
L. B. Burton
Patricia E. Butler
V. Butterfield
Betty R. Butts
Barbara C. Bykowski
Margaret D. Byrd
Phyllis Berger Byrne

C

Mrs. F. Caffey
Gloria M. Cain
Mrs. W. Cain
Patricia Caldwell
Mrs. F. N. Calnon
Doris McManis Camden
Blanche Campbell
Elaine Campbell
Nancy Campbell
S. A. Campiglia
B. Cantwell
Mrs. J. L. Capizzi
Anne Cardwell
M. Carlile
Mrs. David Carlson
E. Carlson
J. Caroll
Janet S. Carroll
Jackie Caruso
Mrs. G. S. Cascio
Mrs. K. Cassidy
Mildred E. Cathcart
D. Caviness
Mrs. K. Cecora
Joanne Chagra
Beatrice Chamberlain
Evelyn R. Chambers
Mary Champion

Gloria Chantland
P. Chaplin
Nelli Chappell
Ann T. Charat
Damiana Chavez
Grace Chicoine
Sandra Robbins Chitty
Star Chrisman
Yvonne Christopher
Frances Clark
Sheryl Clifton
Suzanne S. Coan
Mrs. C. Cochran
Patricia Cochrane
I. Coffey
Mrs. Wayne M. Coffin
Mary Cogar
F. E. Cohen
Linda L. Colle
Mrs. R. Collet
M. Collett
Margarett Collins
Pamila Collins
Mrs. D. A. Collom
Mrs. Harry F. Combs
K. Condon
Mrs. J. Connoley
Maureen A. Connolly
P. Conoley
Bobbie Mae Cooley
Geneva E. Cooley
Marie L. Cooney
Mrs. B. R. Copeland
B. Cordell
Martha H. Corey
Anne M. Corsi
Carl A. Counts
Karen Coxall
Sheila M. Cragg
Janet L. Crisp
Susan Cromartie
Mrs. T. L. Crossley
Norma Crow
Peggy Crump
Georgeann Cukjati
Karren G. Culotta
D. Cummings
Delores E. Cunningham
Jacqueline Cutler
Jeanette A. Czerw

D

Margaret D'Arcangelo

M. Dablow
M. Dahmen
D. R. Dalton
Mrs. J. Daly
Carol Danko
Lillie Davenport
Pauline Davidson
Mrs. J. B. Davis
P. Davis
Claire C. Dawson
Terry M. Day
Lana J. Dean
Eileen A. Dec
Terry Dee
Shirley De LaRosa
June Delehanty
Sonia G. Delijian
J. Maxine Dellas
M. Del Nicki
Mary L. DeMott
Karen Denton
G. DeRossett
Pat Derrico
Lisa DeWillie
M. F. Dexter
C. Diaz
Rebecca Dick-Hurwitz
Mrs. William Diffenbach
Mrs. E. J. Dierking
Donna Rae Dietrich
Barbara DiLalla
Carol S. Dilfer
Rose Dillon
Mrs. H. Dine
Ninette DiPretore
Anne Dirkman
Wanda Dionne
Barbara DiVincenzo
Alice Dodge
Doris Dolphin
Margaret Donnald
Janice P. Doolittle
Phyllis Dorough
I. Douglas
Yvonne P. Douglas
Georgean Dove
Mrs. A. Dryden
Marion Duckworth
Rochelle Dubois
Ann Duffield
John Duffield
LaVerna Duncan
B. S. Durbin

N. Dyer
Kathleen R. Dykhouse
Lucy L. Dykstra

E

Mrs. R. Earhart
Mrs. Jessie M. Easley
Joan Eastman
Alfreda Ebeling
Clara W. Edwards
Genie Edwards
Michelle J. Edwards
Jane Egbert
Sara Ekblad
Angie Elkin
Mrs. W. Eller
Helen Ellett
B. Elliott
K. Elmore
Sandy Elrod
Gladys Embleton
Connie Emerson
Karen Englefield
Mrs. L. English
Annette R. Engravalle
Mrs. E. Enzi
Jack Eppolito
Anne M. Erickson
Theresa Essig
Fanny-Maude Evans
J. Evans
Shirley A. Evans
C. Lorraine Ewart
M. Exner
Mrs. M. Ezrin

F

Maureen Famulare
Mrs. Joseph Farah
Enola M. Fargusson
Y. Farjot-Huber
Mrs. H. Farnham
Helen V. Farrar
Marcia Faulkner
Erika Faust
Hannah J. Featherstron
Gail L. Feinzig
Natalie Felumb
Barbara Ferdinand
Antonette Ferguson
Jacqueline A. Ferguson
Mrs. T. Ferry
Mrs. A. C. Fickett

Kathy B. Fields
Mrs. C. B. Fink
Mrs. M. A. Finke
Conrad Fiorillo
Colette Firmani
Cathie Fisher
Mrs. Marvin Fisher
Rita G. Fitzpatrick
Clarice Flaig
Ruby Flatt
Sema L. Karaoglu Flew
Karen Flynn
Patricia H. Foley
M. Foltz
Mrs. J. F. Ford
Lorraine Forfa
L. Forster
L. Foster
Margaret A. Fowler
Mrs. C. R. Fox
Joanne Fracchia
Terry Tucker Francis
Judy Franzen
Ina Frasier
Ellen Freed
Nita J. Friday
Ina R. Friedman
Mrs. R. J. Friedman
Mary Fritts
Nancy J. Frontiera
Patricia L. Fry
Mrs. J. H. Furst

G

Mrs. J. Gabarron
Mrs. A. W. Galbraith
Nancy Gallagher
Helen L. Garcia
Mrs. Jay Gardner
Sally Gardner
Teresa Gardner
Martha Garrett
V. Gates
V. D. Gauding
Marceline Gearing
Margaret L. Gehlar
Mrs. H. Geisler
Mrs. D. R. Geiss
G. B. Genaro
Mrs. E. Genn
Nita Getman
Eleanor Ghere
P. E. Giesen

Lynne G. Giglia
Mrs. H. E. Giles
L. Gilkey
Audrey Giordano
Mary L. Glassco
Donna L. A. Glazier
V. Gleason
Mrs. Thomas L. Goff
Wilma Golden
M. Goldstein
I. Gonzales
Deborah Gough
P. Grady
Audrey G. Graham
Gloria Graham
Judith Dianne Graham
V. Graham
Lorraine Grant
Jane Grau
Mrs. John L. Gravely
Mrs. F. Gravitter
Kathleen A. Gray
Eleanor Green
Ellen Green
Joyce Green
Diane Greenberg
Mrs. E. E. Greenwood
E. Greer
Dee Grensky
Laurel Griff
Fran Griswold
Nancy L. Grizzi
D. B. Grogan
Mrs. V. O. Groves
Leona McTeer Gulian
Linda L. Gustafson
Betty Gutberlet

H

C. Hadden
Jeanne M. Hagio
Mrs. L. Hahn
Joanne Halataei
Julia Hall
Mrs. C. K. Hallam
Janet Hallstrom
Mrs. J. W. Hallum
Mrs. T. Hamblet
Gloria A. Hamilton
Barbara Hamm
Mrs. C. A. Hammarsten
Sandra Hammer
Mrs. F. A. Hanawalt

Janice C. Handel
Helen N. Hanna
Pam Hanna
Macaire Hannigan
Fridel Hans
Mrs. Bill Hardy
Frances Hargrove
Janet Harlow
Susan Harrington
Margaret J. Harsfall
K. Hartman
Mrs. B. Hayes
Bonnie Hays
Mrs. H. A. Healy
Beverly Heath
Linda S. Heberling
Mrs. P. Heckroth
G. J. Heilman
Dwight D. Heminger
Mrs. W. Hendricks
Mrs. John Hendrickson
Mrs. P. M. Hennesy
K. Henning
Mrs. J. B. Henseon
Louise B. Henson
Wanda Henson
Harriet L. Herer
Mrs. W. Herwig
Adele Hertz
L. Hessler
Elsie L. Hicks
Mrs. R. Jay Hicks
Janet Higby
Ethel Higgins
Mrs. E. D. Higgins
B. Hinton
Karen Hiner
Audrey Hirsch
Shirley Hirth
V. L. Hoare
Nancy Hodge
Rosemary Hoefs
Dorothy Hofbauer
Betty Hoffman
Susan Hofmann
Mrs. E. B. Hogan
Julie Hogan
Mrs. R. J. Hogan
Helen Holland
Marjorie Holland
Mrs. Erwin Hollander
Tamra Hollar
Barbie Hollis

N. Hollis
Mrs. R. Holsinger
S. Holtam
Linda Hooks
Helen Hoover
Gwenda C. Hopkins
Paula K. Hoppe
Mrs. E. G. Hopson
Mrs. F. Horsemann
S. Hortie
Mrs. D. Houchins
George F. Houck
Rosella Houck
Mrs. J. E. Houseworth
Mrs. W. Houston
Anne Howard
Heidi Howard
Hugh Howard
Mrs. H. A. M. Hrizdak
Mrs. C. J. Hromada
Pat Hubbard
Leta Hudson
Wanda N. Hudson
V. Huff
Freda Humiecki
Mrs. W. Hummer
Mrs. C. D. Hunt
Anita Hunter
Margaret L. Hunter
Jennie Hutton
Mrs. J. Hyke

I

E. Susan Iannelli
Linda Ihrig
Mrs. G. G. Ingram
Mrs. Archer F. Irvine

J

Anita A. Jackson
Edith Jackson
Lavina Jackson
Mary Dee Jackson
Frances Jacobs
H. M. James
Nancy James
Rose A. Janniello
Deborah Jarrett
Arlene Jeknavorian
Patricia A. Jenkins
Mrs. Ward C. Jervis
Lois H. Jiminez
Mrs. Barbara Johnson

Diana E. Johnson
Harriet Johnson
Laila Johnson
M. C. Johnson
M. E. Johnson
Marcy Johnson
Pat Johnson
S. Johnson
Mrs. Wally Johnson
Mrs. R. E. Johnstone
Rebecca Johnstone
Joan Joldersma
Mrs. L. R. Jolibois
E. Jones
Eleanor Jones
Mrs. J. H. Jones
Judy Williams Jones
Linda Jones
M. Jones
Pat A. Jones
Sharon Uda Jones
Becky Jordan
Raeona Jordan
I. Jubien
Judy Judd
D. Juenemann
Pat Juenemann
Sue Jukosky
Annabel Jungé

K

Mrs. J. Kaiser, Jr.
Sandra Kaiser
A. Kaiserlian
Deirdre Kane
Julia A. Kapinos
Ralyn Karch
Virginia L. Karis
Marilyn Karns
Betty Ann Karpf
Karen A. Kason
Wilma Jean Kaster
Audrey Kastris
Sheldon M. Kauwell
R. Kay
Virginia Kellan
Midge Kelley
Clara Kelly
Rosalie H. Kelly
Sara N. Kelly
Catherine Kendall

Sarah Kendall
Mrs. M. Kenny
Marge Kent
Cassandra S. Kepka
Herman Kernezy
E. Kerr
Mrs. R. Kersey
Pat Kessler
S. Ketcham
Mrs. S. D. Kettering
Mrs. H. Kidd
Carol Jean Kim
Mrs. J. Kincaid
Lorraine P. Kincaid
Helen Kinder
B. V. King
Judith King
Sandra Jones King
Diana P. Kingham
Mrs. W. Kingsley
Phyllis S. Kirshy
Debbie Kiser
Heidi Kleist
Tanya Klein
B. Klick
June B. Knapp
Mrs. S. L. Knepper
Mrs. G. Koblenz
Cynthia R. Koch
Connie Kochenderfer
L. Koehnlin
Mrs. W. J. Koeppen
Elsie E. Kolberg
Mrs. George Koltiska
Linda Kondo
Susan T. Kondziela
Mrs. K. M. Koons, Jr.
Maurine Korona
Elizabeth Korver
Betty D. Koster
Pearl Kotler
Betty Kovacs
Mrs. T. Kowalski
Mrs. R. Krause
Mrs. A. Kravitz
Sylvia Horner Kreng
Mary M. Kriske
Sharon Kroeber
L. Kroll
Susan Casserly Kruppa
Mrs. G. Krushensky
Mrs. A. Kuden
M. Kunimura

Lee Kunstman
Vera Kushnerov

L
B. Lacey
Deborah Spooner Ladd
F. Ladd
G. C. Ladd
Beverly Ann Lahr
Susan Lakkis
Helen LaMance
I. Lambert
Sue Laney
M. Langer
Sally M. Langley
W. M. Larsen
Denise M. Larson
Anne M. LaRue
Ruth Laser
Mrs. N. B. Laskow
Kari Laughlin
Mrs. D. La Verghetta
L. M. Lawhon
Mrs. Tom D. Ledbetter
P. S. Ledingham
Belva Lee
Mrs. J. Lee
Priscilla R. Lee
Cheryl Ann Leen
E. Legel
C. Leggio
E. Lehmer
Annamarie Leitch
Mr. D. C. Leitch
Esther L. Lense
D. Lent
Kathie Lentz
Mrs. T. E. Leonard
L. Leonhardt
Sheila Leslie
M. Levee
Helene Levin
Dorothy LeWin
Carl L. Lewis
C. Lewis
Mrs. Lee Lewis
Margaret Lewis
Resa Lewis
Dorothy K. Lhamon
Neva Liefer
Marion Lindsay
Frances Littlefield
Helen E. Littrell

Catherine M. Litz
Mrs. D. Livingston
Isobel L. Livingstone
Ritva Ljungquist
Dorothy J. Locke
Earlene R. Long
M. V. Long
P. Lopez
Mrs. D. H. Losch
Lee Louie
Shirley Louthan
Julee M. Lovelace
Jeanne Lowe
Brenda M. Lown
Bobbie Lowthrop
Betty Lubes
Esther Lucas
Theresa Lunceford
Jennie H. Lundquist
Janet Trapp Lunik
Lori A. Lunn
Mrs. R. D. Lunn
Lorraine M. Luplow
S. Lustgarten
Mrs. J. Lutz
Mrs. G. M. Lynes
Mrs. R. Lynne
Marjorie Lyons
Pam Lyons

M
Candice MacDiarmid
Mimi MacGowan
Dorothy Mack
P. Madden
Mrs. R. Mahoney
Ann Malavet
Donna Maldonado
R. Malinowski
Mrs. H. J. Mancz
H. C. Mankevetch
M. Manning
Joan Mannion
Joyce Mansell
J. Mansfield
R. E. Mansfield
E. Maraggio
Mrs. Richard Marchael
Julia Elaine Marsh
Carol H. Marshall
M. L. Martin
Julie Martoccio
Loretta E. Martone

CONTRIBUTORS

Mrs. R. Maruska
Gladys Marx
Chris Marzec
L. Masewicz
Karen P. Mason
Evelyn Maurer
Rita Maurio
Joyce A. May
Sally R. Mayor
Jill L. McCabe
Mrs. Ted McCaffrey
M. McCall
Marsha McCall
Mrs. D. McCarthy
Mrs. C. McClelland
Mrs. C. A. McCullough
Ann McDermott
Mrs. B. McDermott
Catherine McElhenny
Joan C. McElhinney
Mrs. C. W. McGinnis
B. Elizabeth McHugh
Nancy E. McJunkin
L. McKenzie
Ann McLean
Robin McLeod
Mrs. J. L. McMillan
Susan L. McMullin
Eleanor McNamara
G. McSpiritt
Linda McSweeney
Philip J. Meara
Brenda Meehan
Pat Megivern
JoAnn Mehnert
Claudia Mellin
Gerry Mellon
Mabel Melton
Lupe Mendoza-Fernandez
Margaret Menudiado
Anita Mercurio
Fran Merrill
Terri S. Mersereau
Mrs. G. Metzler
Betty Meyer
D. J. Meyer
Mrs. K. Meyer
R. Meyer
G. Michaels
Mrs. H. A. Micol
Mrs. C. Miedema
Cathryn Miller
Mrs. E. Miller

Mrs. F. L. Miller
Georgia P. Miller
L. D. Miller
Mary Jane Miller
Mrs. O. C. Miller
Peggy Miller
Zena D. Miller
F. S. Millham
Helen E. Millham
Anne B. Mills
Mrs. H. Mills
B. J. Milne
Barbara Milos
Rosa Mims
Joanne W. Mitchell
E. Mockler
Max Mockler
Mrs. M. E. Mockler
Stephen Mockler
Judith H. Mofford
S. Molloy
J. Montesano
D. Montgomery
H. Moore
Joyce M. Moore
Judith A. Moore
M. E. Moore
R. Moore
Mrs. B. A. Moorman
M. C. Morehead
Edith Morris
Margaret Joy Morris
Mrs. S. T. Morris
Susan Seville Morris
Carol A. Morrissey
Florence M. Mortimer
Mildred Moschini
Joanne Motes
Nancy E. Mudd
Frieda Muller
T. Muller
Vella C. Munn
Linda Murphy
Mrs. L. Mushaney
D. Musicant
B. Myers

N

Mrs. R. Nageotte
Theresa S. Nagy
Joyce Nakamura
Michelle Namath
Linda Nareau

Anele Narkevicius
Irene Nash
E. G. Neil
Laura Neistadt
A. Nelson
Bonnie Nelson
M. Nelson
H. Newberg
Mrs. V. L. Newell
Bonnie S. Newkirk
Wilma J. Newman
Roberta J. Nicholson
Mary S. Nick
Mrs. B. B. Norris
Mrs. D. Norris
Mrs. R. Novack
Josephine Novello
L. Nowack
Clara L. Null
Mrs. F. Nusbaum

O

E. O'Brien
N. O'Brien
Evelyn M. O'Donnell
Mrs. J. O'Donnell
D. Oelgerking
Thomas E. Oetzel
Mrs. F. B. O'Gara
Joseph Oglesby
Gloria Ogoshi
Mrs. S. Öhlwiler
Carol Oldfield
Mrs. E. S. Olsen
Jean Olson
Barbara J. Orange
Carolyn H. Orendorff
Lynne Orloff-Jones
Mrs. C. Orttel
Helen M. Ossa
Marie Ostertag
Mrs. J. R. Ostrander
Jerry Otero
Elaine Owens
Mrs. E. M. Owczarzak

P

H. Paddock
Erin Page
M. H. Pakkala
Mrs. P. Palmer
Mrs. C.E. Palmquist
Bonnie L. Papke

Mrs. Antje Parker
Mrs. G. Parlet
Mrs. R. Parrella
Mrs. F. E. Parsons
N. K. Parsons
Cynthia S. Patterson
P. Patterson
Linda Paxton
A. Peach
Mrs. G. R. Peak
Jacquelyn Peake
Terry Rogers Peck
Linda L. Peek
S. Scott Peet
Rosemary Pelkey
Pam Pelletier
L. Pennino
Sara Pensyl
Marilyn Peretti
Betty Peters
Mrs. C. Petersen
Mrs. D. E. Petersen
Mrs. J. Peterson
Dianne Petrasek
O. Petrovitz
Linda K. Pfaff
H. Pfaffman
Elsie Phelps
Mrs. Erik A. Phillips, Sr.
Mrs. T. C. Phillips
Sofia Pierangelo
Charlotte Ann Pierce
Eleanor A. Plemmons
Angela Polance
A. Polli
Susie M. Ponzi
Irene N. Pompea
Rebecca Poole
Ronald Porep
G. Potee
Mary A. Powell
Carol J. Powers
Mrs. R. Pribbernon
Mrs. Alton L. Proctor
Ann Purdy

Q
Diane R. Quick
Mildred Quigg
N. Quinn
Eileen Quirk

R
Bernice R. Rader
Marlene Radvansky
Rosemarie Raedy
Julia Randall
Linda Kay Ratts
Mary Ann Ratts
Molly Rauber
Mrs. D. Raveane
Sheila Ray
C. R. Reardon
Mrs. J. Redding
Louise Cowen Reel
Barbara E. Reeves
Mrs. C. F. Regan
Suzanne Reichardt
Jennifer Reid
B. Reitman
Mrs. C. Rhein
Mrs. W. A. Rhodes
Jean O'Kelly Richards
Margaretta Richards
L. Richardson
N. Richmond
Mrs. G. L. Rideout
Frances J. Riley
Hazel F. Risk
Mrs. A. F. Ritchie
Marian K. Ritenour
Pat Ritner
Sherri Riuter
Elizabeth Roberts
Toni Roberts
Euunic Robertson
Leona Robinson
Mrs. R. Rochford
Laurie Rodger
Bette J. Roehsner
Mrs. Orvion Roisum
M'Adele Maton Rollings
Karen Rom
Ann A. Roosevelt
Mrs. D. A. Ross
L. Ross
Patty Ross
Terri Peña Ross
V. Ross
Muriel A. Rossel
Gertrude Rost
Audrey Rosta
Alexis K. Rotella
Jennifer Rousseau
Mrs. P. V. Row

Mrs. A. W. Rowe
Virginia P. Rowe
Florence K. Rudee
Margee Ruggles
Lavone Runge
Audrey Russell
Nina Russell
Peg Russell
Patricia Rutter
Grace Ruttle
B. G. Ryan
H. Ryan
J. N. Ryan
Dorothy Ryder
Joanne Ryder

S
Gail Sabo
Mrs. R. Sachs
A. Safarik
Jeannie Burris Sailors
Laraine Sakerak
Mrs. S. Sanders
Donna Samples
Nancy D. San Carlos
Pat Sandlin
Mrs. M. Sarachan
Mrs. H. Sason
Lynn Saunders
Rosalie M. Savage
M. M. Savoie
K. Sayne
Ruth Schafer
Russel F. Schleicher
Gloria Schlesna
Mrs. E. Schmidt
Mrs. J. D. Schneider
Joy K. Schnell
Sylvia Schoenberger
June Scholl
Marion E. Schoon
Mrs. F. G. Schubert
Grace Schultz
Ruth B. Schumacher
Betty B. Scott
Carol J. Scott
H. L. Scott
Joan M. Scott
Anna A. Sears
Mrs. W. A. Sears
Priscilla Secor
Martha Secosh
Carolyn M. Sedgwick

CONTRIBUTORS

Elsie A. Seglin
Mrs. R. Seidle
Kimberley Sellers
M. Sells
Mrs. A. Sembler
Lynne Senzatimore
L. C. Shackman
Elaine Shadle
N. L. Sharp
Margaret Shauers
Janet S. Shearer
Irene Shelton
Z. Shepard
Anita Harriet Sheridan
Ann Sherman
Sylvia Shermer
Marguerite S. Shields
Anne W. Sienkewicz
Barbara Sietz
Linda m. Sigley
Elizabeth Simcock
G. Simpson
Mrs. C. Sinkel
Mrs. J. B. Sirret
Mary Skeffington
H. V. Skidmore
G. Skinner
Mary L. Skwiot
Dorothy Slate
Mrs. H. E. Slinkman
Mrs. B. Smead, Jr.
Mrs. A. E. Smith
Bryn Smith
Carole A. Smith
Christina Smith
Stephanie Cortner Smith
Gloria G. Smith
Jeannette Smith
Johnnie Ruth Smith
Viola Smith
Norman Smith
Mrs. R. H. Smith
Mrs. V. Elliot Smith
Marlene Smithee
Lola Sneyd
LaVerne Snustab
Mrs. C. Snyder
Ann Sokol
Christine Solomon
Helen Sorokes
Mrs. R. H. Soucie
Mrs. C. Lloyd Spencer
Jean E. Spike

Mrs. J. M. Squires
Mrs. B. Stajick
Mrs. S. Stangine
Donna J. Stankiewicz
Deanne Stanley
Nancy Starkey
C. Steele
Sherry Steiner
Linda Stephanides
Mrs. W. Sterling
Margaret Stevens
Mary Stevens
Carolyn Stewart
Sandy Gordon Stiebel
L. J. Stinson
Sylvia Stolz
Joan L. Stommen
Diane Stone
Mrs. J. W. Stone
Mrs. C. H. Storie
M. C. Stormer
Patricia I. Stratman
Jessie T. Stratton
Sylvia A. Straub
Kay Stockbridge
Shirley L. Strieber
Leona B. Stringer
Dorothy Stutz
Catherine Ann Sullivan
P. A. Sullivan
Shirley Sullivan
Mrs. R. Sunderlin
Ruth W. Sutro
Mrs. C. R. Sweeney
Vera B. Sweeney
Sheree L. Sweet
Eleanor Swift
Mrs. J. Sykora
D. Szymansky

T

Patricia Talley
G. Tate
Eileen Taylor
Judy Taylor
N. Taylor
Mrs. F. C. Thalacker
Mrs. R. Theisen
Anna L. Thomas
Marcia Thomas
Carol Thompkins
A. M. Thompson
Mrs. I. Thompson

M. Thompson
Nancy L. Thompson
D. Thurm
Nancy O. Thorpe
Gwendolyn J. Thyne
Mrs. A. V. Ticner
Bunny M. Tipton
I. Tiritilli
Mrs. J. H. Tolhurst
L. Towler
Margaret Trageser-Kay
Elaine B. Travis
Susan Bella Trimboli
Elizabeth J. Trower
Joan C. Truitt
Mrs. N. Tucker
Jeanne Turney
Rosemary B. Tweet
Mrs. M. M. Tyo

U

Theresa Campos Uppal

V

Eileen Van Albert
Mrs. Birute Vaicaitis
Mrs. L. R. Van Blaricum
H. Vance
Mary Ann Vander Veen
Patricia B. Van Leuvan
Pat Van Vliet
Peggy Van Zandt
Barbara A. Vaughn
Mary Vaughn
Lynn Verrall
Hilde Versaw
Mrs. L. C. Verwoerd
Cecelia Vickery
Victoria Vidak
Jean A. Vighetti
Chris Vineis
Penn Virgin
Patricia Volkerding
E. Von Berge
Norma Voth

W

Melinda B. Wagner
Kim Walker
Mrs. W. G. Walker
E. Beth Wallace
Alana R. Walters
Loretta Walters

272

Rene Walters
Doris Ward
Mrs. G. P. Ward
Leslie Sheldon Wardian
B. Ware
Betty Warkins
Margaret Warren
Mrs. L. Washington
Mrs. E. Waters
Edith V. Watson
L. Watson
Mrs. M. B. Weber
Kathy Webster
Mrs. J. Wedel
Thomas Owen Weeks
B. Wehrli
Sister Ann Petrone Weibel
Carol Welch
J. Welciek
Julia Weller
Dalyce Wells
Joan Werkheiser
Mrs. D. A. Werman
C. L. Werner
Leslie Werner
Ann C. West
K. West
Betty Lou Westrom
Cameron S. White
J. Whitford
E. Whitman
M. B. Whitteker
Mrs. R. Wiegel

Mrs. Karl Wilhelmsen
M. Wilkins
Charlene Williams
J. Williams
Marilyn Williams
Mrs. C. F. Wilson
Kathryn M. Wilson
Mary R. Wilson
Maria Wimpory
Mrs. G. Wingo
Mrs. S. Winskowski
Evelyn Wirtanen
Jo Wise
Donna Wisecamp
Mrs. E. Wisner, Jr.
R. C. Woh
Barbara Wojcik
F. M. Wold
Mrs. Arthur Woldt
Mrs. W. A. Wollard
Claudia L. Womack
Gail E. Wood
Mrs. H. O. Wood
Mrs. W. C. Wood
A. C. Woodbury
Mrs. R. P. Woods
J. L. Woodson
Khuki Woolever
Mrs. R. L. Wooten
Joyce Worsech
Helen Worth
Sheryl Wozniewicz
E. E. Wraith

Linda Wroblewski
Carmen J. Wuitschick
Mrs. L. Wullenwaber

Y
A. Yahn
S. Yablonski
Karla K. Yanotta
Donna Yarmolich
E. Yawin
Helen F. Yawin
Mrs. M. Yeakel
Selma Yerman
Barbara Jean Yonck
Mrs. H. G. Young, Jr.
P. Yundt
Patricia R. Yunkes

Z
Tracey Zarember
P. Zashkoff
A. Zawistoueski
Kim & Alexandra Zeitler
Susan Zeller
Terri Zieve
F. Zimmering
Terry Zimmerman
Mrs. G. A. Zinn
Paula Zinsser
Tre Znera
Kristine Zollinger
C. Zublin
Nan Zyla-Wisensale
...*and many more!*

We also wish to give credit and thanks to the organizations listed below for several hints that appear in this book:

Consumer Information Center
Dahill-Mayflower Moving and Storage Company, Inc.
Household Products Division of the Noxell Corporation
Neighborhood Cleaners Association
Scandia Down Company
Texize

Index

INDEX